S0-BIZ-397

The Scarecrow Author Bibliographies

1. John Steinbeck (Tetsumaro Hayashi). 1973.
2. Joseph Conrad (Theodore G. Ehrsam). 1969.
3. Arthur Miller (Tetsumaro Hayashi). 2d ed. 1976.
4. Katherine Anne Porter (Waldrip & Bauer). 1969.
5. Philip Freneau (Philip M. Marsh). 1970.
6. Robert Greene (Tetsumaro Hayashi). 1971.
7. Benjamin Disraeli (R. W. Stewart). 1972.
8. John Berryman (Richard W. Kelly). 1972.
9. William Dean Howells (Vito J. Brenni). 1973.
10. Jean Anouilh (Kathleen W. Kelly). 1973.
11. E. M. Forster (Alfred Borrello). 1973.
12. The Marquis de Sade (E. Pierre Chanover). 1973.
13. Alain Robbe-Grillet (Dale W. Frazier). 1973.
14. Northrop Frye (Robert D. Denham). 1974.
15. Federico Garcia Lorca (Laurenti & Siracusa). 1974.
16. Ben Jonson (Brock & Welsh). 1974.
17. Four French Dramatists: Eugène Brieux, François de Curel, Emile Fabre, Paul Hervieu (Edmund F. Santa Vicca). 1974.
18. Ralph Waldo Ellison (Jacqueline Covo). 1974.
19. Philip Roth (Bernard F. Rodgers, Jr.). 1974.
20. Norman Mailer (Laura Adams). 1974.
21. Sir John Betjeman (Margaret Stapleton). 1974.
22. Elie Wiesel (Molly Abramowitz). 1974.
23. Paul Laurence Dunbar (Eugene W. Metcalf, Jr.). 1975.
24. Henry James (Beatrice Ricks). 1975.
25. Robert Frost (Lentricchia & Lentricchia). 1976.
26. Sherwood Anderson (Douglas G. Rogers). 1976.
27. Iris Murdoch and Muriel Spark (Tominaga & Schneidermeyer). 1976.
28. John Ruskin (Kirk H. Beetz). 1976.
29. Georges Simenon (Trudee Young). 1976.
30. George Gordon, Lord Byron (Oscar José Santucho). 1976.
31. John Barth (Richard Vine). 1977.
32. John Hawkes (Carol A. Hryciw). 1977.
33. William Everson (Bartlett & Campo). 1977.
34. May Sarton (Lenora Blouin). 1978.
35. Wilkie Collins (Kirk H. Beetz). 1978.
36. Sylvia Plath (Lane & Stevens). 1978.
37. E. B. White (A. J. Anderson). 1978.
38. Henry Miller (Lawrence J. Shifreen). 1979.
39. Ralph Waldo Emerson (Jeanetta Boswell). 1979.
40. James Dickey (Jim Elledge). 1979.
41. Henry Fielding (H. George Hahn). 1979.
42. Paul Goodman (Tom Nicely). 1979.
43. Christopher Marlowe (Kenneth Friedenreich). 1979.
44. Leo Tolstoy (Egan & Egan). 1979.
45. T. S. Eliot (Beatrice Ricks). 1980.
46. Allen Ginsberg (Michelle P. Kraus). 1980.
47. Anthony Burgess (Jeutonne P. Brewer). 1980.
48. Tennessee Williams (Drewey Wayne Gunn). 1980.
49. William Faulkner (Beatrice Ricks). 1980.
50. Lillian Hellman (Mary Marguerite Riordan). 1980.
51. Walt Whitman (Jeanetta Boswell). 1980.
52. Jack Kerouac (Robert J. Milewski). 1981.
53. Herman Melville (Jeanetta Boswell). 1981.
54. Horatio Alger (Scharnhorst & Bales). 1981.
55. Graham Greene (A. F. Cassis). 1981.
56. Henry David Thoreau (Jeanetta Boswell). 1981.

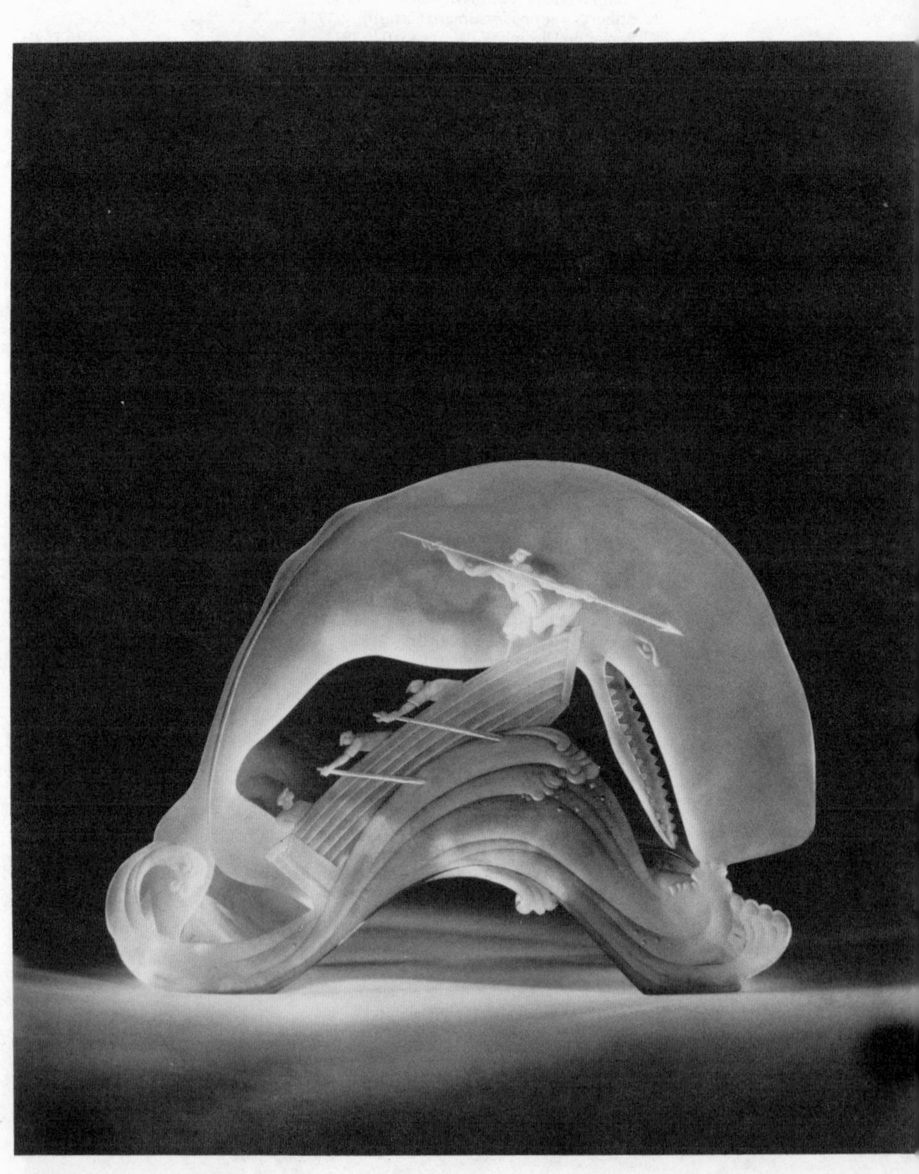

HERMAN MELVILLE AND THE CRITICS

A Checklist of Criticism, 1900-1978

by Jeanetta Boswell

The Scarecrow Author Bibliographies, Number 53

The Scarecrow Press, Inc.
Metuchen, N.J., & London
1981

Frontispiece: "Moby Dick"
Glass design by Donald Pollard
Engraving design by Sidney Waugh
Courtesy, Steuben Glass

Library of Congress Cataloging in Publication Data

Boswell, Jeanetta, 1922-
Herman Melville and the critics.

(The Scarecrow author bibliographies ; no. 53)
Includes indexes.
1. Melville, Herman, 1819-1891--Bibliography.
I. Title.
Z8562.58.B67 [PS2387] 016.813'3 80-25959
ISBN 0-8108-1385-8

Manufactured in the United States of America

To the memory
of my father and mother...

"Here on earth or harbored
in Paradise"

CONTENTS

EXTRACTS

"God keep me from ever completing anything. This whole book is but a draught--nay, but the draught of a draught. Oh, Time, Strength, Cash, and Patience!"

--*Moby-Dick*, Chapter 32

"Out of the trunk, the branches grow; out of them, the twigs. So, in productive subjects, grow the chapters."

--*Moby-Dick*, Chapter 63

"My dear Sir, a presentiment is on me,--I shall at last be worn out and perish, like an old nutmeg-grater, grated to pieces by the constant attrition of the wood, that is, the nutmeg. What I feel most moved to write, that is banned--it will not pay. Yet, altogether, write the other way I cannot. So the product is a final hash, and all my books are blotches."

--Melville's Letter to Hawthorne, June, 1851

"What's the use of elaborating what, in its very essence, is so short-lived as a modern book? Though I wrote the Gospels in this century, I should die in the gutter."

--Melville's Letter to Hawthorne, June, 1851

"He loved to dust his old grammars; it somehow mildly reminded him of his mortality."

--*Moby-Dick*, "Etymology"

"Ring down! The curtain falls and ye
Will go your ways. Yet think of me.
And genie take what's genie given
And long be happy under heaven."

--Melville, "Adieu"

PREFATORY NOTE

In 1849 Melville rather cynically wrote: "All authors should have ghosts capable of revisiting the world to snuff up the stream of praise which begins to rise as the Sexton throws his last shovelful on him--Down goes his body--and up flies his name." Melville's name, however, did not "fly up" for twenty-eight years after his death in 1891. It was not until 1921 that Professor Raymond Weaver, who may rightly be called the "father of Melville criticism," published his slight work Herman Melville: Mariner and Mystic, having already celebrated in print the event of Melville's Centennial (Nation, 109, August 2, 1919). Had Weaver not begun the Melville Revival, it no doubt would have been set going by someone else--the time was right for America to discover a great author of the past: the postwar disillusion; the sad and tragic stories of such young writers as Fitzgerald, Hemingway, and Faulkner; and the general upheaval in values that we glibly refer to as "the lost generation" all contributing to the climate of opinion that gave Melville a generous welcome to the twentieth century.

By 1922-1924 Constable Publishers of London had brought out the first, and as yet the only completed, collected edition of Melville in The Works of Herman Melville, in 16 volumes. Volume 13, edited by Raymond Weaver, contained the hitherto-unpublished story of Billy Budd. Two other "Complete Works" of Melville have been undertaken, the Hendricks House Edition and the Northwestern-Newberry Edition, both of which have achieved a sizable number of volumes, but neither of which has been completed. One suspects that "dollars damn" the ambitious projects.

In 1956 Professor Stanley T. Williams wrote in his introduction to Melville in Floyd Stovall's Eight American Authors that "no complete bibliography of Melville can come into being until after the subsidence of the present wave of biographical and critical writings" and went on to estimate that the time would be about twenty-five years. I am not sure that the wave has subsided, but nevertheless I have undertaken a full-scale listing of secondary Melville materials. A good deal of work has been done in Melville bibliography, including one book-length publication (Ricks and Adams, Herman Melville: A Reference Bibliography, 1973), now out of print. For the most part, however, the bibliographies or checklists have been based on a particular work or encompass a fairly brief segment of time. For example, David Bowman and Ruth Bohan's annotated checklist of criticism on _Mardi_ (1973); Watson G. Branch's annotated bibliography arranged chronologically from 1919 to 1971 on _The Confidence-Man_ (ed. Hershel Parker, 1971); and William H. Shurr's bibliography of criticism on Melville's poetry (_The Mystery of Iniquity_, 1973). Two periodical-published listings are especially thorough: J. Don Vann's checklist of Melville criticism, 1958-1968, in _Studies in the Novel_ (1969), lists chapters of books, articles, and books; Beebe, Hayford, and Roper had previously published a thirty-four-page listing in _Modern Fiction Studies_ (1962).

Two annotated works, of great interest but limited in scope, are James K. Bowen and Richard Vanderbeets's 1971 _Critical Guide_, in which they present well over one hundred pieces of Melville criticism in abstract form. Also in 1971 Theodore Gross and Stanley Wertheim published a book-length work devoted to Hawthorne, Melville, and Stephen Crane, with about two hundred items on Melville fully annotated and evaluated.

Of older works Milton Stern in _The Fine Hammered Steel_ (1957) gave nearly forty pages to bibliography--books, pamphlets, articles, including a great many books on whaling listed by date without publishers given. Also there is the justly-relied-upon _Eight American Authors_ (1956 and revised in 1971), in which some sixty pages of works are scanned with a running commentary. All students, of course, have been grateful to Professor Lewis Leary for his two volumes of _Articles on American Literature_, 1900-1950 and 1950-1967.

Two special-interest works should be mentioned: Marion Sader's _Comprehensive Index to Little Magazines, 1890-1970_, devotes a half-dozen pages to Melville and is useful for locating reviews and relatively little-known periodical works. Warren S. Walker's _Twentieth-Century Short Story Explications_ (1977), has some twenty-five to thirty pages devoted to Melville's short fiction, arranged by title, including discussions in book-length works.

All of these works, plus a good many others, are given in my checklist and are indexed under "Bibliography." Whereas each had something to contribute, I believe mine to be the most complete, although only a fool or a madman would claim total completeness or total accuracy. The Checklist is based largely on materials of the twentieth century written in English. However, I have included a few nineteenth-century and a few foreign-language items. This seems justifiable on the grounds that these pieces have recently been cited in a critical article or book, or the author has other significant work in the twentieth century or in the English language, and I wanted to make the author's contribution look as complete as possible. Regardless of whatever inconsistency may have been created, I felt obliged to include these items. I included one book in German, by Walter Weber, in hopes that someone may notice that it has not been translated into English and will proceed to do so. I believe it would be a valuable contribution to the understanding of Melville's poetry.

There is no way to acknowledge all the debts of gratitude for help in preparing this work: my assistants, Sarah Crouch and Dan Young, who are always willing to spend an afternoon in the library; my family, who keeps "cheering" me on; my three German shepherds, who keep guard on the premises; and friends, who inquire of my progress.

I would also like to acknowledge the gracious cooperation of Miss Chloe Zerwick, who made possible the printing of the beautiful picture of Steuben's "Moby-Dick," and to the interlibrary-loan department of the University of Texas at Arlington, without whom I would be utterly helpless.

Finally there are debts to those who will not see this work: my parents, to whose memory the work is dedicated; Thomas Hill McNeal, the teacher with whom I first read Melville in the early 1940s; to F. O. Matthiessen, whose book _American Renaissance_ (1941) marked the beginning of a life devoted to the study of American literature; and to Herman Melville, who wrote, among other things, _Moby-Dick._

Jeanetta Boswell

Arlington, Texas

April 26, 1980

A NOTE ON USING THIS BOOK

The first 11 numbered entries are of anonymous authorship and are listed chronologically.

Subarrangements under authors' names are chronological.

Abbreviations

Two abbreviations are used throughout:

DA	Dissertation Abstracts
PMLA	Publications of the Modern Language Association

THE CHECKLIST

1 ANONYMOUS (listed chronologically). "Another Significant American Centenary." *Current Opinion*, 67 (September, 1919), 184-185.

2 "Neglected American Classic." *Literary Digest*, 70 (July 16, 1921), 26.

3 *Mardi.* Boston: St. Botolph Society, 1923.

4 "Herman Melville's *Pierre*." *Times Literary Supplement*, October 30, 1930. P. 884.

5 "Manuscript Division Accessions During 1942." *Bulletin of New York Public Library*, 47 (February, 1943), 91-98.

6 "Melville's Journey: The Conflict of Heart and Mind." *Times Literary Supplement*, January 12, 1946. P. 18.

7 "*Billy Budd* Refuses to Fold." *Life Magazine*, March 26, 1951.

8 "An Opera Text." *Times Literary Supplement*, December 18, 1951. P. 785.

9 "Enoch Mudge--Ship Salvation." *Old Dartmouth Historical Society and Whaling Museum Bulletin*, Fall, 1955. Pp. 1-3.

0 "A Monument to Melville." *Times Literary Supplement*, January 21, 1972. Pp. 53-55. Review of Northwestern-Newberry Edition.

11 "W. H. G. Kingston and Melville: A Critical Comparison, by an Englishman Spending the First of April in Pittsfield." *Extracts*, 27 (1976), 8-10.

12 A., S. P. "Toward the Whole Evidence on Melville as Lecturer." *American Notes and Queries*, 2 (October, 1942), 111-112.

13 AARON, Daniel. "Melville and the Missionaries." New England Quarterly, 8 (September, 1935), 404-408.

14 ________. "An English Enemy of Melville." New England Quarterly, 8 (December, 1935), 561-567.

15 ________. The Unwritten War: American Writers and the Civil War. New York: Knopf, 1973. "Melville, the Conflict of Convictions," pp. 75-90.

16 ABCARIAN, Richard. "The World of Love and the Spheres of Fright: Melville's 'Bartleby the Scrivener.'" Studies in Short Fiction, 1 (1964), 207-215.

17 ABEL, Darrell. "'Laurel Twined with Thorn': The Theme of Melville's Timoleon." Personalist, 41 (July, 1960), 330-340.

18 ________. Simplified Approach to Melville. Great Neck, N. Y.: Barron's Educational Series, 1963.

19 ________. "Who Keeps Here His Quiet State." Extracts, 20 (1974), 6.

20 ________. "I Look, You Look, He Looks: Three Critics on Melville's Poetry." Emerson Society Quarterly, 21 (1975), 116-123. Review article.

21 ABRAMS, M. H. "The Correspondent Breeze: A Romantic Metaphor." Kenyon Review, 19 (1957), 113-130. The Aeolian harp in Romantic poetry.

22 ABRAMS, Robert E. "Leviathan's Maw: Melville's Vision of Nothingness." Ph. D. diss., Indiana, 1972. DA, 33 (1973), 6337A.

23 ________. "Typee and Omoo: Herman Melville and the Ungraspable Phantom of Identity." Arizona Quarterly, 31 (1975), 33-50.

24 ________. "'Bartleby' and the Fragile Pattern of the Ego." English Literary History, 45 (1978), 488-500.

25 ADAM, Karl. The Spirit of Catholicism. New York: Macmillan, 1937. Melville, passim.

26 ADAMS, Frederick B. "The Crow's Nest." Colophon, 2 (August, 1936), 148-154.

27 ADAMS, Karen Mary. "Black Images in 19th Century American Painting and Literature: An Iconological Study of Mount, Melville, Homer, and Mark Twain." Ph. D. diss., Emory, 1977. DA, 38 (1978), 7407.

28 ADAMS, Richard P. "Romanticism and the American Renaissance." *American Literature,* 23 (1951), 419-432.

29 ________. "The American Renaissance--an Epistemological Problem." *Emerson Society Quarterly,* 35 (1964), 2-7.

30 ADAMS, Robert Martin. "Masks, Screens, Guises: Melville and Others," in Adams, *Nil: Episodes in the Literary Conquest of Void During the Nineteenth Century.* New York: Oxford University Press, 1966. Pp. 131-148.

31 ADERMAN, R. M. "When Melville Lectured Here." *Historical Messenger,* 9 (June, 1953), 3-5. Refers to Milwaukee.

32 ADKINS, Nelson F. "A Note on Herman Melville's *Typee.*" *New England Quarterly,* 5 (April, 1932), 348-351.

33 ADLER, Joyce Sparer. "Melville on the White Man's War Against the American Indian." *Sciences and Society,* 36 (1972), 417-442.

34 ________. "The Imagination and Melville's Endless Probe for Relation." *American Transcendental Quarterly,* 19 (1973), 37-42.

35 ________. "Melville and the Civil War." *New Letters,* 40 (1973), 99-117.

36 ________. "Melville's *Benito-Cereno:* Slavery and Violence in the Americas." *Science and Society,* 38 (1974), 19-48.

37 ________. "Melville and Harris: Poetic Imaginations Related in Their Response to the Modern World," in Maes-Jelinek, Hena, ed., *Commonwealth Literature and the Modern World.* Brussels: Didier, 1975. Pp. 33-41. Refers to Wilson Harris, born in British Guiana and now living in England.

38 ________. "*Billy-Budd* and Melville's Philosophy of War." *PMLA,* 91 (March, 1976), 266-278.

39 ________. "Melville's *Typee* and *Omoo:* Of 'Civilized War' and 'Savage Peace.'" *Minnesota Review,* 10 (1978), 95-102.

40 AGUIRRE, J. L. "*Moby-Dick* of Herman Melville." *Atlantico,* 5 (1957), 33-48. In Spanish.

41 AIKEN, Conrad. "Herman Melville," a poem. *Wake,* 11 (1952), 16.

42 ALAIMO, Joseph Paul. "A Natural History of American Virtue: Melville's Critique of the Transcendental Hero." Ph. D. diss., University of Minnesota, 1974. *DA,* 35 (1975), 5385A.

43 ALBERT, Theodore Gibbs. "1. The Law vs Clarissa Harlowe. 2. The Pastoral Argument of The Sound and the Fury. 3. Melville's Savages." Ph.D. diss., Rutgers, 1976. DA, 37 (1976), 3601A.

44 ALBRECHT, Robert C. "White Jacket's Intentional Fall." Studies in the Novel (North Texas State), 4 (1972), 17-26.

45 ______. "The Thematic Unity of Melville's 'The Encantadas.'" Texas Studies in Literature and Language, 14 (1972), 463-477.

46 ALDRICH, Herbert L. Arctic Alaska and Siberia, or Eight Months with the Arctic Whalemen. Chicago and New York: Rand, McNally, 1889. Excerpt reprinted in McCormick, ed., Life on a Whaler (1960), pp. 85-93.

47 ALEXIS, Gerhard T. "Two Footnotes on a Faceless Whale." American Notes and Queries, 11 (1973), 99-100.

48 ALLEN, Don Cameron. "Symbolic Color in the Literature of the English Renaissance." Philological Quarterly, 15 (1936), 81-92.

49 ALLEN, Gay Wilson, et al., eds. American Poetry. New York: Harper and Row, 1965. "Melville's Poetry," pp. 479-501; Notes, pp. 1159-1166.

ALLISON, Denis see LAPE, Denis A.

50 ALMY, Robert F. "J. N. Reynolds: A Brief Biography with Particular Reference to Poe and Symmes." Colophon, 2 (Winter, 1937), 227-245.

51 ALTER, Robert. "The Apocalyptic Temper." Commentary, 41 (June, 1966), 61-66.

52 ______. "The Self-Conscious Novel in Eclipse," in Alter, Partial Magic. Berkeley: University of California Press, 1975. Pp. 84-137.

53 ALTIZER, Thomas J. J. The Gospel of Christian Atheism. Philadelphia: Westminster, 1966. Melville, passim. See article by Daniel C. Noel (1970).

54 ______. The Descent into Hell. Philadelphia: Lippincott, 1970. Melville, p. 190 and passim.

55 ______. "Theology and Contemporary Sensibility," in Beardslee, William, ed., America and the Future of Theology. Philadelphia: Westminster, 1977. Melville, p. 30 and passim.

56 ALTSCHULER, Glenn C. "Whose Foot on Whose Throat? A Re-examination of Melville's Benito-Cereno." College Language Association Journal, 18 (March, 1975), 383-392.

57 AMENT, William S. "Bowdler and the Whale: Some Notes on the First English and American Editions of _Moby-Dick._" _American Literature_, 4 (March, 1932), 39-47.

58 ______. "Some Americanisms in _Moby-Dick._" _American Speech_, 7 (June, 1932), 365-367.

59 _AMERICAN LITERATURE_, 26 (January, 1954), Melville number.

60 _AMERICAN TRANSCENDENTAL QUARTERLY_, 7 (Summer, 1970), Melville number; contains 18 articles, half of them on the short stories.

61 _THE AMERICAN WRITER IN ENGLAND_: An Exhibition Arranged in Honor of the Sesquicentennial of the University of Virginia. Charlottesville: University Press of Virginia, 1969. Melville, pp. 50-54.

62 AMES, Nathaniel. _A Mariner's Sketches_. Providence, R.I.: Cong, Marshall, and Hammond, 1830.

63 ANDERSEN, Marilyn. "Melville's Jackets: _Redburn_ and _White-Jacket_." _Arizona Quarterly_, 26 (Summer, 1970), 173-181.

64 ANDERSON, Betty C. "The Melville-Kierkegaard Syndrome." _Rendezvous_, 3 (1968), 41-53.

65 ANDERSON, Charles Roberts. "A Reply to Herman Melville's _White Jacket_ by Rear Admiral Thomas O. Selfridge, Sr." _American Literature_, 7 (May, 1935), 123-144.

66 ______. "With Herman Melville in the South Seas." Ph.D. diss., Columbia, 1935.

67 ______. "Contemporary American Opinions of _Typee_ and _Omoo_." _American Literature_, 9 (March, 1937), 1-25.

68 ______. "The Romance of Scholarship: Tracking Melville in the South Seas." _Colophon_, 3 (Spring, 1938), 259-279.

69 ______. _Melville in the South Seas_. New York: Columbia University Press, 1939. Reprinted New York: Dover; London: Constable, 1966.

70 ______. "Melville's English Debut." _American Literature_, 11 (March, 1939), 23-38. Comments on _Typee_.

71 ______. "The Genesis of 'Billy Budd.'" _American Literature_, 12 (November, 1940), 328-346.

72 ______. "Melville's South Sea Romance." _The Rising Generation_, 115 (1969), 478-482, 564-568. Only English essay in Japanese publication.

73 ________, ed. Journal of a Cruise to the Pacific Ocean, 1842-1844, in the Frigate United States. Durham, N.C.: Duke University Press, 1937.

74 ANDERSON, David D. "Melville and Mark Twain in Rebellion." Mark Twain Journal, 11 (Fall, 1961), 8-9.

75 ________. "Melville Criticism: Past and Present." Midwest Quarterly, 2 (Winter, 1961), 169-184.

76 ANDERSON, Quentin. "Second Trip to Byzantium." Kenyon Review, 11 (Summer, 1949), 516-520.

77 ________, ed. with Introduction. Moby-Dick. New York: Collier, 1962.

78 ANDRE, Robert. "L'expérience d'autrui chez Melville." Cahiers du Sud, 54 (December, 1962--January, 1963), 270-279. In French.

79 ________. "Melville et Shakespeare." Critique, 20 (August-September, 1964), 705-715. In French.

80 ANDREWS, Deborah C. "A Note on Melville's The Confidence-Man." Emerson Society Quarterly, 63 (1971), 27-28.

81 ________. "Attacks of Whales on Ships: A Checklist." Extracts, 18 (1974), 3-19.

82 ANSON, George. A Voyage Around the World in the Years 1740-1744. London: c. 1820. New edition with Introduction by Williams and Glyndur. London: Oxford University Press, 1974. Text edition.

83 APPLEBAUM, Noha. "Nature's Cunning Alphabet: Multiplicity and Perceptual Ambiguity in Hawthorne and Melville." Ph.D. diss., Washington University, 1974. DA, 36 (1975), 295A-296A.

84 ARBUR, Rosemarie. "Melville's Moby-Dick." Explicator, 36 (1977), item 28.

85 ARCHER, Lewis F. "Coleridge's Definition of the Poet and the Works of Herman Melville and William Faulkner." Ph.D. diss., Drew, 1966. DA, 28 (1967), 1810A-1811A.

86 ARIZONA QUARTERLY, 26 (Summer, 1970). Special Melville issue, contains 7 essays: See Anderson, Marilyn; Frederick, John T.; Fulwiler, Toby; Kinnamon, Jon M.; Lowance, Mason I., Jr.; Rucker, Mary E.; and Witherington, Paul.

87 ARMS, George. "Moby-Dick and 'The Village Blacksmith.'" Notes and Queries, 192 (May 3, 1947), 187-188.

88 ARNOLD, Edward Vernon. *Roman Stoicism*. New York: Macmillan, 1911. Reprinted London: Routledge and Kegan Paul, 1958. Melville, passim.

89 ARVIN, Newton. "A Note on the Background of Billy-Budd." *American Literature*, 20 (March, 1948), 51-55.

90 ———. "Melville and the Gothic Novel." *New England Quarterly*, 22 (March, 1949), 33-48.

91 ———. "Melville's Shorter Poems." *Partisan Review*, 16 (October, 1949), 1034-1046.

92 ———. "Melville's *Mardi*." *American Quarterly*, 2 (Spring, 1950), 71-81.

93 ———. *Herman Melville*. New York: William Sloane Associates, 1950. Reprinted New York: Viking, 1957. American Men of Letters series.

94 ———. "The Whale," chapter from *Herman Melville* (pp. 143-193), reprinted in Rahv, Philip, ed., *Literature in America* (1957), pp. 168-188.

95 ———. "Melville's *Clarel*." *Hudson Review*, 14 (Summer, 1961), 298-300. Review of *Clarel*, edited by Walter Bezanson (1960).

96 ———. "*Mardi*, *Redburn*, *White-Jacket*," in Chase, ed., *Melville: A Collection* (1962), pp. 21-38.

97 ———, ed. with Introduction. *Moby-Dick*. New York: Holt, Rinehart, 1948. Rinehart edition.

98 ASALS, Frederick. "Satire and Skepticism in 'The Two Temples.'" *Books at Brown*, 24 (1971), 7-18.

99 ASCHAFFENBURG, Walter, and Jay Leyda. "Bartleby: Genesis of an Opera, 1," in Vincent, Howard P., ed., *Melville Annual*, No. 1 (1965), pp. 25-41.

100 ASHLEY, Clifford Warren. *The Yankee Whaler*. Boston: Houghton Mifflin, 1926. Reprinted Garden City, N.Y.: Halcyon House, 1942.

101 ———. "A Possible Verse Parody of *Moby-Dick*." *American Notes and Queries*, 2 (July, 1942), 62-63.

102 ASPIZ, Harold. "Phrenologizing the Whale." *Nineteenth-Century Fiction*, 23 (1968), 18-27.

103 ASQUINO, Mark L. "Hawthorne's 'Village Uncle' and Melville's *Moby-Dick*." *Studies in Short Fiction*, 10 (1973), 413-414.

104 AUDEN, W. H. New Year Letter: In Verse. London: Faber and Faber, 1941. Melville and Whitman, pp. 70 and 152.

105 _______. "Herman Melville," in Auden, Collected Poems. New York: Random House, 1945. Pp. 146-147.

106 _______. "The Christian Tragic Hero." New York Times Book Review, 50 (December 16, 1945), pp. 1, 21.

107 _______. The Enchafèd Flood: The Romantic Iconography of the Sea. New York: Random House, 1950. Reprinted Charlottesville: University Press of Virginia, 1979. Melville, pp. 93-149.

108 AUGUSTIN, Hermann. "Johann Jacob Bachofen und Herman Melville." Schweizer Monatshefte, 46 (1967), 1124-1146. In German.

109 AULT, Nelson A. "The Sea Imagery in Herman Melville's Clarel." Research Studies (State College of Washington), 27 (June, 1959), 72-84.

110 AUSBAND, Stephen C. "The Whale and the Machine: An Approach to Moby-Dick." American Literature, 47 (May, 1975), 197-211.

111 AUSTIN, Allen. "The Three-Stranded Allegory of Moby-Dick." College English, 26 (February, 1965), 344-349.

112 AVALLONE, C. Sherman. "Melville's 'Piazza.'" Emerson Society Quarterly, 22 (1976), 221-231.

113 AYO, Nicholas. "Bartleby's Lawyer on Trial." Arizona Quarterly, 28 (1972), 27-38.

114 BAAR, Stephen R. "From Novel to Film: The Adaptation of American Renaissance Symbolic Fiction." Ph.D. diss., Utah, 1973. DA, 34 (1974), 4186A. The Scarlet Letter, The House of the Seven Gables, and Moby-Dick.

115 BABCOCK, C. Merton. "Melville's Backwoods Seamen." Western Folklore, 10 (April, 1951), 126-133.

116 _______. "The Language of Melville's 'Isolatoes.'" Western Folklore, 10 (October, 1951), 285-289.

117 _______. "Melville's World Language." Southern Folklore Quarterly, 16 (September, 1952), 177-182.

118 _______. "Melville's Proverbs of the Sea." Western Folklore, 11 (October, 1952), 254-265.

119 ______. "Melville's 'Moby Dictionary.'" Word Study, 29 (December, 1953), 7-8.

120 ______. "The Vocabulary of Moby-Dick." American Speech, 28 (1953), 91-101.

121 ______. "Herman Melville's Whaling Vocabulary." American Speech, 29 (October, 1954), 161-174.

122 ______. "Some Expressions from Herman Melville." Publications of the American Dialect Society, 31 (April, 1959), 3-13.

123 BABIN, James L. "Herman Melville and the Idea of Order." Ph.D. diss., Duke, 1969. DA, 31 (1970), 2372A.

124 ______. "Melville and the Deformation of Being: From Typee to Leviathan." Southern Review, 7 (1971), 89-114.

125 BACH, Bert Coates. "Narrative Point of View in the Fiction of Herman Melville after Moby-Dick." Ph.D. diss., New York University, 1965. DA, 27 (1966), 2494A.

126 ______. "Melville's Israel Potter: A Re-evaluation of Its Reputation and Meaning." Cithara, 7 (1967), 39-50.

127 ______. "Melville's Theatrical Mask: The Role of Narrative Perspective in His Short Fiction." Studies in the Literary Imagination, 2 (1969), 43-55.

128 ______. "Melville's Confidence-Man: Allegory, Satire, and the Irony of Intent." Cithara, 8 (1969), 28-36.

129 ______. "Narrative Technique and Structure in Pierre." American Transcendental Quarterly, 7 (1970), 5-8.

130 BADAL, James Jessen, Jr. "Studies in the Tragic Attitude." Ph.D. diss., Case Western Reserve, 1975. DA, 37 (1976), 961A-962A. Includes Melville.

131 BADER, A. L. "Marryat's 'The Ocean Wolf.'" Philological Quarterly, 16 (January, 1937), 80-82.

132 BAENDER, Paul. "Reflections upon the CEAA by a Departing Editor." Resources for American Literary Study, 4 (1974), 131-144.

133 BAGLEY, Carol Lenore. "Melville's Trilogy: Symbolic Precursor of Freudian Personality Structure in the History of Ideas." Ph.D. diss., Washington State, 1966. DA, 27 (1966), 1778A.

134 BAIM, Joseph. "The Confidence Man as 'Trickster.'" American Transcendental Quarterly, 1 (1969), 81-83.

135 BAIRD, James. "Herman Melville and Primitivism." Ph.D. diss., Yale, 1947.

136 _______. "Noble Polynesian." Pacific Spectator, 4 (Autumn, 1950), 452-465.

137 _______. Ishmael: A Study of the Symbolic Mode in Primitivism. Baltimore: Johns Hopkins University Press, 1956. Reprinted New York: Harper and Row, 1960.

138 _______. "Typee as Paradigm: Prefiguration of Melville's Later Work." Extracts, 15 (1973), 2. Abstract of lecture read at Spring meeting of Melville Society.

139 BAKER, Carlos. "Of Art and Artifacts." New York Times Book Review, 52 (August 10, 1947), 2.

140 BAKKAR, J. "Beyond Slavery: A Study of 'Benito Cereno.'" Dutch Quarterly Review (Amsterdam), 7 (1977).

141 BALFOUR, M. C., ed. Omoo. London: John Lane, 1904. Appendix, "Tahiti in 1842: As Melville Saw It," pp. 447-452.

142 BALL, Roland C. "American Re-interpretation of European Romantic Themes: The Rebel-Hero in Cooper and Melville," in Jost, François, ed., Proceedings of the IVth Congress of the International Comparative Literature Association, 2 vols. (Fribourg, Switzerland, 1964). The Hague: Mouton, 1966. Pp. 1113-1121.

143 BANK, Stanley, ed. with Introduction. American Romanticism: A Shape for Fiction. New York: Capricorn, 1969. "Herman Melville: Pasteboard Masks," pp. 289-345. Includes selections from Melville's works and reprints article by Fitz-James O'Brien, "Our Young Authors--Melville" (Putnam's Magazine, 1853).

144 BANTA, Martha. "The Man of History and the Mythy Man in Melville." American Transcendental Quarterly, 10 (1971), 3-11. Franklin in Israel Potter and Emerson in The Confidence-Man.

145 _______. "About America's 'White Terror': Melville, James, Poe, etc." in Frank, Luanne, ed., Literature and the Occult: Essays in Comparative Literature. Arlington: University of Texas at Arlington Publications in Literature, 1977. Pp. 31-53.

146 BARBARROW, George. "Leyda's Melville--A Reconsideration." Hudson Review, 7 (Winter, 1955), 585-593.

147 BARBER, John W., ed. History of the Amistad Captives.

American Transcendental Quarterly, 22 (1974), 109-120. Facsimile reprinting; refers to work relating a slave-revolt.

148 BARBER, Patricia. "Melville's Self-Image as a Writer and the Image of the Writer in Pierre." Massachusetts Studies in English, 3 (1972), 65-71.

149 ________. "Melville's House in Brooklyn." American Literature, 45 (1973), 433-434.

150 ________. "What If Bartleby Were a Woman?" in Diamond, A., and L. R. Edwards, eds., The Authority of Experience: Essays in Feminist Criticism. Amherst: University of Massachusetts Press, 1977. Pp. 212-223, 298-300.

151 ________, ed. "Two New Melville Letters." American Literature, 49 (1977), 418-421.

152 BARBOUR, James. "The Writing of Moby-Dick." Ph.D. diss., UCLA, 1970. DA, 31 (1971), 6538A.

153 ________. "The Town-Ho's Story: Melville's Original Whale." Emerson Society Quarterly, 21 (1975), 111-115.

154 ________. "The Composition of Moby-Dick." American Literature, 47 (November, 1975), 343-360. Foerster Prize article.

155 ________ and Leon Howard. "Carlyle and the Conclusion of Moby-Dick." New England Quarterly, 49 (1976), 214-224.

156 BARITZ, Loren. City on a Hill: A History of Ideas and Myths in America. New York: Wiley, 1964. "The Demonic: Herman Melville," pp. 271-331.

157 BARNET, Sylvan. "The Execution in Billy-Budd." American Literature, 33 (January, 1962), 517-519.

158 BARNETT, Louise K. "Bartleby as Alienated Worker." Studies in Short Fiction, 11 (Fall, 1974), 379-385.

159 ________. Ignoble Savage: American Literary Racism, 1790-1890. Westport, Conn.: Greenwood, 1975. Melville, pp. 166-184 and passim.

160 BARNEY, Stephen A. Allegories of History, Allegories of Love. Hamden, Conn.: Shoe String, 1979. Includes study of Melville's The Confidence-Man.

161 BARRETT, Laurence N. "Fiery Hunt: A Study of Herman Melville's Theories of the Artist." Ph.D. diss., Princeton, 1949.

162 ———. "The Differences in Melville's Poetry." PMLA, 70 (September, 1955), 606-623.

163 BARRY, Sister Marie. "The Problem of Shifting Voice and Point of View in Herman Melville's Early Novels and Moby-Dick." Ph.D. diss., Catholic University, 1951.

164 BARTLETT, I. H. The American Mind in the Mid-Nineteenth Century. New York: Crowell, 1967. "The Democratic Imagination," pp. 94-113, includes Melville.

165 BASILE, Joseph Lawrence. "The Meridians of Melville's Wicked World." South Dakota Review, 11 (1973), 62-76.

166 BATTENFELD, David H. "The Source for the Hymn in Moby-Dick." American Literature, 27 (November, 1955), 393-396.

167 ———. "'I Seek for Truth': A Comparative Study of Herman Melville's Moby-Dick and Pierre." Ph.D. diss., Stanford, 1958. DA, 18 (1958), 1426-1427.

168 BAYM, Max I. A History of Literary Aesthetics in America. New York: Ungar, 1973. Melville, pp. 68-70.

169 BAYM, Nina. "The Erotic Motif in Melville's Clarel." Texas Studies in Language and Literature, 16 (1974), 315-328.

170 BEACH, Joseph Warren. "Hart Crane and Moby-Dick." Western Review, 20 (Spring, 1956), 183-196.

171 BEALE, Thomas P. The Natural History of the Sperm Whale. London: Van Voorst. Reprinted London: Holland, 1973.

172 BEATTY, Lillian. "Typee and Blithedale: Rejected Ideal Communities." Personalist, 37 (Autumn, 1956), 367-378.

173 BEAVER, Harold L. "Whale or Boojum: An Agony," in Guiliano, Edward, ed., Lewis Carroll Observed: A Collection of Unpublished Photographs, Drawings, Poetry, and New Essays. New York: Potter, 1976. Pp. 111-131. Refers to Moby-Dick and Carroll's Hunting of the Snark.

174 ———. "Time on the Cross: White Fiction and Black Messiahs." Yearbook of English Studies, 8 (1978), 40-53. Discusses Melville and Harriet Beecher Stowe.

175 ———, ed. Moby-Dick. London: Penguin English Library, 1972.

176 ———, ed. "Billy Budd, Sailor" and Other Stories. London: Penguin English Library, 1972.

177 ________, ed. Redburn. London: Penguin English Library, 1972.

178 BECK, Horace P. "Melville as a Folklore Recorder in Moby-Dick." Keystone Folklore, 18 (February, 1973), 75-88.

179 BECKWITH, Toni H. L. "Truth and Truth-Telling in Moby-Dick." Ph.D. diss., Brown, 1973. DA, 34 (1974), 5955A.

180 BEEBE, Maurice, Harrison Hayford, and Gordon Roper. "Criticism of Herman Melville: A Selected Checklist." Modern Fiction Studies, 8 (1962), 312-346.

181 BEECHEY, Frederick W. Narrative of a Voyage to the Pacific and the Bering Straits. Philadelphia: Carey and Lea, 1832. Reprinted London: Colburn and Bentley, 1931. Also reprinted New York: Da Capo, 1969.

182 BEHARRIEL, Stanley R. "The Head and the Heart in Herman Melville." Ph.D. diss., Wisconsin, 1954.

183 BEIDLER, Philip D. "Billy Budd: Melville's Valedictory to Emerson." Emerson Society Quarterly, 24 (1978), 215-228.

184 BEJA, Morris. "Bartleby and Schizophrenia." Massachusetts Review, 19 (1978), 555-568.

185 BELCHER, Sir Edward. Narrative of a Voyage Around the World, 1836-1842. London: Colburn, 1843. Reprinted Los Angeles: Dawson's, 1970.

186 BELGION, Montgomery. "Heterodoxy on Moby-Dick? Sewanee Review, 55 (Winter, 1947), 108-125.

187 ________, ed. Moby-Dick. London: Cresset, 1946.

188 BELL, Michael Davitt. "The Glendinning Heritage: Melville's Literary Borrowings in Pierre." Studies in Romanticism, 12 (1973), 741-762.

189 ________. "Melville's Redburn: Initiation and Authority." New England Quarterly, 46 (December, 1973), 558-572.

190 ________. "Melville and 'Romance': Literary Nationalism and Fictional Form." American Transcendental Quarterly, 24 (1974), 56-62.

190a BELL, Millicent. "Pierre Bayle and Moby-Dick." PMLA, 66 (September, 1951), 626-648.

191 ________. "Melville and Hawthorne at the Grave of St. John (A Debt to Pierre Bayle)." Modern Language Notes, 47 (February, 1952), 116-118.

192 ________. "The Irreducible Moby-Dick." Emerson Society Quarterly, 28 (1962), 4-6.

193 BELLIS, George D. "Moby-Dick and a Philosophy of Will." Ph.D. diss., Catholic University, 1970. DA, 32 (1971), 2050A-2051A.

194 BENDER, Bert. "Melville's Shock of Genius and His Three Tales of the Shocked Unrecognized." Forum (Houston), 13 (1976), 24-30.

195 ________. "Moby-Dick, an American Lyrical Novel." Studies in the Novel, 10 (1978), 346-356.

196 BENET, William Rose. "Poet in Prose." Saturday Review of Literature, 30 (August 2, 1947), 17.

197 BENNETT, Arnold. The Savour of Life. London: Cassell; New York: Doubleday, Doran, 1928. Melville's Pierre, pp. 305-307.

198 BENNETT, Frederick Debell. Narrative of a Whaling Voyage Around the Globe, 1833-1836. London: Bentley, 1840. Reprinted New York: Da Capo, 1970.

199 BENNETT, John Frederick. "Herman Melville's Humanitarian Thought: A Study in Moral Idealism." Ph.D. diss., Wisconsin, 1956. DA, 16 (1965), 961.

200 ________. The Struck Leviathan: Poems on "Moby-Dick." Columbia: University of Missouri Press, 1970. Bennett says, "These poems, written as interior monologues by major and minor characters in Melville's Moby-Dick, serve as comments on the action of the novel or they are individual expressions as each character responds to his own world of experience, thought, and feeling."

201 BENOIT, Raymond. Single Nature's Double Name. Atlantic Highlands, N.J.: Humanities, 1973; The Hague: Mouton, 1973. Melville, pp. 22, 58, and passim.

202 ________. "Norman Mailer's Moby-Dick." Notes on Modern American Literature, 1 (1977), item 26.

203 BENSON, Carl Maltby, ed. Moby-Dick. Introduction by A. S. W. Rosenbach. New York: Doubleday, Doran, 1928.

204 BENSON, James D., and William S. Greaves. "The White and the Gold: Equative Clauses and the Symbolism of Melville's Moby-Dick." Linguistics in Literature, 2 (1977), 44-67.

205 BENZIGER, James. Images of Eternity: Studies in the Poetry

of Religious Vision from Wordsworth to T. S. Eliot. Carbondale: Southern Illinois University Press, 1964. Melville, passim.

206 BERCOVITCH, Sacvan. "Melville's Search for National Identity: Son and Father in Redburn, Pierre, and Billy-Budd." College Language Association Journal, 10 (March, 1967), 217-228.

207 ________. The American Jeremiad. Madison: University of Wisconsin Press, 1978. Melville, passim.

208 BERGLER, Edmund. "A Note on Herman Melville." American Imago, 11 (Winter, 1954), 385-397.

209 BERGMANN, Johannes Dietrich. "The Original Confidence Man: The Development of the American Confidence Man in the Sources and Backgrounds of Herman Melville's The Confidence-Man: His Masquerade." Ph.D. diss., Connecticut University, 1968. DA, 30 (1969), 678A-679A.

210 ________. "The Original Confidence Man." American Quarterly, 21 (Fall, 1969), 20-21.

211 ________. "'Bartleby' and The Lawyer's Story." American Literature, 47 (November, 1975), 432-436. Refers to a novel by James Maitland, 1853.

212 ________. "The New York Morning News and Typee." Extracts, 31 (1977), 1-4.

213 ________. "New Great Traditions." Melville Society Extracts, 36 (1978), 13-14. Review article.

214 BERGSTROM, Robert E. "The Impulsive Counter-Change: The Development and Artistic Expression of Melville's Religious Thought, 1846-1857." Ph.D. diss., Duke, 1968. DA, 30 (1969), 272A-273A.

215 ________. "The Top-Most Grief: Rejection of Ahab's Faith." Essays in Literature (Denver), 2 (1975), 171-180.

216 BERINGHAUSE, A. F. "Melville and Chrétien de Troyes." American Notes and Queries, 2 (October, 1963), 20-21. Refers to a French poet of the late twelfth century.

217 BERKELEY, David S. "Figurae Futurarum in Moby-Dick." Bucknell Review, 21 (1973), 108-123. Use of foreshadowing devices.

218 BERKELMAN, R. G. "Moby-Dick: Curiosity or Classic?" English Journal (college edition), 27 (November, 1938), 742-755.

219 BERLIND, Bruce. "Notes on Melville's Shorter Poems." Hopkins Review, 3 (Summer, 1950), 24-35.

220 BERNARD, Kenneth. "Melville's Mardi and the Second Loss of Paradise." Lock Haven Review, 7 (1965), 23-30.

221 BERNSTEIN, John A. "Pacificism and Rebellion in the Writings of Herman Melville." Ph.D. diss., University of Pennsylvania, 1961. DA, 23 (1962), 221-222.

222 ________. "'Benito Cereno' and the Spanish Inquisition." Nineteenth-Century Fiction, 16 (March, 1962), 345-350.

223 ________. Pacifism and Rebellion in the Writings of Herman Melville. The Hague: Mouton, 1964.

224 BERRYMAN, Charles. From Wilderness to Wasteland: The Trial of the Puritan God in the American Imagination. Port Washington, N.Y.: Kennikat, 1979. Contains material on Emerson, Hawthorne, and Melville.

225 BERTHOFF, Warner. "Certain Phenomenal Men: The Example of Billy-Budd." Journal of English Literary History, 26 (1960), 334-351.

226 ________. The Example of Melville. Princeton, N.J.: Princeton University Press, 1962.

227 ________. "Herman Melville: The Confidence Man," in Cohen, Henig, ed., Landmarks of American Writing (1969), pp. 121-133.

228 ________. "Melville's Later Fiction," in Berthoff, ed., Fictions and Events. New York: Dutton, 1971. Pp. 219-242.

229 ________, ed. with Introduction. Great Short Works of Herman Melville. New York: Harper and Row, 1970.

230 BERTHOLF, Robert J. "Charles Olson and the Melville Society." Extracts, 10 (1972), 3-4.

231 ________. "Melville and Olson: The Poetics of Form." Extracts, 17 (1974), 5-6.

232 ________. "On Olson, His Melville." Io (Plainsfield, Vt.), 22 (1976), 5-36.

233 BETTS, William W., Jr. "Moby-Dick: Melville's Faust." Lock Haven Bulletin, 1 (1959), 31-44.

234 BEUM, Robert. "Melville's Course." Dalhousie Review, 45 (1965), 17-33.

235 BEVERLEY, Gordon. "Herman Melville's Confidence." London Times Literary Supplement, November 11, 1949. P. 733. A letter on The Confidence-Man.

236 BEWLEY, Marius. "A Truce of God for Melville." Sewanee Review, 61 (Autumn, 1953), 682-700. Review-essay on Lawrance Thompson's Melville's Quarrel with God (1952).

237 _______. The Eccentric Design: Form in the Classic American Novel. New York: Columbia University Press, 1959. "Melville and the Democratic Experience," pp. 187-219. Reprinted in Chase, Richard V., ed., Melville: A Collection of Criticism (1962), pp. 91-115.

238 BEZANSON, Walter Everett. "Herman Melville's Clarel." Ph.D. diss., Yale, 1943. DA, 30 (1969), 2520A.

239 _______. "Moby-Dick, Work of Art," in Hillway, Tyrus, ed., Centennial Essays (1951), pp. 30-58.

240 _______. "Melville's Clarel: The Complex Passion." English Literary History, 21 (1954), 146-159.

241 _______. "Melville's Reading of Arnold's Poetry." PMLA, 69 (June, 1954), 365-391.

242 _______. "The Context of Melville's Fiction." Emerson Society Quarterly, 28 (1962), 9-12.

243 _______, ed. with Introduction. Clarel: A Poem and Pilgrimage in the Holy Land. New York: Hendricks House, 1960. 117-page introduction.

244 BICKLEY, Robert Bruce. "Literary Influences and Techniques in Melville's Short Fiction: 1853-1856." Ph.D. diss., Duke, 1969. DA, 30 (1970), 4935A.

245 _______. "The Minor Fiction of Hawthorne and Melville." American Transcendental Quarterly, 14 (1972), 149-152.

246 _______. The Method of Melville's Short Fiction. Durham, N.C.: Duke University Press, 1975.

247 _______. "Three More Musical Compositions Inspired by Melville's Works." Extracts, 26 (1976), 10.

248 BIER, Jesse. "Melville's 'The Fiddler' Reconsidered." American Transcendental Quarterly, 14 (1972), 2-4.

249 BIGELOW, Gordon E. "The Problem of Symbolist Form in Melville's 'Bartleby the Scrivener.'" Modern Language Quarterly, 31 (1970), 345-358.

250 BIGLER, Clair Ellsworth, Jr. "A Study of Recurring Imagery of Unusual Height, Depth, and Mass in the Writings of Herman Melville: 1838-1857." Ph.D. diss., University of Wisconsin (Madison), 1974. DA, 35 (1975), 7246A.

251 BILLSON, James. "Works of Herman Melville." Nation (London), 19 (June 11, 1921), 396-397.

252 ________. "Some Melville Letters." Nation (American), 29 (August 13, 1921), 712-713.

253 BILLY, Ted. "Eros and Thanatos in 'Bartleby.'" Arizona Quarterly, 31 (1975), 21-32.

254 BINGHA, Hiram. A Residence of Twenty Years in the Sandwich Islands. New York: Converse, 1847. Reprinted New York: Praeger, 1969.

255 BIRD, Christine M. "Melville's Debt to Cooper's Sea Novels." Ph.D. diss., Tulane, 1972. DA, 33 (1973), 4332A.

256 BIRDSALL, Richard D. "Berkshire's Golden Age." American Quarterly, 8 (Winter, 1956), 328-355.

257 BIRRELL, Augustine. "The Great White Whale." Athenaeum (London), January 28, 1921. Pp. 99-100.

258 ________. "Immortal White Whale." Living Age, 308 (March 12, 1921), 659-661. Reprinted in Gay, Robert Malcolm, ed., Fact, Fancy, and Opinion. Boston: Little, Brown, 1923. Pp. 47-51.

259 BIRSS, John Howard. "Melville's Marquesas." Saturday Review of Literature, 8 (January 2, 1932), 429.

260 ________. "Letter of Tribute to James Fenimore Cooper from Melville." Notes and Queries, 162 (January 16, 1932), 39.

261 ________. "A Book Review of Herman Melville." New England Quarterly, 5 (April, 1932), 346-348. Review of Cooper's The Red Rover.

262 ________. "A Note on Melville's Mardi." Notes and Queries, 162 (June 4, 1932), 404.

263 ________. "An Obscure Melville Letter." Notes and Queries, 163 (October 15, 1932), 275.

264 ________. "Moby Dick Under Another Name." Notes and Queries, 164 (March 25, 1933), 206. Refers to a pamphlet, Pehe Nûe, The Tiger Whale of the Pacific; contains a picture of Moby-Dick.

265 ________. "Whitman and Herman Melville." Notes and Queries, 164 (April 22, 1933), 280.

266 ________. "A Satire on Melville in Verse." Notes and Queries, 165 (December 9, 1933), 402.

267 ________. "Herman Melville Lectures in Yonkers." American Book Collector, 5 (February, 1934), 50-52.

268 ________. "Herman Melville and Blake." Notes and Queries, 166 (May 5, 1934), 311.

269 ________. "Herman Melville and the Atlantic Monthly." Notes and Queries, 167 (September 29, 1934), 223-224.

270 ________. "'Travelling': A New Lecture by Herman Melville." New England Quarterly, 7 (December, 1934), 725-728.

271 ________. "International Copyright: A New Letter of Herman Melville." Notes and Queries, 173 (December 4, 1937), 402.

272 ________. "Melville and James Thomson ('B. V.')." Notes and Queries, 174 (March 5, 1938), 171-172.

273 ________. "Toward the Whole Evidence on Melville as a Lecturer." American Notes and Queries, 3 (April, 1943), 11-12.

274 ________. "'The Story of Toby,' a Sequel to Typee." Harvard Library Bulletin, 1 (Winter, 1947), 118-119.

275 ________. "Another, but Later, Redburn." American Notes and Queries, 6 (January, 1947), 150.

276 ________. "'A Mere Sale to Effect,' with Letters of Herman Melville." New Colophon, 1 (July, 1948), 239-255. Letters of 1846-1852.

277 BIXBY, William. Rebel Genius: The Life of Herman Melville. New York: McKay, 1970.

278 BLACK, Stephen Ames. "On Reading Psychoanalytically." College English, 39 (1977), 267-274. Teaching Moby-Dick.

279 BLACK, Walter E. "Failure Redeemed: Melville's Reworkings of Mardi, Pierre, and Clarel." Ph.D. diss., Denver, 1972. DA, 34 (1973), 3334A.

280 BLACKMUR, Richard P. "The Craft of Herman Melville: A Putative Statement." Virginia Quarterly Review, 14 (Spring, 1938), 266-282. Also in Blackmur, The Expense

of Greatness. New York: Arrow, 1940. Pp. 139-166. Reprinted in Blackmur, The Lion and the Honeycomb: Essays in Solicitude and Critique. New York: Harcourt, Brace, 1955. Pp. 124-144. Also reprinted in Chase, Richard V., ed., Melville: A Collection (1962), pp. 75-90.

281 ______, ed. American Short Novels. New York: Crowell, 1960. Contains "Billy-Budd," with notes.

282 BLAIR, John G. "Puns and Equivocation in Melville's The Confidence-Man." American Transcendental Quarterly, 22 (1974), 91-95.

283 ______. The Confidence Man in Modern Fiction. New York: Barnes and Noble, 1979.

284 BLAKE, Nancy. "Mourning and Melancholia in 'Bartleby.'" Delta English Studies, 7 (1978), 155-168.

285 BLANCH, R. J. "Captain Ahab: The Outsider." The English Record, 18 (1967), 10-14.

286 BLANCK, Jacob. "News from the Rare Book Sellers." Publishers' Weekly, 152 (August 23, 1947), 122.

287 ______. Bibliography of American Literature, 6 vols. + . New Haven: Yale University Press, 1955--present. Melville, Vol. VI (1973), pp. 152-181. Lists primary source material.

288 BLANKENSHIP, Russell. American Literature as an Expression of the National Mind. New York: Holt, 1931. Reissued in a revised edition, New York: Holt, Rinehart, and Winston, 1958.

289 BLANSETT, Barbara Ruth Nieweg. "From Dark to Dark: Mardi, a Foreshadowing of Pierre." The Southern Quarterly, 1 (April, 1963), 213-227.

290 ______. "Melville and Emersonian Transcendentalism." Ph.D. diss., University of Texas, 1963. DA, 24 (1964), 2904.

291 BLAU, Richard M. "Melville in the Valley of the Bones." American Transcendental Quarterly, 10 (1971), 11-16.

292 ______. "The Body as Ground of Being in Four Novels of Herman Melville." Ph.D. diss., Yale, 1973. DA, 34 (1974), 7220A-7221A. Includes Typee, White-Jacket, Moby-Dick, and Pierre.

293 BLOOM, Edward. "The Allegorical Principle." English Literary History, 18 (1951), 163-190.

294 BLUEFARB, Sam. "The Sea-Mirror and Maker of Character in Fiction and Drama." English Journal, 48 (December, 1959), 501-510.

295 BLUESTEIN, Gene. The Voice of the Folk: Folklore and American Literary Theory. Amherst: University of Massachusetts Press, 1972. Melville, pp. 36-46.

296 ________. "The Brotherhood of Sinners: Literary Calvinism." New England Quarterly, 50 (1977), 195-213.

297 BLUESTONE, George, producer, and John Haag, actor. "Bartleby," a movie based on Melville's story, 1962.

298 ________. "Bartleby: The Tale and the Film," in Vincent, Howard P., ed., Melville Annual, No. 1 (1965), pp. 45-54.

299 BOAS, George. Romanticism in America (Baltimore: Johns Hopkins Univ. Press, 1940). Reprinted New York: Russell and Russell, 1961. Melville, passim.

300 BOBB, Earl Victor. "Education, the Protagonist, and the Nature of Knowledge in Melville and Twain." Ph.D. diss., University of Oregon, 1977. DA, 38 (1977), 3495A-3496A.

301 BODE, Carl. The Half-World of American Culture. Preface by C. P. Snow. Carbondale: Southern Illinois University Press, 1965. "Foreign Parts and Exotic Places: 1840-1860," pp. 33-53.

302 ________, ed. The Young Rebel in American Literature: Seven Lectures. London: Heinemann, 1959; New York: Praeger, 1959.

303 BOGGS, John C., Jr. "Modern Egotism and Melville's Imagery: Effects of a Naturalistic Perspective on Symbolic Relationships in the Prose Fiction of Herman Melville." Ph.D. diss., Columbia, 1970. DA, 32 (1971), 421A.

304 BOHRER, Rand Edward. "The Universal Cannibalism of the Seas: The Development of Melville's Mythology of Alienation." Ph.D. diss., Yale, 1976. DA, 37 (1977), 4349A.

305 BOIES, Jack Jay. "Herman Melville: Nihilist." Ph.D. diss., University of Wisconsin, 1959. DA, 20 (1959), 1022-1023.

306 ________. "Existential Nihilism and Herman Melville." Transactions of the Wisconsin Academy of Science, Arts, and Letters, 50 (1961), 307-320.

307 ________. "The Whale Without Epilogue." Modern Language Quarterly, 24 (1963), 172-176.

308 ———. "Melville's Quarrel with Anglicanism." *Emerson Society Quarterly*, 33 (1963), 75-79.

309 ———. "Sailor's Snug Harbor." *Extracts*, 14 (1973), 2-3.

310 BOLITHO, Hector, and John Mulgan. "Wainewright and Herman Melville," in *Emigrants: Early Travellers to the Antipodes*. New York: Selwyn and Blount, 1939. Pp. 155-167.

311 BOLLAS, Christopher Kim. "Melville's Lost Self: 'Bartleby.'" *American Imago*, 31 (1974), 401-411. Reprinted in Tennenhouse, Leonard, ed., *The Practice of Psychoanalytic Criticism*. Detroit: Wayne State University Press, 1976. Pp. 226-236.

312 ———. "Melville's Man: The Character of Breakdown." Ph.D. diss., State University of New York (Buffalo), 1977. *DA*, 38 (1977), 1385A.

313 BOLLER, Paul F., Jr. *American Transcendentalism, 1830-1860: An Intellectual Inquiry*. New York: Putnam, 1974. Melville, pp. 139-140 and passim; Melville and Emerson, pp. 164-167.

314 BOLLINGER, Lee C. "The Homer of the Pacific: Melville's Art and the Ambiguities of Judging Evil." *Michigan Law Review*, 75 (1977), 823-844. Discusses three books on judicial injustice. See also work by Robert M. Cover (1975).

315 BOND, William H. "Melville and *Two Years Before the Mast*." *Harvard Library Bulletin*, 7 (1953), 362-365.

316 *BOOKS AT BROWN*, 24 (1971). Special Melville issue.

317 BOOTH, Edward Townsend. *God Made the Country*. New York: Knopf, 1946. "Berkshire Loam: Melville," pp. 220-245.

318 BOOTH, Thornton Y. "*Moby-Dick*: Standing Up to God." *Nineteenth-Century Fiction*, 17 (June, 1962), 33-43.

319 BOOTH, Wayne C. *The Rhetoric of Fiction*. Chicago: University of Chicago Press, 1961. Melville's "Billy-Budd," pp. 156-215.

320 BORGES, Jorge Luis. "Prologue to Herman Melville's 'Bartleby.'" *Review*, 17 (1976), 24-25.

321 BORTON, John. "Herman Melville: The Philosophical Implications of Literary Techniques in *Moby-Dick*." Amherst College Honors Thesis, No. 6, Amherst, Massachusetts, 1961.

322 BOUDREAU, Gordon V. "Herman Melville: Master Mason of the Gothic." Ph.D. diss., Indiana University, 1967. DA, 28 (1968), 5007A-5008A.

323 ________. "Of Pale Ushers and Gothic Piles: Melville's Architectural Symbology." Emerson Society Quarterly, 18 (1972), 67-82.

324 BOWDEN, Edwin. The Dungeon of the Heart: Human Isolation and the American Novel. New York: Macmillan, 1961. Melville, pp. 156-172.

325 BOWEN, James K. "Crazy Ahab and Kierkegaard's Melancholy Fantastic." Research Studies, 40 (March, 1969), 60-64.

326 ________. "Alienation and Withdrawal Are Not the Absurd: Renunciation and Preference in 'Bartleby the Scrivener.'" Studies in Short Fiction, 8 (1971), 633-635.

327 ________. "England's 'Bachelors' and America's 'Maids': Melville on Withdrawal and Sublimation." Revue des Langues Vivantes, 38 (1972), 631-634.

328 ________, and Richard Vanderbeets, compilers. A Critical Guide to Herman Melville. Glenview, Ill. Scott, Foresman, 1971. Abstracts 40 years of Melville criticism.

329 BOWEN, Merlin R. "Redburn and the Angle of Vision." Modern Philology, 52 (November, 1954), 100-109.

330 ________. "Self and Experience in the Writings of Herman Melville." Ph.D. diss., University of Chicago, 1957.

331 ________. The Long Encounter: Self and Experience in the Writings of Herman Melville. Chicago: University of Chicago Press, 1960.

332 ________. "Tactics of Indirection in Melville's The Confidence-Man." Studies in the Novel, 1 (Winter, 1969), 401-420.

333 ________, ed. Redburn. New York: Rinehart, Winston, 1971. Rinehart edition.

334 BOWMAN, David H., and Ruth L. Bohan. "Herman Melville's Mardi: A Voyage Thither: An Annotated Checklist of Criticism." Resources for American Literary Study, 3 (1973), 27-72. Lists published criticism, 1849-1971.

335 BOYNTON, Percy H. Contemporary Americans. Chicago: University of Chicago Press, 1924. Melville, passim.

336 ________. More Contemporary Americans. Chicago: University of Chicago Press, 1927. Melville, pp. 29-50. Revised and reprinted as Literature and American Life.

337 BRACK, O. M., Jr., ed. American Humor: Essays Presented to John C. Gerber. Scottsdale, Ariz.: Arete, 1977. "Melville's The Confidence-Man: A Structure of Satire," by Alexander Kern, pp. 27-41.

338 BRACK, Vida K., and O. M. Brack. "Weathering Cape Horn: Survivors in Melville's Minor Short Fiction." Arizona Quarterly, 28 (1972), 61-73.

339 BRADLEY, Donald W. "Character as Thematic Embodiment in the Fiction of Herman Melville." Ph.D. diss., University of California (Riverside), 1973. DA, 35 (1974), 440A-441A.

340 BRADT, David R. "From Fiction to Film: An Analysis of Aesthetic and Cultural Implications in the Adaptations of Two American Novellas." Ph.D. diss., Washington State, 1973. DA, 35 (1974), 3671A-3672A. Refers to "Billy-Budd" and Miss Lonelyhearts.

341 BRANCH, E. Douglas. The Sentimental Years: 1836-1860. New York: Appleton-Century, 1934. Melville, passim.

342 BRANCH, Watson G. "The Confidence Man: His Masquerade: An Edition with Introduction and Notes." Ph.D. diss., Northwestern, 1970. DA, 31 (1971), 3496A.

343 ________. "The Mute as 'Metaphysical Scamp,'" in Parker, ed., The Confidence-Man (1971), pp. 316-319.

344 ________. "An Annotated Bibliography of Melville's The Confidence-Man," in Parker, ed., The Confidence-Man (1971), pp. 363-376.

345 ________. "The Genesis, Composition, and Structure of The Confidence-Man." Nineteenth-Century Fiction, 7 (1973), 424-448.

346 ________. "Melville's 'Incompetent' World in Billy-Budd, Sailor." Melville Society Extracts, 34 (1978), 1-2.

347 ________, ed. Melville: The Critical Heritage. London and Boston: Routledge and Kegan Paul, 1974. Invaluable collection of reviews and notices of Melville's works when they were published.

348 BRANDES, Georg. Main Currents in Nineteenth-Century Literature, 6 vols. New York: Macmillan, 1904. American literature not discussed; listed as source for English and European background material.

349 BRASHERS, H. C. "Ishmael's Tattoos." Sewanee Review, 70 (Winter, 1962), 137-154.

350 BRASWELL, William. "A Note on 'The Anatomy of Melville's Fame.'" American Literature, 5 (January, 1934), 360-364. Refers to an article by O. W. Riegel (1931).

351 ______. "Herman Melville and Christianity." Ph.D. diss., University of Chicago, 1934.

352 ______. "The Satirical Temper of Melville's Pierre." American Literature, 7 (January, 1936), 424-438.

353 ______. "Melville as a Critic of Emerson." American Literature, 9 (November, 1937), 317-334.

354 ______. "Melville's Use of Seneca in Mardi." American Literature, 12 (March, 1940), 98-104.

355 ______. Melville's Religious Thought: An Essay in Interpretation. Durham, N.C.: Duke University Press, 1943. Reprinted New York: Pageant, 1959.

356 ______. "The Early Love Scenes of Melville's Pierre." American Literature, 22 (November, 1950), 283-289.

357 ______. "Melville's Opinion of Pierre." American Literature, 23 (May, 1951), 246-250.

358 ______. "Melville's Billy-Budd as 'An Inside Narrative.'" American Literature, 29 (May, 1957), 133-146.

359 ______. "The Main Theme of Moby-Dick." Emerson Society Quarterly, 28 (1962), 15-17.

360 BRAUDE, W. G. "Melville's Moby-Dick." Explicator, 21 (November, 1962), item 23.

361 BRAUN, Julie A. "Spiritual Journey: Herman Melville's Use of Carlyle's Sartor Resartus, 1846-1857." Ph.D. diss., UCLA, 1967. DA, 28 (1968), 4622A.

362 BRAWLEY, Benjamin Griffith. "The Negro in Fiction." Dial, 60 (May 11, 1916), 445-450.

363 ______. The Negro in Literature and Art in the United States. New York: Duffield, 1929. Reprinted St. Clair Shores, Mich.: Scholarly Press, 1972. Melville, passim.

364 BRAY, Richard T. "Melville's Mardi: An Approach Through Imagery." Ph.D. diss., Wisconsin, 1969. DA, 30 (1970), 5401A.

365 BREDAHL. Axel Carl Jr. "Melville's Angles of Vision: The Function of Shifting Perspectives in the Novels of Herman

Melville." Ph.D. diss., Pittsburgh, 1979. *DA*, 31 (1970), 1263A.

366 ———. *Melville's Angles of Vision*. Gainesville: University of Florida Humanities Monograph, No. 37.

367 BREINIG, Helmbrecht. "The Destruction of Fairyland: Melville's *Piazza* in the Tradition of the American Imagination." *English Literary History*, 35 (June, 1968), 254-283.

368 ———. "Symbol, Satire, and the Will to Communicate in Melville's 'The Apple-Tree Table.'" *American Studies*, 22 (1977), 269-285.

369 BREIT, Harvey, et al. "*Moby-Dick*." *Invitation to Learning*, 2 (Spring, 1952), 41-47.

370 BRENT, Julia Deaner. "Thomas Carlyle and the American Renaissance: The Use of Sources and the Nature of Influence." Ph.D. diss., George Washington, 1975. *DA*, 36 (1975), 884A-885A.

371 BRIDGEMAN, Richard. "Melville's Roses." *Texas Studies in Literature and Language*, 8 (Summer, 1966), 235-244.

372 BRIGGS, C. F. *Working a Passage*. New York: John Allen, 1844. Reprinted New York: Garrett, 1970.

373 BRITTEN, Benjamin. *Billy-Budd: An Opera in Four Acts*. Libretto, E. M. Forster and Eric Crozier. London: Boosey and Hawkes, 1952; New York, 1953.

374 BRODHEAD, Richard H. "Polysensum: Hawthorne, Melville, and the Form of the Novel." Ph.D. diss., Yale, 1972. *DA*, 33 (1973), 6863A.

375 ———. *Hawthorne, Melville, and the Novel*. Chicago: University of Chicago Press, 1976. "The Uncommon Long Cable: *Moby-Dick*," pp. 134-162; "The Fate of Candor," pp. 163-193.

376 ———. "*Mardi*: Creating the Creative," in Pullin, ed., *Perspectives* (1978), pp. 29-53.

377 BRODTKORB, Paul, Jr. "Melville's Symbology." Ph.D. diss., Yale, 1963.

378 ———. *Ishmael's White World: A Phenomenological Reading of Moby-Dick*. New Haven: Yale University Press, 1965.

379 ———. "The Definitive *Billy-Budd*: 'But Aren't It All Sham?'" *PMLA*, 82 (December, 1967), 602-612.

380 ________. "The Confidence Man: The Con Man as Hero." Studies in the Novel, 1 (Winter, 1969), 421-435.

381 BRODWIN, Stanley. "Herman Melville's Clarel: An Existential Gospel." PMLA, 86 (1971), 375-387.

382 ________. "Melville's Clarel, continued." PMLA, 87 (1972), 310-312. A reply to Chamberlain, PMLA, January, 1972.

383 BROOKS, Cleanth, and Robert Penn Warren. Understanding Poetry, 4th edition. Holt, Rinehart, and Winston, 1976. Melville poems, pp. 125, 170, 238.

384 ________, et al., eds. An Approach to Literature, 3rd edition. New York: Appleton-Century, 1952. Melville poem, "Commemorative of a Naval Battle," pp. 344-345.

385 BROOKS, Van Wyck. "A Reviewer's Notebook" (column). Freeman, 4 (October 26, 1921 and December 21, 1921), 166-167, 358-359.

385a ________. "A Reviewer's Notebook." Freeman, 6 (February 14, 1923), 550-551.

386 ________. "A Reviewer's Notebook." Freeman, 7 (May 9, May 16, and May 30, 1923), 214-215, 238-239, and 286-287.

387 ________. Emerson and Others. London: Cape; New York: Dutton, 1927. Melville, pp. 171-205.

388 ________. The Flowering of New England: 1815-1865. New York: Dutton, 1937. Melville, passim.

389 ________. The World of Washington Irving. New York: Dutton, 1944. Melville, passim.

390 ________. "Melville in the Berkshires." Tiger's Eye, 1 (October, 1947), 47-52.

391 ________. The Times of Melville and Whitman. New York: Dutton, 1947. "Melville, the Traveller," pp. 142-161; Everyman's Library edition, pp. 145-164. "Melville in the Berkshires," pp. 162-175; Everyman's Library edition, pp. 165-179. "After the Civil War," pp. 234-257; Everyman's Library edition, pp. 241-265.

392 ________, ed. Omoo. New York: Heritage, 1967.

393 BROPHY, Robert J. "Benito Cereno, Oakum, and Hatchets." American Transcendental Quarterly, 1 (1969), 89-90.

394 BROUWER, Fred E. "Melville's The Confidence-Man as Ship

of Philosophers." Southern Humanities Review, 3 (Spring, 1969), 158-165.

395 BROWER, K. "Moby-Dick, Man, and Environment," in Schwartz, W., ed., Voices for the Wilderness. New York: Ballantine, 1969. Pp. 176-178.

396 BROWN, Cecil M. "The White Whale." Partisan Review, 36 (1969), 453-459.

397 BROWN, E. K. "Hawthorne, Melville, and 'Ethan Brand.'" American Literature, 3 (March, 1931), 72-75.

398 BROWN, Herbert Ross. The Sentimental Novel in America: 1789-1860. Durham, N.C.: Duke University Press, 1940. Melville, passim.

399 BROWN, James Temple. "Whalemen, Vessels, Apparatus and Methods of the Whale Fishery," in The Fisheries and Fishing Industries of the United States, 4 vols. ed. by George Brown Goode. Washington, D.C.: United States Government Printing Office, 1884-1887. Section 5, Vol. II, 218-293.

400 ________. "Stray Leaves from a Whaleman's Log." Century Magazine, 45 (February, 1893), 507-517. Excerpt reprinted in McCormick, ed., Life on a Whaler (1960), pp. 94-98.

401 BROWN, John Mason. "Review of the play Billy-Budd." Saturday Review of Literature, 28 (March 17, 1951), 3.

402 ________. "Hanged from the Yardarm," in As They Appear. New York: McGraw-Hill, 1952. Pp. 186-192. Compares Melville's work with the play.

403 BROWN, Sterling A. The Negro in American Fiction. Washington, D.C.: Association of Negro Folk Education, 1937. "Benito Cereno," pp. 11-13.

404 ________. "A Century of Negro Portraiture in American Literature." Massachusetts Review, 7 (Winter, 1966), 72-97.

405 BROWNE, J. Ross. Etchings of a Whaling Cruise, with Notes of a Sojourn on the Island of Zanzibar. To Which Is Appended a Brief History of the Whale Fishery, Its Past and Present Condition. New York: Harper Brothers, 1846. Reprinted New York: Harper and Row, 1972. Excerpt reprinted in McCormick, ed., Life on a Whaler (1960), pp. 45-52.

406 BROWNE, Ray Broadus. "Billy-Budd: Gospel of Democracy." Nineteenth-Century Fiction, 17 (March, 1963), 321-337.

407 ______. "Popular Theater in Moby-Dick," in Browne, Donald M. Winkleman, and Allen Hayman, eds., New Voices in American Studies. West Lafayette, Ind.: Purdue University Press, 1966. Pp. 89-101.

408 ______. "The Affirmation of 'Bartleby,'" in Wilgus, D. K., ed., Folklore International: Essays in Traditional Literature, Belief, and Custom in Honor of Wayland Hand. Hatboro, Pa.: Folklore Associates, 1967. Pp. 11-21.

409 ______. "Israel Potter: Metamorphosis of Superman," in Browne, ed., Frontiers of American Culture. West Lafayette, Ind.: Purdue University Press, 1968. Pp. 88-98.

410 ______. "Two Views of Commitment: 'The Paradise of Bachelors' and 'The Tartarus of Maids.'" American Transcendental Quarterly, 7 (1970), 43-47.

411 ______. Melville's Drive to Humanism. West Lafayette, Ind.: Purdue University Press, 1971.

412 ______. "Whalelore and Popular Print in Mid-Nineteenth Century America: Sketches Toward a Profile," in Salzman, Jack, ed., Prospects: Annual of the American Cultural Studies, Vol. I. New York: Franklin, 1975. Pp. 29-40.

413 ______, and Donald Pizer, eds., Themes and Directions in American Literature: Essays in Honor of Leon Howard. West Lafayette, Ind.: Purdue Research Foundation, 1969. "Ishmael, Writer and Art Critic," by Howard P. Vincent, pp. 69-79.

414 BRUCCOLI, Matthew J., ed. The Profession of Authorship in America, 1800-1870: The Papers of William Charvat. Columbus: Ohio State University Press, 1968. "Melville," by William Charvat, pp. 204-261.

415 ______, ed. The Chief Glory of Every People: Essays on Classic American Writers. Carbondale: Southern Illinois University Press, 1973. "Herman Melville, 1972," by Jay Leyda, pp. 161-171.

416 BRUMM, Ursula. "The Figure of Christ in American Literature." Partisan Review, 24 (Summer, 1957), 403-413.

417 ______. American Thought and Religious Typology, trans. by John Hoaglund. New Brunswick, N.J.: Rutgers University Press, 1970. "Herman Melville: 'The Lexicon of Holy Writ,'" pp. 162-187; "Herman Melville: The Terminology of the Symbolic Connections," pp. 187-197.

418 BRUNER, Margaret R. "The Gospel According to Herman Melville: A Reading of The Confidence Man: His Masquerade." Ph.D. diss., Vanderbilt, 1971. DA, 32 (1972), 6368A.

419 BUCHLOH, Paul Gerhard, and Hartmut Kruger, eds. Herman Melville: A Collection of Criticism. Darmstadt, Germany: Wissenschaftliche Buchgesellschaft, 1974. 470 pages of critical essays, all but one in English.

420 BUCHO, Luella M. "Melville and Captain Delano's Narrative of Voyages: The Appeal of the Preface." American Notes and Queries, 16 (1978), 157-160.

421 BUCKLEY, Vincent. "The White Whale as Hero." Melbourne Critical Review, 9 (1966), 3-21.

422 BUELL, Lawrence. The Last Word on The Confidence-Man." Illinois Quarterly, 35 (1972), 15-29.

423 _______. Literary Transcendentalism: Style and Vision in the American Renaissance. Ithaca, N.Y.: Cornell University Press, 1973. Melville, passim.

424 BULLEN, Frank T. The Cruise of the "Cachalot" Round the World After Sperm Whales. New York: Appleton-Century, 1899. Excerpt reprinted in McCormick, ed., Life on a Whaler (1960), pp. 1-38.

425 BUNGERT, Hans. "William Faulkner on Moby-Dick: An Early Letter." Studi Americani (Rome, Italy), 9 (1964), 371-375.

426 BURBANK, Rex, and Jack B. Moore, eds. The Literature of the American Renaissance: An Anthology. Columbus, Ohio: Merrill, 1969. Includes Melville, poetry, pp. 222-243 with notes; fiction, pp. 336-378 with notes.

427 BURGESS, Robert H. "Whalers, Whales, and Pigs: A Sea Superstition." Extracts, 15 (1973), 10-11.

428 _______. "'The Sea Serpent' Meets the 'Corinthian.'" Extracts, 17 (1974), 11.

429 BURKE, Kenneth. "'Ethan Brand': A Preparatory Investigation." Hopkins Review, 5 (Winter, 1952), 45-65.

430 BURNAM, Tom. "Tennyson's 'Ringing Grooves' and Captain Ahab's Grooved Soul." Modern Language Notes, 68 (June, 1952), 423-424.

431 BURNS, Graham. "The Unshored World of Moby-Dick." Melbourne Critical Review, 13 (1970), 68-83.

432 BURNS, Nancy Schreiber. "Crises of Confidence: A Study of the Confidence Man as Metaphor in Melville's Novels." Ph.D. diss., Claremont Graduate School, 1978. DA, 39 (1978), 1561A.

433 BURNS, Robert A. "Moby-Dick: Cannibalism and 'The Mystery.'" Extracts: An Occasional Newsletter, 24 (1975), 5-7.

434 BURNSHAW, Stanley, ed. Varieties of Literary Experience. New York: New York University Press, 1962. "Moby-Dick: An Hamitic Dream," by Edward Dahlberg, pp. 183-213.

435 BUSCH, Frederick. "The Whale as Shaggy Dog: Melville and 'The Man Who Studied Yoga.'" Modern Fiction Studies, 19 (1973), 193-206.

436 ______. "Thoreau and Melville as Cellmates." Modern Fiction Studies, 23 (1977), 239-242. A study of "Bartleby" and "Civil Disobedience."

437 BUSH, C. W. "The Stupendous Fabric: The Metaphysics of Order in Melville's Pierre and Nathanael West's Miss Lonelyhearts." Journal of American Studies (Manchester, England), 1 (October, 1967), 269-274.

438 BUSH, Oakleigh R., ed. Over the Carnage Rose Prophetic a Voice: The American Civil War in Prose and Verse. Bossum, Netherlands: Paul Brand, 1965. Title quotation is from Whitman; contains material from Whitman and Melville.

439 BUTLER, John F. Exercises in Literary Understanding. Chicago: Scott, Foresman, 1956. Melville, pp. 22-25.

440 CABAS, Victor Nicholas, Jr. "The Broken Staff: A Generic Study of the Problem of Authority in Beowulf, The Tempest, and Moby-Dick." State University of New York, 1975. DA, 36 (1976), 6654A.

441 CAHALAN, James Fee. "A Concordance to Herman Melville's Moby-Dick." Ph.D. diss., University of Pennsylvania, 1977. DA, 39 (1978), 1561A-1562A.

442 CAHOON, Herbert. "Herman Melville and W. H. Hudson." American Notes and Queries, 8 (December, 1949), 131-132.

443 ______. "Herman Melville: A Checklist of Books and Manuscripts in the Collection of the New York Public Library." Bulletin of the New York Public Library, 55 (June and July, 1951), 264-275, 325-338.

444 ______, Thomas V. Lange, and Charles Ryskamp, compilers. American Literary Autographs: From Washington Irving to Henry James. New York: Dover, 1977. Melville, p. 55.

445 CAIRNS, William B. A History of American Literature. New York and London: Oxford University Press, 1912. Melville, pp. 368-370.

446 CALHOUN, Dorothy C. "Typee: A Fifteen Minute Radio Play," in Kozlenko, William, ed., One Hundred Non-Royalty One-Act Plays. New York: Greenbury, 1940.

447 CALLAN, Richard J. "The Burden of Innocence in Melville and Mark Twain." Renascence, 17 (1965), 191-194.

448 CALLOW, James T., and Robert J. Reilly. Guide to American Literature from Its Beginnings Through Walt Whitman. New York: Barnes and Noble, 1976. Contains long bibliography.

449 CAMBON, Glauco. "Ishmael and the Problem of Formal Discontinuities in Moby-Dick." Modern Language Notes, 76 (June, 1961), 516-523.

450 _______. "Space, Experiment, and Prophecy," in Cambon, The Inclusive Flame: Studies in Modern American Poetry. Bloomington: Indiana University Press, 1963. Melville's poetry, pp. 3-52. Original Italian publication in 1956.

451 CAMERON, Kenneth Walter. "More Grist for Melville's Moby-Dick." Emerson Society Quarterly, 1 (1955), 7-8. Hereafter ESQ in Cameron listings.

452 _______. "Billy-Budd and an Execution at Sea." ESQ, 2 (1956), 13-15. Reprints article of 19th Century.

453 _______. "A Note on the Corpusants in Moby-Dick." ESQ, 19 (1960), 22-24.

454 _______. "Emerson and Melville Lecture in New Haven, 1856-1857." ESQ, 19 (1960), 85-96.

455 _______. "Etymological Significance of Melville's Pequod." ESQ, 29 (1962), 3-4.

456 _______. "Melville's Oath as Inspector of Customs, 1866." ESQ, 47 (1967), 129. Reproduction of document.

457 _______. "Melville, Cooper, Irving, and Bryant on International Matters." ESQ, 51 (1968), 112.

458 _______. "Scattered Melville Manuscripts." American Transcendental Quarterly, 1 (1969), 63-64. Hereafter ATQ in Cameron listings.

459 _______. "A Melville Letter and Stray Books from His Library." ESQ, 63 (1971), 47-49.

460 _______. "Starbuck, Moby, and the Wreck of the Ann Alexander." ATQ, 14 (1972), 99-100. Reproduces Boston Daily Evening Traveller, November 3, 1851, news story of sinking of the ship.

461 _______. "Uncollected Melville Letter." ATQ, 14 (1972), 111.

462 _______. "Another Newspaper Anticipation of Billy-Budd." ATQ, 14 (1972), 167-168. See also item above. Reproduces an account of an execution at sea, 1846.

463 _______. "Broadside of 'Billy in the Darbies.'" ATQ, 19 (1973), 42.

464 _______. "Melville and National Matters." ATQ, 20 (1973), 183-192. See similar item above.

465 CAMP, James Edwin. "An Unfulfilled Romance: Image, Symbol, and Allegory in Herman Melville's Clarel." Ph.D. diss., University of Michigan, 1965. DA, 27 (1966), 472A.

466 CAMPBELL, Harry Modean. "The Hanging Scene in Melville's Billy-Budd." Modern Language Notes, 64 (June, 1951), 378-381.

467 _______. "The Hanging Scene in Billy-Budd: A Reply to Mr. Giovannini." Modern Language Notes, 70 (November, 1955), 497-500.

468 CAMPBELL, Marie A. "A Quiet Crusade: Melville's Tales of the Fifties." American Transcendental Quarterly, 7 (1970), 8-12.

469 CAMUS, Albert. "Herman Melville," in Camus, Lyrical and Critical Essays, ed. with Notes by Philip Thody; trans. from French by Ellen Conroy Kennedy. New York: Knopf, 1968. Pp. 288-294.

470 CANADAY, Nicholas, Jr. "Herman Melville and Authority: A Study of Thematic Unity." Ph.D. diss., University of Florida, 1957. DA, 17 (1957), 2007.

471 _______. "A New Reading of Melville's Benito Cereno," in McNeir, Waldo, and Leo B. Levy, eds., Studies in American Literature. Baton Rouge: Louisiana University Press, 1960. Pp. 49-57.

472 _______. "The Theme of Authority in Melville's Omoo and Typee." Ball State University Forum, 4 (Fall, 1963), 38-41.

473 _______. Melville and Authority. Gainesville: University of

Florida Press, 1968. University of Florida Humanities Monograph.

474 ________. "Melville's Pierre: At War with Social Convention." Papers on Language and Literature, 5 (1969), 51-62.

475 ________. "Harry Bolton and Redburn: The Old World and New," in Kirby, Thomas A. and William J. Olive, eds., Essays in Honor of Esmond Linworth Marilla. Baton Rouge: Louisiana State University Press, 1970. Pp. 291-298.

476 ________. "Melville's 'The Encantadas': The Deceptive Enchantment of the Absolute." Papers on Language and Literature, 10 (1974), 58-69.

477 CANBY, Henry Seidel. "Conrad and Melville." Literary Review, 2 (1922), 383-394. Reprinted in Canby, Definitions, First Series: Essays in Contemporary Criticism. New York: Harcourt, Brace, 1922. Pp. 257-268.

478 ________. Classic Americans: Eminent American Writers from Irving to Whitman. New York: Harcourt, Brace, 1931. Reprinted New York: Russell and Russell, 1959. Chapter 6, "Hawthorne and Melville," pp. 226-262.

479 CANFIELD, Francis X. "Herman Melville's Vision of Conflict." Ph.D. diss., Ottaway, 1951.

480 ________. "Moby-Dick and the Book of Job." Catholic World, 174 (January, 1952), 254-260.

481 CANNADY, Joan, ed. Black Images in American Literature. New Rochelle, N.Y.: Hayden, 1977. Contains "Benito Cereno," with Introduction and notes.

482 CANNON, Agnes Dicken. "Melville's Use of Sea Ballads and Songs." Western Folklore, 23 (January, 1964), 1-16.

483 ________. "Melville's Concept of the Poet and Poetry." Ph.D. diss., University of Pennsylvania, 1968. DA, 29 (1969), 2207A.

484 ________. "Melville's Concept of the Poet and Poetry." Arizona Quarterly, 31 (1975), 315-339.

485 ________. "On Translating Clarel," in Robillard, ed., Symposium on Melville's Poetry (1976), pp. 160-180.

486 CANNON, Margaret H. "The Sole Survivor: A Romantic Motif." Ph.D. diss., University of North Carolina (Chapel Hill), 1970. DA, 31 (1971), 6004A-6005A.

487 CARABER, Andrew J., Jr. "Melville's The Confidence-Man." Explicator, 29 (1970), item 9.

488 CARDWELL, Guy A. "Melville's Gray Story: Symbols and Meaning in Benito-Cereno." Bucknell Review, 8 (May, 1959), 154-167.

489 _______. "A Surprising World: Amasa Delano in Kentucky." Mark Twain Journal, 16 (1973), 12-13.

490 CARGILL, Oscar. Intellectual America: Ideas on the March. New York: Macmillan, 1941. Melville, passim.

491 CARLISLE, Ervin Frederick. "Captain Amasa Delano: Melville's American Fool." Criticism, 7 (Fall, 1965), 349-362.

492 CARLSON, Thomas G. "1. Melville's Fictive Voices Before Moby-Dick. 2. The Othello of Edwin Booth: A Reassessment. 3. The Political Theme in Shakespeare's The Tempest." Ph.D. diss., Rutgers, 1971. DA, 33 (1972), 1675A-1676A.

493 _______. "Who's Afraid of Moby-Dick? An Approach to Teaching Ishmael's Autobiography." Interpretations, 5 (1973), 10-19.

494 _______. "Ishmael as Art Critic: Double Metrical Irony in Moby-Dick." Extracts, 20 (1974), 2-4.

495 _______. "Fictive Voices in Melville's Reviews, Letters, and Prefaces." Interpretations, 6 (1974), 39-46.

496 CAROTHERS, Robert L. "Melville's Cenci: A Portrait of Pierre." Ball State University Forum, 10 (1969), 53-59.

497 _______. "Herman Melville and the Search for the Father: An Interpretation of the Novels." Ph.D. diss., Kent State, 1969. DA, 30 (1970), 4445A.

498 _______, and John L. Marsh. "The Whale and the Panorama." Nineteenth-Century Fiction, 26 (1971), 319-328.

499 CARPENTER, Frederick Ives. "Puritans Preferred Blonds: The Heroines of Melville and Hawthorne." New England Quarterly, 9 (June, 1936), 253-272.

500 _______. "Melville: The World in a Man-of-War." University of Kansas City Review, 19 (Summer, 1953), 257-264.

501 _______. American Literature and the Dream. New York: Philosophical Library, 1955. Melville, pp. 73-82, 203-205.

502 CARTER, Angela. "Redburn: His First Voyage." Antigonish Review, 1 (1970), 103-105.

503 CARTER, Everett. The American Idea: The Literary Response to American Optimism. Chapel Hill: University of North Carolina Press, 1977. Melville, pp. 176-196.

504 CARUSO, Domenick. "A Contemporary Re-Creation of Moby-Dick: An Approach to Creative Writing." Ph.D. diss., New York University, 1975. DA, 36 (1976), 8031A.

505 CASPER, Leonard. "The Case Against Captain Vere." Perspective, 5 (Summer, 1952), 146-152.

506 CATE, Herma R. "Shakers in American Fiction." Tennessee Folklore Society Bulletin, 41 (1975), 19-24.

507 CAVANAUGH, Miriam Katherine. "The Romantic Hero in Byron, Hawthorne, and Melville." Ph.D. diss., University of Massachusetts, 1978. DA, 39 (1978), 1563A.

508 CAWELTI, John G. "Some Notes on the Structure of The Confidence-Man." American Literature, 29 (November, 1957), 278-288.

509 CECCHI, Emilio. "Two Notes on Melville." Sewanee Review, 68 (July-September, 1960), 398-406. First published in Italian: "Moby-Dick," 1931; Israel Potter, 1945.

510 CERVO, Nathan A. "Melville's Bartleby--Imago Dei." American Transcendental Quarterly, 14 (1972), 152-156.

511 CHABOT, C. Barry. "Melville's The Confidence-Man: A 'Poisonous' Reading." Psychoanalytic Review, 63 (1976), 571-585.

512 CHAFFEE, Patricia A. "The Lee Shore: Volition, Time, and Death in the Fiction of Herman Melville." Ph.D. diss., Indiana, 1971. DA, 32 (1972), 4556A.

513 ________. "The Kedron in Melville's Clarel." College Language Association Journal, 18 (March, 1975), 374-382.

514 ________. "Paradox in Mardi." American Transcendental Quarterly, 29 (1976), 80-83.

515 CHAMBERLAIN, Safford C. "Melville's Clarel." PMLA, 87 (1972), 103-104. Attacks Brodwin's article, PMLA, 1971.

516 CHANDLER, Alice. "The Name Symbolism of Captain Vere." Nineteenth Century Fiction, 21 (June, 1967), 86-89.

517 ________. "Captain Vere and the 'Tragedies of the Palace.'" Modern Fiction Studies, 13 (Summer, 1967), 259-261.

518 CHAPIN, Henry, ed. The Apple-Tree Table and Other Sketches. Princeton, N.J.: Princeton University Press, 1922.

519 _______, ed. John Marr and Other Poems. Princeton, N.J.: Princeton University Press, 1922.

520 CHAPMAN, Sara. "Melville and Saul Bellow in the Real World: Pierre and Augie March." West Virginia University Philological Papers, 18 (1971), 51-57.

521 CHARTERS, Ann. Olson/Melville: A Study in Affinity. Berkeley, Calif.: Oyez, 1971. Charles Olson criticism of Melville.

522 CHARVAT, William. "Melville's Income." American Literature, 15 (November, 1943), 251-261. Reprinted among other materials in Bruccoli, ed., The Profession of Authorship (1968), pp. 204-261.

523 _______. "James T. Fields and the Beginnings of Book Promotion, 1840-1855." Huntington Library Quarterly, 8 (1944), 75-94.

524 _______. "Melville and the Common Reader." Studies in Bibliography, 12 (1959), 41-57. Earlier version of article reprinted as "Melville," among other materials in Bruccoli, ed., The Profession of Authorship (1968), pp. 204-261.

525 CHASE, F. H. Lemuel Shaw. Boston: Houghton Mifflin, 1918. Refers to Judge Shaw, Melville's father-in-law.

526 CHASE, Owen. Narrative of the Most Extraordinary and Distressing Shipwreck of the Whaleship Essex. New York: Gilley, 1821. Edited by Bruce R. McElderry, and reprinted New York: Corinth, 1963.

527 CHASE, Richard V. "An Approach to Melville." Partisan Review, 14 (1947), 284-294. Reprinted in Zabel, Morton D., Literary Opinion in America, 3rd edition. New York: Harper and Row, 1962. Also reprinted in Malin, Irving, ed., Psychoanalysis and American Fiction. New York: Dutton, 1965. Pp. 111-120.

528 _______. "Dissent on Billy-Budd." Partisan Review, 15 (1948), 1212-1218.

529 _______. Quest for Myth. Baton Rouge: Louisiana State University Press, 1948. Reprinted New York: Greenwood, 1969.

530 _______. Herman Melville: A Critical Study. New York: Macmillan, 1949.

531 ______. "Melville's Confidence Man." Kenyon Review, 11 (Winter, 1949), 122-140.

532 ______. The American Novel and Its Tradition. Garden City, N.Y.: Doubleday, Anchor, 1957. "Melville and Moby-Dick," pp. 89-115. Reprinted in Anderson, Quentin, ed., The Proper Study. New York: St. Martins, 1962. Pp. 528-544. Also reprinted in Chase, ed., Melville: A Collection (1962), pp. 49-61.

533 ______, ed. Selected Tales and Poems by Herman Melville. New York: Holt, Rinehart, and Winston, 1950. Rinehart edition.

534 ______, ed. Melville: A Collection of Critical Essays. Englewood Cliffs, N.J.: Prentice-Hall, 1962.

535 CHASLES, Philarête. "Voyages rêals et fantastiques d'Herman Melville." Revue des deux mondes, (May 15, 1849), 541-570. In French.

536 ______. Anglo-American Literature and Manners, trans. from French by Donald MacLeon. New York: Scribner, 1852. Melville, pp. 118-146.

537 CHATFIELD, E. Hale. "Levels of Meaning in Melville's 'I and My Chimney.'" American Imago, 19 (Summer, 1962), 163-169.

538 CHEEVER, Rev. Henry T. The Whale and His Captors; or, The Whaleman's Adventures, and the Whale's Biography, As Gathered on the Homeward Cruise of the "Commodore Preble." New York: Harper and Brothers, 1850. Excerpt reprinted in McCormick, ed., Life on a Whaler (1960), pp. 62-64.

539 CHEIKEN, Miriam Quen. "Captain Vere: Darkness Made Visible." Arizona Quarterly, 34 (1978), 293-310.

540 CHESLER, Pearl Canick. "A Correspondent Coloring: Dickens and Melville in Their Time." Ph.D. diss., Columbia, 1973. DA, 37 (1976), 294A.

541 CHILDS, Charles D. "'Thar She Blows': Some Notes on American Whaling Pictures." Antiques, July, 1941. Pp. 20-23.

542 CHITTICK, V. L. O. "The Way Back to Melville: Sea Chart of a Literary Revival." Southwest Review, 40 (Summer, 1955), 238-248.

543 ______. "A Footnote to Tales of the Sea." Dalhousie Review, 36 (August, 1956), 275-278. Relates to Melville and "Song of Myself."

544 ________. "Haliburton Postscript I: Ring-Tailed Yankee." Dalhousie Review, 37 (Spring, 1957), 19-36.

545 CHITWOOD, William Oscar Jr. "Symbolism in Melville's Typee and Omoo." Ph.D. diss., University of Alabama, 1974. DA, 35 (1975), 7250A-7251A.

546 CHRISTENSEN, Kirsten H. "Primitivity, Development, and Isolation in Herman Melville's Works, Primarily Billy-Budd and Moby-Dick." Extracta (University of Copenhagen), 3 (1971), 55-60. Abstract of a longer article.

547 CHRISTY, Wallace McVay. "The Shock of Recognition: A Psycho-Literary Study of Hawthorne's Influence on Melville's Short Fiction." Ph.D. diss., Brown, 1970. DA, 31 (1971), 6543A.

548 CHUN, Woo Y. "Thought and Structure in Melville's Moby-Dick and His Later Works." Ph.D. diss., Ohio State, 1973. DA, 34 (1974), 7184A.

549 CHURCH, Albert. Whale Ships and Whaling. New York: Norton, 1938.

550 CIFELLI, Edward H. "Melville's Billy-Budd." Explicator, 31 (1973), item 60.

551 ________. "Billy-Budd: Boggy Ground to Build On." Studies in Short Fiction, 13 (1976), 463-469.

552 CLARK, Harry Hayden. "Changing Attitudes in Early American Literary Criticism," in Stovall, Floyd, ed., The Development of American Literary Criticism. Chapel Hill: University of North Carolina Press, 1955. Melville and others, pp. 15-73.

553 ________. American Literature: Poe Through Garland. New York: Appleton-Century-Crofts, 1971. Melville, pp. 65-73.

554 CLARK, Marden J. "Blending Cadences: Rhythm and Structure in Moby-Dick." Studies in the Novel, 8 (1976), 158-171. E. M. Forster's concept of larger rhythms.

555 CLARK, Michael. "Melville's Typee: Fact, Fiction, and Esthetics." Arizona Quarterly, 34 (1978), 351-370.

556 CLARKE, Katherine Ann. "'Pour saluer Melville,' Jean Giono's Prison Book." French Review, 35 (1962), 478-483. In English.

557 CLAVERING, Rose. "The Conflict Between the Individual and Social Forces in Herman Melville's Works: Typee to Moby-Dick." Ph.D. diss., New York University, 1954. DA, 18 (1958), 2137-2138.

558 CLAYCOMBE, Julia R. "Carlo: The 'Third Twin' in Melville's *Redburn*." *Extracts*, 27 (1976), 10-12.

559 CLIVE, Geoffrey. "'Teleological Suspension of the Ethical' in Nineteenth-Century Literature." *Journal of Religion*, 34 (April, 1954), 75-87. Reprinted in shorter form in Clive, *The Romantic Enlightenment*. New York: Meridian, 1960. Pp. 161-165.

560 CLUBB, M. D. "The Second Personal Pronoun in *Moby-Dick*." *American Speech*, 35 (December, 1960), 252-260.

561 COAN, Titus. *Life in Hawaii ... 1835-1881*. New York: Randolph, 1882.

562 COCHRAN, Robert. "Babo's Name in 'Benito Cereno': An Unnecessary Controversy?" *American Literature*, 48 (1976), 217-219.

563 COCKCROFT, George P. "The Two Herman Melville's." Ph.D. diss., Columbia, 1964.

564 CODMAN, John. *Sailor's Life and Sailor's Yarns*. New York: Francis, 1847.

565 COHEN, Hennig. "Wordplay on Personal Names in the Writings of Herman Melville." *Tennessee Studies in Literature*, 8 (1963), 85-97.

566 ________. "Melville and Webster's *The White Devil*." *Emerson Society Quarterly*, 33 (1963), 33.

567 ________. "New Melville Letters: Four Letters to Julius Rockwell of Pittsfield." *American Literature*, 38 (January, 1967), 556-559.

568 ________. "Another Book Read by Melville: Broughton's *Popular Poetry of the Hindoos*." *Papers of the Bibliographical Society of America*, 61 (April, 1967), 266-267.

569 ________. "Melville's Tomahawk Pipe: Artifact and Symbol." *Studies in the Novel*, 1 (1969), 397-400.

570 ________. "Recognition of Herman Melville, ca. 1910." *Extracts*, 11 (1972), 10.

571 ________. "Melville's Surgeon Cuticle and Surgeon Cutbush." *Studies in the Novel*, 5 (1973), 251-253. A study of *White-Jacket*.

572 ________. "A Comic Mode of the Romantic Imagination: Poe, Hawthorne, Melville," in Rubin, Louis, ed., *The Comic Imagination in American Literature*. New Brunswick, N.J.: Rutgers University Press, 1973. Pp. 85-99.

573 ________. "Hawthorne's Israel Potter." Extracts, 14 (1973), 9-10.

574 ________. "'The Famous Tales' Anthologies: Recognition of Melville, 1899." Papers of the Bibliographical Society of America, 68 (April, 1974), 179-180.

575 ________. "Melville to Mrs. Gifford, 1888." College Literature, 2 (1975), 229.

576 ________. "The Singing, Stammering Motif in Billy-Budd." Western Folklore, 34 (January, 1975), 54-55.

577 ________. "Of Rama and Queequeg." Extracts, 30 (1977), 12.

578 ________. "Bannadonna's Bell Ritual." Melville Society Extracts, 36 (1978), 7-8.

579 ________, ed. The Battle Pieces of Herman Melville. New York: Yoseloff, 1963.

580 ________, ed. Selected Poems of Herman Melville. Carbondale: Southern Illinois University Press, 1964. Also published in New York: Anchor, 1964. Contains good notes on poems, pp. 176-259.

581 ________, ed. The Confidence Man. New York: Holt, Rinehart, and Winston, 1964. Rinehart edition.

582 ________, ed. White-Jacket. New York: Holt, Rinehart and Winston, 1967. Rinehart edition.

583 ________, ed. The American Culture. Boston: Houghton Mifflin, 1968. Melville, passim.

584 ________, ed. Landmarks of American Writing. New York: Basic, 1969. "The Confidence Man," by Warner Berthoff, pp. 121-133.

585 COLCORD, Lincoln. "Notes on Moby-Dick." Freeman, 5 (August 23 and 30, 1922), 559-562, 585-587.

586 COLLINS, Carvel. "Melville's Moby-Dick." Explicator, 4 (February, 1946), item 27.

587 ________. "Melville's Mardi." Explicator, 12 (May, 1954), item 42.

588 COLTON, Walter. Deck and Port; or Incidents of a Cruise in the U.S. Frigate "Congress" to California. New York: Barnes, 1850.

589 COLUM, Padraic. "Moby-Dick as an Epic: A Note." Measure, 13 (March, 1922), 16-18.

590 ______. "Epic of the Sea," in Colum, A Half-Day's Ride. New York: Macmillan, 1932. Pp. 175-179.

591 COLVIN, Sir Sidney, ed. The Letters of Robert Louis Stevenson to His Family and Friends. New York and London: Scribner, 1899. Melville, passim.

592 COLWELL, James L., and Gary Spitzer. "'Bartleby' and 'The Raven': Parallels of the Irrational." Georgia Review, 23 (1969), 37-43.

593 COMBS, Barbara S. "The Confidence-Man as Apocalyptic Vision." Ph.D. diss., Ohio State, 1972. DA, 33 (1973), 4336A-4337A.

594 CONARROE, Joel O. "Melville's Bartleby and Charles Lamb." Studies in Short Fiction, 5 (1968), 113-118.

595 CONDON, Richard A. "The Broken Conduit: A Study of Alienation in American Literature." Pacific Spectator, 8 (Autumn, 1954), 326-332.

596 CONNOLLEY, Thomas E. "A Note on the Name Symbolism in Melville." American Literature, 25 (1954), 489-490.

597 CONNOR, C. H. "Moby-Dick." CEA Critic, 10 (October, 1948), 3.

598 CONNOR, John Joseph. "The Quixotic Novel from the Point of View of the Narrative." Ph.D. diss., University of Florida, 1977. DA, 38 (1978), 6700A-6701A.

599 CONNOR, Marian. "The Abysm and the Star: A Study of the Poetry of Herman Melville." Ph.D. diss., Boston University Graduate School, 1977. DA, 38 (1977), 2122A.

600 COOK, Albert S. "Romance as Allegory: Melville and Kafka," in Cook, The Meaning of Fiction. Detroit: Wayne State University Press, 1960. Pp. 242-259.

601 COOK, Charles H., Jr. "Ahab's 'Intolerable Allegory.'" Boston University Studies in English, 1 (1955-1956), 45-52. Reprinted in Stern, ed., Discussions of Moby-Dick (1960), pp. 60-65.

602 COOK, Dayton G. "The Apocalyptic Novel: Moby-Dick and Doktor Faustus." Ph.D. diss., Colorado, 1973. DA, 35 (1974), 2260A-2261A.

603 COOK, Reginald L. "Big Medicine in Moby-Dick." Accent, 8 (Winter, 1948), 102-109. Reprinted in Stern, ed., Discussions of Moby-Dick (1960), pp. 19-24. Also reprinted in Vickery, John B., ed., Myth and Literature: Contem-

porary Theory and Practice. Lincoln: University of Nebraska Press, 1966. Pp. 193-199.

604 ________, ed. Themes, Tones, and Motifs in the American Renaissance: A Symposium. Hartford, Conn.: Transcendental, 1968. Melville, pp. 43-60: "The Extraordinary Man as Idealist in the Novels by Hawthorne and Melville," by Paul McCarthy, pp. 43-51; "Moby-Dick Millennial Attitudes and Politics," by Milton R. Stern, pp. 51-60.

605 ________. "The Grotesque in the Fiction of Herman Melville." Ph.D. diss., University of Michigan, 1972. DA, 33 (1973), 6305A.

606 COOK, Richard M. "The Grotesque and Melville's Mardi." Emerson Society Quarterly, 21 (1975), 103-110.

607 ________. "Evolving the Inscrutable: The Grotesque in Melville's Fiction." American Literature, 49 (1978), 544-559.

608 COONAN, Michael. "Spending Light: A Consideration of Refractory, Binomial Pluralism in Herman Melville's Fictional First-Half Days." Ph.D. diss., University of Pittsburgh, 1976. DA, 38 (1977), 260A-261A.

609 COREY, James R. "Herman Melville and the Theory of Evolution." Ph.D. diss., Washington State, 1968. DA, 29 (1969), 3093A.

610 COSTELLO, Jacqueline A., and Robert J. Kloss. "The Psychological Depths of Melville's 'The Bell-Tower.'" Emerson Society Quarterly, 19 (1973), 254-261.

611 COSTNER, Martha Izora. Goldsmith's Citizen of the World and Melville's The Confidence Man. Comanche, Okla.: Privately printed, 1971. 35-page pamphlet.

612 COUCH, H. N. "Melville's Moby-Dick and the Phaedo." Classical Journal, 28 (February, 1933), 367-368.

613 COULON, Claude. "Pour une dramaturgie de Melville dans 'Bartleby.'" Delta English Studies, 7 (1978), 131-141.

614 COULTER, John. Adventures in the Pacific. London: Longmans, Brown, 1845.

615 COURNOS, John. A Modern Plutarch. London: Butterworth; Indianapolis: Bobbs-Merrill, 1928. "Melville, the Seeker," pp. 78-95; "A Comparison of Melville with Rimbaud and Doughty," pp. 127-134.

616 COURSEN, H. R. "Nature's Center." College English, 24 (March, 1963), 467-469.

617 COVER, Robert M. "Prelude: Of Creon and Captain Vere," in Cover, Justice Accused: Antislavery and the Judicial Process. New Haven: Yale University Press, 1975. Pp. 1-7.

618 COWAN, James C. "Lawrence's Criticism of Melville." Extracts, 17 (1974), 6-9.

619 COWAN, John Bainard. "Moby-Dick as Allegory of the Allegorical Process." Ph.D. diss., Yale, 1975. DA, 36 (1976), 7419A.

620 COWAN, Michael H. City of the West: Emerson, America, and the Urban Metaphor. New Haven: Yale University Press, 1967. Melville, passim.

621 ________. "The Americanness of Norman Mailer," in Adams, Laura, ed., Will the Real Norman Mailer Please Stand Up? Port Washington, N.Y.: Kennikat, 1974. Melville, pp. 95-112 and passim.

622 COWAN, S. A. "In Praise of Self-Reliance: The Role of Bulkington in Moby-Dick." American Literature, 38 (January, 1967), 547-556.

623 COWEN, Wilson Walker. "Herman Melville's Marginalia," 11 vols. Ph.D. diss., Harvard, 1965.

624 ________. "Melville's 'Discoveries': A Dialogue of the Mind with Itself," in Parker, ed., The Recognition of Herman Melville (1967), pp. 333-346.

625 ________. "Melville's Marginalia: Hawthorne," in Myerson, ed., Studies: 1978 (1978), pp. 279-302.

626 COWIE, Alexander. The Rise of the American Novel. New York: American Book Company, 1948. Melville, pp. 363-411.

627 ________. "Symbols Ahoy!" CEA Critic, 2 (January, 1949), 7-8. Review of Chase, Herman Melville (1949).

628 COWLEY, Malcolm. "Mythology and Melville." New Republic, 73 (October 30, 1950), 125. Review of Chase, Herman Melville (1949).

629 COX, James T., et al. "Textual Studies in the Novel: A Selected Checklist, 1950-1974." Studies in the Novel, 7 (1975), 445-471. Lists 20 items on Melville.

630 COXE, Louis O., and Robert Chapman. Billy-Budd: A Play in Three Acts. Foreword by Brooks Atkinson from The New York Times. Princeton, N.J.: Princeton University Press, 1951. Reprinted New York: Hill and Wang, 1962.

631 ________. "Herman Melville's 'The Encantadas,'" in Coxe, Louis O., Enabling Acts. Columbia: University of Missouri Press, 1976. Pp. 143-149.

632 CRAMER, Maurice B. "Billy-Budd and Billy-Budd." Journal of General Education, 10 (April, 1957), 78-91. Refers to novel and to the play by Coxe.

633 CRANE, Hart. "At Melville's Tomb," a poem. Poetry, 29 (October, 1926), 25. Also published in Calender, 3 (April, 1926--January, 1927), 105. Reprinted in Collected Poems and Selected Letters and Prose of Hart Crane. New York: Liveright, 1933.

634 ________. "Letter from Hart Crane to Harriet Monroe," in Horton, Philip, Hart Crane: The Life of an American Poet. New York: Norton, 1937. Reprinted New York: Viking, 1957. Pp. 329-334. Letter relates to Melville poem above.

635 CRAVEN, H. T. "Tahiti from Melville to Maugham." Bookman, 50 (November-December, 1919), 262-267.

636 CREEGER, George Raymond. "Color Symbolism in the Works of Herman Melville, 1846-1852." Ph.D. diss., Yale, 1952. DA, 25 (1953), 6620.

637 ________. "The Symbolism of Whiteness in Melville's Prose Fiction." Jahrbuch für Amerikastudien (Frankfurt, Germany), 5 (1960), 147-163.

638 CRISE, Stelio. "Ahab, Pizârool, Quark." James Joyce Quarterly, 7 (1969), 65-69.

639 CRISP, Frank. The Adventure of Whaling. London: Macmillan, 1954.

640 CRONKHITE, George Ferris. "Literature as Livelihood: The Attitude of Certain American Writers Toward Literature as a Profession from 1820 to the Civil War." Ph.D. diss., Harvard, 1948.

641 CROSS, Richard K. "Moby-Dick and Under the Volcano: Poetry from the Abyss." Modern Fiction Studies, 20 (Summer, 1974), 149-156. Refers to a novel by Malcolm Lowry.

642 CROWLEY, William G. "Melville's Chimney." Emerson Society Quarterly, 14 (1959), 2-6.

643 CUDDY, Lois Arlene. "Elegy and the American Tradition: Subjective Lyrics on Life and Experience." Ph.D. diss., Brown, 1975. DA, 37 (1976), 273A-274A. Includes Whitman and Melville.

644 CULHANE, Mary. "Thoreau, Melville, Poe and the Romantic Quest." Ph.D. diss., Minnesota, 1945.

645 CUNLIFFE, Marcus. The Literature of the United States. Harmondsworth, Middlesex: Penguin, 1954. Melville, pp. 105-119.

646 CURL, Vega. Pasteboard Masks: Fact as Spiritual Symbol in the Novels of Hawthorne and Melville. Cambridge: Harvard University Press, 1931. Based on honors thesis, Radcliffe, 1931.

647 CURLE, Richard. Collecting American First Editions: Its Pitfalls and Pleasures. Indianapolis: Bobbs-Merrill, 1930. Melville, pp. 129-130, 208-210, and passim.

648 CURNOW, Wystan Tremayne. "The Poetry of Herman Melville," in Australasian Universities Language and Literature Association: Proceedings and Papers on the 13th Congress held at Monash University, August 12-18, 1970, ed. by J. R. Ellis. Melbourne: AULLA and Monash University Press, 1971. Abstract of talk, pp. 147-148.

649 ________. "Melville's Poetry to 1876." Ph.D. diss., University of Pennsylvania, 1972. DA, 33 (1972), 1719A-1720A. Battle-Pieces and Clarel.

650 ________. "Romanticism and Modern American Criticism." Studies in Romanticism, 12 (1973), 777-799.

651 CURRAN, Ronald T. "Insular Types: Puritanism and Primitivism in Mourning Becomes Electra." Revue des Langues Vivantes (Brussels), 41 (1975), 371-377.

652 DAHL, Curtis. "Moby-Dick and the Reviews of The Cruise of the Cachelot." Modern Language Notes, 67 (November, 1952), 471-472.

653 ________. "Moby-Dick's Cousin Behemoth." American Literature, 31 (March, 1959), 21-29.

654 ________. "Jonah Improved: Sea-Sermons on Jonah." Extracts, 19 (1974), 6-9.

655 ________. "The Minnow and the Whale: Ely's 'There She Blows' and Melville's Moby-Dick." Log of Mystic Seaport (Marine Historical Association, Mystic, Conn.), 24 (1972), 8-13.

656 ________. "Of Foul Weather and Bulkingtons." Extracts, 30 (1977), 10-11. Relates to Moby-Dick.

657 ________. "Three Fathers, Many Sons." Methodist History (Lake Junaluska, N.C.), 15 (1977), 234-250. Relates to Father Mapple in Moby-Dick.

658 DAHLBERG, Edward. Can These Bones Live? New York: Harcourt, Brace, 1941. Revised with a new Preface by Herbert Read, and reprinted New York: New Directions, 1960. Melville, pp. 122-127.

659 ________. "Can These Bones Live?" in Dahlberg, Sing O' Barren. London: Routledge and Kegan Paul, 1947. Pp. 27-67.

660 ________. "Laurels for Borrowers." Freeman, 2 (1951), 187-190.

661 ________. "Moby-Dick: An Hamitic Dream." Literary Review, 4 (August, 1960), 87-118. Reprinted in Burnshaw, ed., Varieties of Literary Experience (1962), pp. 183-213. Also reprinted in Dahlberg, Alms for Oblivion. Minneapolis: University of Minnesota Press, 1964. Pp. 115-142.

662 DAIKER, Donald A. "The Motif of the Quest in the Works of Herman Melville." Ph.D. diss., Indiana, 1969. DA, 30 (1970), 4979A.

663 ________. "Marx's Garden and Melville's 'Green, Gentle, and Most Docile Earth.'" American Examiner: A Forum of Ideas (Michigan State), 4 (1975), 5-7.

664 DALE, T. R. "Melville and Aristotle: The Conclusion of Moby-Dick as a Classical Tragedy." Boston University Studies in English, 3 (Spring, 1957), 45-50.

665 DAMON, S. Foster. "Pierre, the Ambiguous." Hound and Horn, 2 (January-March, 1929), 107-118.

666 ________. "Why Ishmael Went to Sea." American Literature, 2 (November, 1930), 281-283.

667 DANA, Richard Henry. The Seaman's Friend. New York: Dayton and Saxton, 1841. Reprinted New York: Library Editions, 1970.

668 ________. Two Years Before the Mast. New York: Harper Brothers, 1842. Reprinted New York: Harper and Row, 1965.

669 D'ARCY, Martin C. The Nature of Belief. London: Sheed and Ward, 1931. Melville, passim; see pp. 193-207. Reprinted Dublin: Clonmore and Reynolds, 1958.

670 DAUBER, Kenneth. "Criticism of American Literature." Diacritics, 8 (1977), 55-66.

671 DAUNER, Louise. "The 'Case' of Tobias Pearson: Hawthorne and the Ambiguities." American Literature, 21 (January, 1950), 464-472. Relates to Pierre.

672 D'AVANZO, Mario L. "Melville's 'Bartleby' and Carlyle," in Vincent, ed., Melville Annual, No. 1 (1965), pp. 113-139.

673 ______. "'The Cassock' and Carlyle's 'Church-Clothes.'" Emerson Society Quarterly, 50 Supplement (1968), 74-76.

674 ______. "Melville's 'Bartleby' and John Jacob Astor." New England Quarterly, 41 (1968), 259-264.

675 ______. "Ahab, the Grecian Pantheon, and Shelley's Prometheus Unbound: The Dynamics of Myth in Moby-Dick." Books at Brown, 24 (1971), 19-44.

676 ______. "Pierre and the Wisdom of Keats' Melancholy." Extracts, 16 (1973), 6-9.

677 ______. "'A Bower in the Arsacides' and Solomon's Temple." Arizona Quarterly, 34 (1978), 317-326.

678 ______. "'Undo It, Cut It, Quick': The Gordian Knot in 'Benito Cereno.'" Studies in Short Fiction, 15 (1978), 192-194.

679 DAVIDSON, Cathy N. "Courting God and Mammon: The Biographers Impasse in Melville's 'Bartleby the Scrivener.'" Delta English Studies, 6 (1978), 47-59.

680 DAVIDSON, Frank. "Melville, Thoreau, and 'The Apple-Tree Table.'" American Literature, 25 (January, 1953), 479-488.

681 ______. "'Bartleby': A Few Observations." Emerson Society Quarterly, 27 (1962), 25-32.

682 DAVIES, Margaret. "Rimbaud and Melville." Revue de Littérature Comparée, 43 (1969), 479-488.

683 DAVIS, Frank M. "Herman Melville and the Nineteenth-Century Church Community." Ph.D. diss., Duke, 1966. DA, 27 (1967), 3866A-3867A.

684 DAVIS, Merrell R. "Melville's Midwestern Lecture Tour, 1859." Philological Quarterly, 20 (January, 1941), 46-57.

685 ______. "The Flower Symbolism in Mardi." Modern Language Quarterly, 2 (December, 1941), 625-638.

686 ______. "Herman Melville's Mardi: The Biography of a Book." Ph.D. diss., Yale, 1947. DA, 30 (1969), 1522A-1523A.

687 ______. Melville's Mardi: A Chartless Voyage. New Haven: Yale University Press, 1952. Reprinted Hamden, Conn.: Shoe String, 1967.

688 ______, and William H. Gilman, eds. Melville's Letters. New Haven: Yale University Press, 1960.

689 DAVISON, Richard Allan. "Melville's Mardi and John Skelton." Emerson Society Quarterly, 43 (1966), 86-87.

690 ______. "Redburn, Pierre, and Robin: Melville's Debt to Hawthorne?" Emerson Society Quarterly, 47 (1967), 32-34.

691 DAY, A. Grove. "Hawaiian Echoes in Melville's Mardi." Modern Language Quarterly, 18 (March, 1957), 3-8.

692 ______, ed. Melville's South Seas: An Anthology. New York: Hawthorn, 1970.

693 DAY, Frank L. "Herman Melville's Use of The Rebellion Record in His Poetry." M.A. thesis, University of Tennessee, 1959.

694 ______. "Melville and Sherman March to the Sea." American Notes and Queries, 2 (May, 1964), 134-136.

695 DAYTON, Abram C. Last Days of Knickerbocker Life in Old New York. New York: Harlan, 1882. Reprinted New York: Putnam, 1897.

696 D'AZEVEDO, Warren. "Revolt on the San Dominick." Phylon, 17 (1956), 129-140.

697 DEA, Eugene M. "Evolution and Atheism in Clarel." Extracts, 26 (1976), 3-4.

698 DEAN, John. "Shakespeare's Influence on Moby-Dick, or, Where There's a Will, There's a Whale." Cahiers Elisabethains: Etudes sur la Pré-Renaissance et la Renaissance Anglaise, 13 (1978), 41-48.

699 DEAN, Paul. "Herman Melville: Four Views of American Commercial Society." Revue des Langues Vivantes, 34 (1968), 504-507.

700 ______. "Herman Melville: The Quality of Balance." Serif, 7 (1970), 12-17.

701 DELANO, Reuben. Wanderings and Adventures of Reuben Delano, Being a Narrative of Twelve Years Life in a Whale Ship! Boston: Redding, 1846. Excerpt reprinted in McCormick, ed., Life on a Whaler (1960), pp. 65-75.

702 DELLAVEDOVA, Benjamin Robert. "The Carnivorous Word: A Study in Herman Melville." Ph.D. diss., University of Tulsa, 1977. DA, 38 (1977), 1386A.

703 DE MOTT, Robert J., and Sanford E. Marovitz, eds. Artful Thunder: Versions of the Romantic Tradition in American Literature in Honor of Howard P. Vincent. Kent, Ohio: Kent State University Press, 1975.

704 DENNY, Margaret, and William H. Gilman, eds. The American Writer and the European Tradition. Minneapolis: University of Minnesota Press, 1952. "American Writers as Critics of Nineteenth-Century Society," by Willard Thorp, pp. 90-105.

705 DENTON, Lynn W. "Melville's Jerusalem--'Wreck Ho--the Wreck!'" Harvard Theological Review, 67 (April, 1974), 184-186.

706 DE ONIS, José. "Melville y el mundo hispânico." Cuadernos, 70 (March, 1963), 53-60. In Spanish.

707 ________. "Messianic Nationalism in the Literature of the Americas: Melville and the Hispanic World," in Jost, François, ed., Proceedings of the IVth Congress of the International Comparative Literature Association (Fribourg, Switzerland, 1964). The Hague: Mouton, 1966. Pp. 229-236.

708 ________. Melville y el mundo hispânico. Rio Piedras, Cuba: Editorial Universitaria, 1974. See review by A. Rodriguez-Seda in Canadian Review of Comparative Literature, 4 (1975), 112-114. Author is Cuban.

709 DETTLAFF, Shirley M. "Hebraism and Hellenism in Melville's Clarel: The Influence of Arnold, Goethe, and Schiller." Ph.D. diss., USC, 1978. DA, 39 (1978), 2910A.

710 DEVERS, James. "Melancholy, Myth, and Symbol in Melville's 'Benito Cereno': An Interpretative Study." Ph.D. diss., UCLA, 1968. DA, 29 (1969), 2671A.

711 DE VOTO, Bernard. "Editions of Typee." Saturday Review of Literature, 5 (November 24, 1928), 406.

712 ________. Mark Twain's America. Boston: Little, Brown, 1932. Melville, pp. 312-313 and passim.

713 DEW, Marjorie C. "Benito Cereno: Melville's Vision and Revision of the Source." Paper presented to the Melville Society at the 1964 MLA. Published in Gross, ed., A Benito Cereno Handbook (1965), pp. 178-184.

714 ________. "The Attorney and the Scrivener: Quoth the Raven 'Nevermore,'" in Vincent, ed., Melville Annual, No. 1 (1965), pp. 94-103.

715 ________. "Herman Melville's Existential View of the Universe." Ph.D. diss., Kent State, 1966. DA, 28 (1967), 672A.

716 ________. "The Prudent Captain Vere." American Transcendental Quarterly, 7 (1970), 81-85.

717 ________. "Black-Hearted Melville: 'Geniality' Reconsidered," in De Mott, ed., Artful Thunder (1975), pp. 177-194.

718 DIAMOND, Arlyn, and Lee R. Edwards, eds. The Authority of Experience: Essays in Feminist Criticism. Amherst: University of Massachusetts Press, 1977. "What if Bartleby Were a Woman?" by Patricia Barber, pp. 212-223, 298-300.

719 DICHMANN, Mary E. "Absolutism in Melville's Pierre." PMLA, 67 (September, 1952), 702-715.

720 DILLINGHAM, William B. "'Neither Believer Nor Infidel': Themes of Melville's Poetry." Personalist, 46 (October, 1965), 501-516.

721 ________. "The Narrator of Moby-Dick." English Studies, 49 (February, 1968), 20-29.

722 ________. "Melville's Long Ghost and Smollett's Count Fathom." American Literature, 42 (1970), 232-235. Refers to Omoo and The Adventures of Count Fathom.

723 ________. An Artist in the Rigging: The Early Work of Herman Melville. Athens: University of Georgia Press, 1972.

724 ________. Melville's Short Fiction: 1853-1856. Athens: University of Georgia Press, 1977.

725 DILLISTONE, Frederick W. The Novelist and the Passion Story. London: Collins, 1960; New York: Sheed and Ward, 1961. Melville, pp. 45-68.

726 DIX, William S. "Herman Melville and the Problem of Evil." Rice Institute Pamphlet, 35 (July, 1948), 81-107.

727 DOBBYN, Dermot. "The Birthplace of Moby-Dick." Catholic World, 185 (September, 1957), 431-435. Refers to the Bible.

728 DONAHUE, Jane (see also Eberwein, Jane Donahue). "Mel-

ville's Classicism: Law and Order in His Poetry." Papers on Language and Literature, 5 (Winter, 1969), 63-72.

729 DONALDSON, Scott. "Damned Dollars and a Blessed Company: Financial Imagery in Moby-Dick." New England Quarterly, 46 (June, 1973), 279-283.

730 DONOGHUE, Denis. "In the Scene of Being: Melville." Hudson Review, 14 (Summer, 1961), 232-246.

731 ______. Connoisseurs of Chaos: Ideas of Order in Modern American Poetry. New York: Macmillan, 1965. Melville, pp. 76-99.

732 ______. Thieves of Fire. New York: Oxford University Press, 1973. "Thieves of Fire: Melville," pp. 87-107.

733 DONOW, Herbert S. "Herman Melville and the Craft of Fiction." Modern Language Quarterly, 25 (June, 1964), 181-186.

734 DOUBLEDAY, Neal F. "Jack Easy and Billy Budd." English Language Notes, 2 (1964), 39-42. Refers to Marryat's novel.

735 DOW, Eddy. "Van Wyck Brooks and Lewis Mumford: A Confluence in the 'Twenties.'" American Literature, 45 (1973), 407-422.

736 DOW, Janet. "Ahab: The Fisher King." Connecticut Review, 2 (1969), 42-49.

737 DOWNS, Robert Bingham. "Saga of the White Whale," in Downs, Famous American Books. New York: Macmillan, 1970. Pp. 107-114.

738 DREW, Philip. "Appearance and Reality in Melville's The Confidence Man." Journal of English Literary History, 31 (December, 1964), 418-442.

739 ______. "The Two-Headed Symbol." Listener, 74 (1965), 300-301.

740 DRUMMOND, C. Q. "Nature: Meek Ass or White Whale?" Sage (University of Wyoming), 1 (1966), 71-84.

741 DRURY, Donald. "Additions to The Melville Log by Jay Leyda." Extracts, 31 (1977), 4-9.

742 ______. "Some Middle Lives of Melville." Extracts, 32 (1977), 12. Note on Raymond M. Weaver.

743 DRYDEN, Edgar Afton. "Herman Melville's Narrators and

the Art of Fiction." Ph.D. diss., Johns Hopkins, 1965. DA, 26 (1966), 3298-3299.

744 ________. Melville's Thematics of Form: The Great Art of Telling the Truth. Baltimore: Johns Hopkins University Press, 1968.

745 DUBAN, James. "Melville and Christianity: His Masquerade." Ph.D. diss., Cornell, 1976. DA, 37 (1977), 5825A-5826A.

746 ________. "The Spenserian Maze of Melville's Pierre." Emerson Society Quarterly, 23 (1977), 217-225.

747 ________. "The Translation of Pierre Bayle's An Historical and Critical Dictionary Owned by Melville." Papers of the Bibliographical Society of America, 71 (1977), 347-351.

748 DUBLER, Walter. "Themes and Structure in Melville's The Confidence Man." American Literature, 33 (November, 1961), 307-319.

749 DUERKSEN, Roland A. "Caleb Williams, Political Justice, and Billy Budd." American Literature, 38 (November, 1966), 372-376.

750 ________. "The Deep Quandary in Billy Budd." New England Quarterly, 41 (March, 1968), 51-66.

751 DUFFIELD, Brainerd. "Moby-Dick: A Modern Adaptation." Line, 1 (April-May, 1948), 32-40.

752 DUFFY, Charles. "A Source for the Conclusion of Melville's Moby-Dick." Notes and Queries, 181 (November 15, 1941), 278-279.

753 ________. "Toward the Whole Evidence on Melville as a Lecturer." American Notes and Queries, 2 (July, 1942), 58.

754 DURAND, Régis. "Le Cadre de la fiction ('Bartleby' de Herman Melville)." Delta English Studies, 6 (1978), 95-107.

755 DURHAM, Philip. "Prelude to the Constable Edition of Melville." Huntington Library Quarterly, 21 (May, 1958), 285-289.

756 DUSSINGER, Gloria R. "The Romantic Concept of the Self, Applied to the Works of Emerson, Whitman, Hawthorne, and Melville." Ph.D. diss., Lehigh, 1973. DA, 34 (1974), 5963A.

757 DUYCKINCK, Evert. "Review of Moby-Dick." The Literary World, November 15 and 22, 1851. Reprinted in Branch, ed., Melville: The Critical Heritage (1974), 264-268.

758 ________, and George L. Duyckinck, eds. Cyclopedia of American Literature, 2 vols. New York: Scribner, 1855. Melville, Vol. II, pp. 672-676. Revision issued in 1866; reprinted several times.

759 DYER, Susan Athearn. "Plinlimmon's Theme: The Aspirations and Limitations of Man in the Novels of Herman Melville." Ph.D. diss., Duke, 1977. DA, 38 (1978), 4824A-4825A.

760 E., T. T. "Melville's Billy Budd." Explicator, 2 (1943), item 14.

761 EASTWOOD, David R. "O'Brien's Fiddler--or Melville's?" American Transcendental Quarterly, 29 (1976), 39-46.

762 EBERWEIN, Jane Donahue. "Joel Barlow and The Confidence-Man." American Transcendental Quarterly, 24 (1974), 28-29.

763 ________. "Fishers of Metaphor: Mather and Melville on the Whale." American Transcendental Quarterly, 26 supplement (1975), 30-31.

764 EBERWEIN, Robert T. "The Impure Fiction of Billy-Budd." Studies in the Novel, 6 (Fall, 1974), 318-326.

765 EBY, Cecil D., Jr. "William Starbuck May and Herman Melville." New England Quarterly, 35 (1962), 515-520.

766 ________. "Another Breaching of 'Mocha Dick.'" English Language Notes, 4 (June, 1967), 277-279.

767 EBY, E. H. "Herman Melville's 'Tartarus of Maids.'" Modern Language Quarterly, 1 (March, 1940), 95-100.

768 ECKARDT, Sister Mary Ellen. "An Interpretive Analysis of the Patterns of Imagery in Moby-Dick and Billy Budd." Ph.D. diss., Notre Dame, 1962. DA, 23 (1962), 2134.

769 ________. "Duplicate Imagery in Moby-Dick." Modern Fiction Studies, 8 (Autumn, 1962), 252-264.

770 ________. "Parallels in Contrast: A Study of Melville's Imagery in Moby-Dick and Billy-Budd." Studies in Short Fiction, 2 (Spring, 1965), 284-290.

771 EDDY, Fern Darlene Mathis. "A Dark Similitude: Melville and the Elizabethan-Jacobean Perspective." Ph.D. diss., Rutgers, 1967. DA, 28 (1967), 626A.

772 ________. "Melville's Response to Beaumont and Fletcher: A New Source for The Encantadas." American Literature, 40 (1968), 374-380.

773 ________. "Melville's Sicilian Moralist." English Language Notes, 8 (1971), 191-200. On Melville's interest in the sculptures of Gaetano Giulo Zumba.

774 ________. "Bloody Battles and High Tragedies: Melville and the Theatre of the 1840's." Ball State University Forum, 13 (1972), 34-45.

775 EDGAR, Pelham. The Art of the Novel. New York: Macmillan, 1933. Melville, pp. 130-135.

776 EDINGER, Edward F. Melville's Moby-Dick: A Jungian Commentary: An American Nekyia. New York: New Directions, 1978.

777 EHRLICH, Heyward. "A Note on Melville's 'Men Who Dive.'" Bulletin of the New York Public Library, 69 (December, 1965), 661-664.

778 ________. "'Diving and Ducking Moralities': A Rejoinder." Bulletin of the New York Public Library, 70 (December, 1966), 552-553.

779 EIGNER, Edwin M. "The Romantic Unity of Melville's Omoo." Philological Quarterly, 46 (1967), 95-108.

780 ________. The Metaphysical Novel in England and America: Dickens, Bulwer-Lytton, Melville, and Hawthorne. Berkeley: University of California Press, 1978.

781 EISIMINGER, Sterling. "Melville's Small Debt to Poe." American Notes and Queries, 15 (1977), 70-71.

782 EKNAR, Reidar. "The Encantadas and Benito Cereno--On Sources and Imagination in Melville." Moderna Sprak (Sweden), 60 (1966), 258-273.

783 ________, ed. Billy-Budd. Stockholm, Sweden: Raben and Sjögren, 1955.

784 ELDER, Marjorie J. "Transcendental Symbolists: Hawthorne and Melville." Ph.D. diss., University of Chicago, 1964.

785 ________. Nathaniel Hawthorne: Transcendental Symbolist. Athens: Ohio University Press, 1969. Melville, passim.

786 ELDRIDGE, Herbert G. "'Careful Disorder': The Structure of Moby-Dick." American Literature, 39 (May, 1967), 145-162.

787 ELIOT, Alexander. "Melville and Bartleby." Furioso, 3 (Fall, 1947), 11-21.

788 ELLIOTT, Harrison. "A Century Ago an Eminent Author Looked upon Paper and Papermaking." Paper Making, 21 (1952), 55-58. Refers to "The Tartarus of Maids."

789 ELLIOTT, Patrick F. "Herman Melville's Tragic Vision: An Essay in Theological Criticism." Ph.D. diss., University of Chicago, 1965.

790 ELLIS, Theodore. "Another Broadside into Mardi." American Literature, 41 (November, 1969), 419-422.

791 ELLIS, William (1794-1872). Narrative of a Tour Through Hawaii, with remarks on the history, traditions, manners, customs, and language of the inhabitants of the Sandwich Islands. London: Printed for the author by Fisher, Son, and P. Jackson, 1826.

792 ________. A Defense of the Missions in the South Seas. London: Fisher, Son, and P. Jackson, 1827.

793 ________. A Vindication of the South Seas Missions. London: Fisher, Son, and P. Jackson, 1831.

794 ________. Polynesian Researches. London: Fisher and Son, 1833.

795 ________. History of Madagascar. Comprising also the progress of the Christian mission established in 1818; and an authentic account of the persecution and recent martyrdom of the native Christians. London: Fisher, Son, and Company, 1838.

796 ________. The History of the London Missionary Society. London: Fisher and Son, 1844.

797 ELLISON, Jerome. "How to Catch a Whale: Evil, Melville, and the Evolution of Consciousness." Michigan Quarterly Review, 6 (Spring, 1967), 85-89.

798 EMERSON SOCIETY QUARTERLY, 28 (1962), 2-30. Special Melville supplement, ed. Carl F. Strauch.

799 EMERY, Allan Moore. "The Alternatives of Melville's 'Bartleby.'" Nineteenth-Century Fiction, 31 (1976), 170-187.

800 ________. "Parables of Perception: A Contextual Approach to Melville's Short Fiction, 1853-1856." Ph.D. diss., Cornell, 1976. DA, 38 (1977), 1387A.

801 EMMERS, Amy Puett. "Melville's Closet Skeleton: A New

Letter About the Illegitimacy Incident in Pierre," in Myerson, ed., Studies: 1977 (1978), pp. 339-344.

802 ENGEL, Leonard. "Melville and the Young American Movement." Connecticut Review, 4 (1971), 91-101.

803 ENGSTROM, Alfred G. "The Single Tear: A Stereotype of Literary Sensibility." Philological Quarterly, 42 (January, 1963), 106-109.

804 ENNSSLEN, Klaus. "Melville's 'Benito Cereno,'" in Kleine Beitrage..., ed. Hans Galinsky and Hans-Joachim Lang. Heidelburg, Germany: Winter, 1961. Pp. 27-33.

805 ENSOR, Allison R. "The Downfall of Poor Richard: Benjamin Franklin as Seen by Hawthorne, Melville, and Mark Twain." Mark Twain Journal, 17 (1975), 14-18.

806 ERSKINE, John. Leading American Novelists. New York: Holt, 1910. Reprinted Freeport, N.Y.: Books for Libraries, 1966. Melville, passim, pp. 179-274.

807 ________. The Delight of Great Books. Indianapolis: Bobbs-Merrill, 1928. Melville, pp. 223-240.

808 ________. "A Whale of a Story." Delineator, October, 1929. P. 15.

809 ESTRIN, Mark W. "Dramatizations of American Fiction: Hawthorne and Melville on Stage and Screen." Ph.D. diss., New York University, 1969. DA, 30 (1970), 3428A.

810 ________. "Robert Lowell's Benito-Cereno." Modern Drama, 15 (1973), 411-426.

811 EVANS, William A. "The Boy and the Shadow: The Role of Pip and Fedallah in Moby-Dick." Studies in the Literary Imagination, 2 (1969), 77-81.

EXTRACTS: An Occasional Newsletter see MELVILLE SOCIETY.

812 FABRICANT, Carole. "Tristram Shandy and Moby-Dick: A Cock and Bull Story and a Tale of a Tub." Journal of Narrative Technique (Ypsilanti, Eastern Michigan University Press), 7 (1977), 57-69.

813 FADIMAN, Clifton. "Herman Melville." Atlantic, 172 (October, 1943), 88-91.

814 ________, ed. with Introduction. Moby-Dick, or the Whale. New York: Heritage, 1955. Text based on the Limited Editions Club Publication, 1950. Illustrations by Boardman Robinson.

815 FAGAN, David Lloyd. "The Voyage to Easter: Melville's Resolution of Doubt and Belief." Ph.D. diss., Florida State, 1975. DA, 36 (1975), 3712A.

816 FAGIN, N. Bryllion. "Herman Melville and the Interior Monologue." American Literature, 6 (January, 1935), 433-434.

817 FAIGELMAN, Steven H. "The Development of Narrative Consciousness in Moby-Dick." Ph.D. diss., Cornell, 1967. DA, 28 (1967), 2243A-2244A.

818 FANNIN, Alice. "Through a Glass Darkly: Masks, Veils, and Masquerades as Obstacles to Perception in the Major Novels of Herman Melville." Ph.D. diss., University of Kentucky, 1975. DA, 37 (1977), 5826A.

819 FARNSWORTH, Robert M. "Herman Melville's Use of Point of View in His First Seven Novels." Ph.D. diss., Tulane, 1957. DA, 19 (1959), 3294-3295.

820 ________. "Israel Potter: Pathetic Comedy." Bulletin of the New York Public Library, 65 (1961), 125-132.

821 ________. "Ishmael to the Royal Masthead." University of Kansas City Review, 28 (Spring, 1962), 183-190.

822 ________. "From Voyage to Quest in Melville." Emerson Society Quarterly, 28 (1962), 17-20.

823 ________. "Slavery and Innocence in 'Benito Cereno.'" Emerson Society Quarterly, 44 (1967), 94-96.

824 FARRELL, James T. "James T. Farrell and Moby-Dick: A Reflection." Extracts, 25 (1976), 7.

825 FARWELL, Harold F., Jr. "The Relation of Point of View and Style in Four Early Novels of Herman Melville." Ph.D. diss., Wisconsin, 1969. DA, 31 (1970), 2912A.

826 FAST, Howard. "American Literature and the Democratic Tradition." College English, 8 (March, 1947), 279-284.

827 FEIDELSON, Charles, Jr. "The Idea of Symbolism in American Writing, with Particular Reference to Emerson and Melville." Ph.D. diss., Yale, 1948.

828 ________. Symbolism and American Literature. Chicago: Uni-

versity of Chicago Press, 1953. "Toward Melville: Some Versions of Emerson," pp. 162-212.

829 ______. "The World of Melville." Show, 3 (July, 1963), 47-55.

830 ______, ed. with Introduction and Annotation. Moby-Dick. New York and Indianapolis: Bobbs-Merrill, 1964. Contains maps and illustrations by Joseph P. Ascherl, pp. xxvii-xxxvii.

831 ______, and Paul Brodtkorb, eds. Interpretations of American Literature. New York: Oxford University Press, 1959. "Seven Moby Dicks," by John Parke, pp. 84-101.

832 FELHEIM, Marvin. "Meaning and Structure in 'Bartleby.'" College English, 23 (February, 1962), 369-370, 375-376.

833 FELTENSTEIN, Rosalie. "Melville's 'Benito-Cereno.'" American Literature, 19 (November, 1947), 245-255.

834 FENTON, Charles A. "'The Bell-Tower': Melville and Technology." American Literature, 23 (May, 1951), 219-232.

835 FERGUSON, De Lancey. "The Legacy of Letters." American Scholar, 29 (Summer, 1960), 406-418.

836 FERGUSON, Terrance John. "'The Test of Greatness': The Grotesque in Melville's Major Novels." Ph.D. diss., University of Toronto, 1977. DA, 39 (1978), 2271A-2272A.

837 FERRIS, M. L. D. "Herman Melville." Bulletin of the Society of American Authors, 6 (Summer, 1901), 289-293.

838 FIEDLER, Leslie A. "Come Back to the Raft Ag'in, Huck Honey!" Partisan Review, 14 (1948), 664-671. Reprinted in Fiedler, An End to Innocence (1955), pp. 142-151. Relates to Queequeg and Ishmael; homosexuality and the Negro.

839 ______. "Out of the Whale." The Nation, 169 (November 19, 1949), 494-495.

839a ______. An End to Innocence. Boston: Beacon, 1955. Melville, pp. 142-151 and passim.

840 ______. No! In Thunder: Essays on Myth and Literature. Boston: Beacon, 1960; London: Eyre and Spottiswoode, 1963. Melville, passim.

841 ______. Love and Death in the American Novel. New York: Criterion, 1960. Reprinted New York: Meridian, 1962.

"*Moby-Dick*: The Baptism of Fire and the Baptism of Sperm," pp. 520-552. Revised edition printed New York: Stein and Day, 1966.

842 ______. "The Failure of Sentiment and the Evasion of Love," in *Love and Death in the American Novel*. Revised edition. New York: Stein and Day, 1966. Pp. 337-390.

843 ______. "Ishmael's Trip." *The Listener* (London), 78 (August 3, 1967), 134-136. Reprinted as "The Shape of *Moby-Dick*," in Fiedler, *Collected Essays* (1971), pp. 312-318.

844 ______. *The Return of the Vanishing American*. New York: Stein and Day, 1968. Melville, passim.

845 ______. *The Collected Essays of Leslie Fiedler*, 2 vols. New York: Stein and Day, 1971. "The Shape of *Moby-Dick*," Vol. II, pp. 312-318.

846 ______, ed. *The Art of the Essay*. New York: Crowell, 1958.

847 FIELD, Maunsell Bradhurst. *Memories of Many Men and of Some Women*. New York: Harper and Brothers, 1874. Melville, pp. 198-202.

848 FIELDS, James T. *Yesterdays with Authors*. Boston: Osgood, 1872. Melville, passim.

849 FIENE, Donald M. "Bartleby, the Christ." *American Transcendental Quarterly*, 7 (1970), 18-23.

850 ______. "Chronological Development in Summary of Criticism of 'Bartleby,'" in Vincent, ed., *Melville Annual*, No. 1 (1965), pp. 140-190.

851 FIESS, Edward. "Byron and Byronism in the Mind and Art of Herman Melville." Ph.D. diss., Yale, 1951. *DA*, 25 (1965), 4145.

852 ______. "Melville as a Reader and Student of Byron." *American Literature*, 24 (May, 1952), 186-195.

853 ______. "Byron's Dark Blue Ocean and Melville's Rolling Sea." *English Language Notes*, 3 (1966), 274-278.

854 FINE, Ronald E. "Herman Melville and the Rhetoric of Psychological Fiction." Ph.D. diss., University of Rochester, 1966. *DA*, 27 (1966), 1364A.

855 FINEMAN, Daniel David. "On Errands of Life: Vitality and Language in the Novels of Herman Melville." Ph.D. diss., Princeton, 1976. *DA*, 37 (1977), 5826A-5827A.

856 FINHOLT, Richard David. "The Murder of *Moby-Dick*: Mad Metaphysics as Salvation Psychology in American Fiction." Ph.D. diss., Northern Illinois University (De Kalb), 1975. *DA*, 36 (1976), 7420A.

857 ———. *American Visionary Fiction: Mad Metaphysics as Salvation Psychology*. Port Washington, N.Y.: Kennikat, 1978. "The Murder of *Moby-Dick*," pp. 5-82.

858 FINKELSTEIN, Dorothee Metlitsky Grdseloff. "A Note on the Origin of Fedallah in *Moby-Dick*." *American Literature*, 27 (November, 1955), 396-403.

859 ———. "Herman Melville and the Near East." Ph.D. diss., Yale, 1957.

860 ———. *Melville's Orienda*. New Haven: Yale University Press, 1961.

861 FINKELSTEIN, Sidney. "Six Ways of Looking at Reality." *Mainstream*, 13 (December, 1960), 31-42.

862 FIRCHOW, Peter E. "Bartleby: Man and Metaphor." *Studies in Short Fiction*, 5 (Summer, 1968), 342-348.

863 FIREBAUGH, Joseph J. "Humorist as Rebel: The Melville of *Typee*." *Nineteenth-Century Fiction*, 9 (1954), 108-120.

864 FISCHER, Douglas R. "Relativism in Melville's *Piazza Tales*." Ph.D. diss., Princeton, 1974. *DA*, 36 (1975), 1502A.

865 FISHER, Marvin. "Melville's 'Bell-Tower': A Double Thrust." *American Quarterly*, 18 (1966), 200-207.

866 ———. "Melville's 'Jimmy Rose': Truly Risen?" *Studies in Short Fiction*, 4 (1966), 1-11.

867 ———. "Focus on Herman Melville's 'The Two Temples': The Denigration of the American Dream," in Madden, David, ed., *American Dreams, American Nightmares*. Carbondale: Southern Illinois University Press, 1970. Pp. 76-86.

868 ———. "Melville's 'Tartarus': The Deflowering of New England." *American Quarterly*, 23 (1971), 79-100.

869 ———. "Bug and Humbug in Melville's 'Apple-Tree Table.'" *Studies in Short Fiction*, 8 (1971), 459-466.

870 ———. "'Poor Man's Pudding': Melville's Meditation on Grace." *American Transcendental Quarterly*, 13 (1972), 32-35.

871 ______. "Melville's 'Brave Officer.'" Extracts, 14 (1973), 7-8.

872 ______. "Bartleby: Melville's Circumscribed Scrivener." Southern Review, 10 (January, 1974), 59-79.

873 ______. "Melville's 'The Fiddler': Succumbing to the Drummer." Studies in Short Fiction, 11 (1974), 153-160.

874 ______. "Prospect and Perspective in Melville's Piazza." Criticism, 16 (Summer, 1974), 203-216.

875 ______. "Portrait of the Artist in America: 'Hawthorne and His Mosses.'" Southern Review, 11 (January, 1975), 156-166.

876 ______. "'Benito Cereno': Old World Experience, New World Expectations, and Third World Realities." Forum (Houston), 13 (1976), 31-36.

877 ______. Going Under: Melville's Short Fiction and the American 1850's. Baton Rouge: Louisiana State University Press, 1977.

878 FISHER, R. E. "The American Repudiation of Melville's Pierre." Moderna Sprak (Sweden), 55 (Fall, 1961), 233-240.

879 FISKE, John C. "Herman Melville in Soviet Criticism." Comparative Literature, 5 (Winter, 1953), 30-39.

880 FITCH, George H. Great Spiritual Writers of American Literature. San Francisco: Elder, 1916. Melville, passim.

881 FITE, Olive La Rue. "The Interpretation of Herman Melville's Billy Budd." Ph.D. diss., Northwestern, 1956. DA, 17 (1957), 354.

882 ______. "Billy Budd, Claggart, and Schopenhauer." Nineteenth-Century Fiction, 23 (1968), 336-343.

883 FITZROY, Robert, ed. Narrative of HMS Adventure and Beagle, 1826-1836. London: Colburn, 1839. Reprinted New York: AMS, 1966.

884 FLANAGAN, John T. "The Spirit of the Times Reviews Melville." Journal of English and Germanic Philology, 64 (January, 1965), 57-64.

885 FLECK, Richard F. "Stone Imagery in Melville's Pierre." Research Studies, 42 (1974), 127-130.

886 FLETCHER, Richard M. "Melville's Use of Marquesan." American Speech, 39 (1964), 135-138.

887 FLEURDORGE, Claude. "'Bartleby': A Story of Broadway." Delta English Studies, 7 (1978), 65-109.

888 FLIBBERT, Joseph T. "Melville and the Art of Burlesque." Ph.D. diss., Illinois (Urbana-Champaign), 1970. DA, 31 (1971), 6602A.

889 ______. Melville and the Art of Burlesque. Amsterdam, Netherlands: Rodopi, 1974.

890 FLOAN, Howard R. The South in Northern Eyes: 1831-1861. Austin: University of Texas Press, 1958. Melville, pp. 131-147.

891 FLOYD, Nathaniel M. "Billy Budd: A Psychological Autopsy." American Imago, 34 (1977), 28-49.

892 FOERSTER, Norman. Nature in American Literature. New York: Macmillan, 1923. Reprinted New York: Russell and Russell, 1958. Melville, passim. See also Emerson, Thoreau, Whitman.

893 ______, ed. The Reinterpretation of American Literature. New York: Harcourt, Brace, 1928. "American Literary History and American Literature," by Harry Hayden Clark, pp. 181-213.

894 ______, and Robert P. Falk, eds. Eight American Writers: An Anthology. New York: Norton, 1963. "Herman Melville," ed. with Introduction by Leon Howard, pp. 781-970.

895 FOGLE, Richard Harter. "The Monk and the Bachelor: Melville's 'Benito Cereno.'" Tulane Studies in English, 3 (1953), 155-178.

896 ______. "Organic Form in American Criticism: 1840-1870," in Stovall, Floyd, ed., The Development of American Literary Criticism. Chapel Hill: University of North Carolina Press, 1955. Pp. 75-111.

897 ______. "Billy Budd: Acceptance or Irony?" Tulane Studies in English, 8 (1958), 107-113.

898 ______. "Melville and the Civil War." Tulane Studies in English, 9 (1959), 61-89.

899 ______. "Melville's Clarel: Doubt and Belief." Tulane Studies in English, 10 (1960), 101-116.

900 ______. "Billy-Budd: The Order of the Fall." Nineteenth-Century Fiction, 15 (December, 1960), 189-205.

901 ______. "The Themes of Melville's Later Poetry." Tulane Studies in English, 11 (1961), 65-86.

902 ________. "Melville's Poetry." Tulane Studies in English, 12 (1962), 81-86.

903 ________. "Benito Cereno," in Chase, ed., Melville: A Collection (1962), pp. 116-124. Short version of 1953 article.

904 ________. The Permanent Pleasure. Athens: University of Georgia Press, 1974. Includes new material and the following previously published essays: "The Themes of Melville's Later Poetry," pp. 137-164; "Melville's Clarel," pp. 165-183; "Melville's Poetry," pp. 184-190; "Billy-Budd: Acceptance or Irony?" pp. 191-209.

905 ________, ed. Melville's Shorter Tales. Norman: University of Oklahoma Press, 1960.

906 FOLEY, Mary. "The Digressions in Billy-Budd," in Stafford, ed., Melville's Billy-Budd and the Critics (1961 and 1968), pp. 161-164.

907 FOLEY, Patrick Kevin. American Authors: 1795-1895. Boston: Publishers' Printing Company, 1897.

908 FORREY, Robert. "Herman Melville and the Negro Question." Mainstream, 15 (February, 1962), 28-29.

909 FORSTER, E. M. Aspects of the Novel. New York: Harcourt, Brace, 1927. Reprinted New York: Harvest, 1954. Melville, pp. 138-143 and 199-206.

910 ________. "Letter" (explains his libretto to Britten's opera). The Griffin, 1 (1951), 4-6.

911 ________, and Eric Crozier. "Libretto," for Benjamin Britten's Billy-Budd: An Opera in Four Acts. London: Boosey and Hawkes, 1951.

912 FORSYTHE, Robert S. "Mr. Lewis Mumford and Melville's Pierre." American Literature, 2 (November, 1930), 286-289.

913 ________. "Herman Melville in Honolulu." New England Quarterly, 8 (March, 1935), 99-105.

914 ________. "Herman Melville's 'The Town-Ho's Story.'" Notes and Queries, 168 (May 4, 1935), 314.

915 ________. "Herman Melville in the Marquesas." Philological Quarterly, 15 (January, 1936), 1-15.

916 ________. "Herman Melville's Father Murphy." Notes and Queries, 172 (April 10 and 17, 1937), 254-258, 272-276.

917 _______. "An Oversight by Herman Melville." Notes and Queries, 172 (April 24, 1937), 296.

918 _______. "Herman Melville in Tahiti." Philological Quarterly, 16 (October, 1937), 344-357.

919 _______. "More upon Herman Melville in Tahiti." Philological Quarterly, 17 (January, 1938), 1-17.

920 _______. "Review of Willard Thorp's Herman Melville." American Literature, 11 (1939), 92-95.

921 _______. "Emerson and Moby-Dick." Notes and Queries, 177 (December 23, 1939), 457-458.

922 _______, ed. with Introduction by John B. Moore. Pierre. New York: Knopf, 1930. Reissued 1941.

923 FOSTER, Charles H. "Something in Emblems: A Reinterpretation of Moby-Dick." New England Quarterly, 34 (March, 1961), 3-35.

924 FOSTER, Edward Francis. "A Study of the Grim Humor in the Works of Poe, Melville, and Twain." Ph.D. diss., Vanderbilt, 1956. DA, 17 (1957), 1761-1762.

925 FOSTER, Elizabeth S. "Herman Melville's The Confidence Man: Its Origins and Meaning." Ph.D. diss., Yale, 1942.

926 _______. "Melville and Geology." American Literature, 17 (March, 1945), 50-65.

927 _______. "Another Note on Melville and Geology." American Literature, 22 (January, 1951), 479-487.

928 _______. "Historical Note," in Hayford, Harrison, et al., eds., Mardi. Evanston and Chicago: Northwestern University Press and Newberry Library, 1970. Pp. 657-681.

929 _______, ed. with Introduction. The Confidence-Man: His Masquerade. New York: Hendricks House, 1954.

930 FOSTER, Richard J. "Melville and Roguery: A Study of the Relation of Melville's Writing to Picaresque Fiction." M.A. thesis, Oberlin, 1950.

931 _______, ed. Six American Novelists of the Nineteenth-Century. Minneapolis: University of Minnesota Press, 1968. "Herman Melville," by Leon Howard, pp. 82-117. Reprint of six University Minnesota Pamphlets on American Writers.

932 FRACCHIA, Charles A. "Melville in San Francisco." Extracts, 25 (1976), 2-3.

933 FRANKLIN, Howard Bruce. "Herman Melville's Mythology." Ph.D. diss., Stanford, 1961. DA, 22 (1962), 3644.

934 ________. "'Apparent Symbol of Despotic Command': Melville's 'Benito-Cereno.'" New England Quarterly, 34 (December, 1961), 462-477.

935 ________. The Wake of the Gods: Melville's Mythology. Stanford, Calif.: University of Stanford Press, 1963.

936 ________. "Redburn's Wicked End." Nineteenth-Century Fiction, 20 (September, 1965), 190-194.

937 ________. "Herman Melville and Science Fiction," in Franklin, Future Perfect: American Science Fiction in the Nineteenth-Century. New York: Oxford University Press, 1966. Pp. 144-150. Revised edition, 1978.

938 ________. "The Island Worlds of Darwin and Melville." The Centennial Review, 11 (Summer, 1967), 353-370.

939 ________. "Herman Melville: Artist of the Workers' World," in Rudich, Norman, ed., Weapons of Criticism: Marxism in America and the Literary Tradition. Palo Alto, Calif.: Ramparts, 1976. Pp. 287-309.

940 ________, ed. Mardi: A Voyage Thither. New York: Capricorn, 1964.

941 ________, ed. with Introduction. The Confidence Man: His Masquerade. Indianapolis: Bobbs-Merrill, 1967.

942 FRANKLIN, Samuel Rhoades. Memories of a Rear-Admiral. New York and London: Harper and Brothers, 1898.

943 FRANZOSA, John Carl. "Darwin and Melville: Why a Tortoise?" American Imago, 33 (1976), 361-379.

944 FRASCONI, Antonio, ed. with Woodcut Photography. On the Slain Collegians. New York: Farrar, Straus, and Giroux, 1971.

945 FREAR, W. F. Anti-Missionary Criticism with Reference to Hawaii. Honolulu: Hawaii Advertiser, 1935.

946 FREDERICK, Joan. "Variations upon a Theme: The Use of Physical Disabilities in Melville's Fiction." Ph.D. diss., University of Tennessee, 1973. DA, 34 (1974), 5099A.

947 FREDERICK, John T. "Symbol and Theme in Melville's Israel Potter." Modern Fiction Studies, 8 (Autumn, 1962), 265-275.

948 _______. "Melville's Early Acquaintance with Bayle." American Literature, 39 (1968), 545-547.

949 _______. The Darkened Sky: Nineteenth-Century American Novelists and Religion. Notre Dame, Ind.: Notre Dame University Press, 1969. Melville, pp. 79-122.

950 _______. "Melville's Last Long Novel: Clarel." Arizona Quarterly, 26 (1970), 151-157.

951 FREDERIX, Pierre. Herman Melville. Paris, France: Gallimard, 1950. In French; has not been translated.

952 FREEMAN, F. Barron. "A Critical and Variorum Edition of Melville's Billy-Budd from the Original Manuscripts." Ph.D. diss., Harvard, 1942.

953 _______. "The Enigma of Melville's 'Daniel Orme.'" American Literature, 16 (November, 1944), 208-211.

954 _______, ed. with Introduction. Herman Melville's Billy-Budd. Cambridge: Harvard University Press, 1948.

955 FREEMAN, John. Herman Melville. London and New York: Macmillan, 1926.

956 FREIBERG, Louis. "The Westminster Review and American Literature, 1824-1885." American Literature, 24 (1953), 310-329.

957 FREIBERT, Sister Lucy Marie. "Meditative Voice in the Poetry of Herman Melville." Ph.D. diss., Wisconsin, 1970. DA, 31 (1971), 2875A.

958 _______. "Andrew Marvell and Melville's Bellipotent." Extracts, 21 (1975), 7-8.

959 _______. "A Checklist of Musical Compositions Inspired by Herman Melville's Works." Extracts, 23 (1975), 3-5.

960 FREIMARCK, Vincent. "Mainmast as Crucifix in Billy-Budd." Modern Language Notes, 72 (November, 1957), 496-497.

961 _______, and Bernard Rosenthal. Race and the American Romantics. New York: Schocken, 1971. "Herman Melville: 'Better Present Woes for Some,'" pp. 51-52.

962 FRENCH, Brandon. "Lost at Sea," in Peary, Gerald, and Roger Shatzin, eds., The Classic American Novel and the Movies. New York: Ungar, 1977. Pp. 52-61. About Moby-Dick. Also contains an article about Billy-Budd, by Robert L. Nadeau, pp. 124-131.

963 FREUND, Philip. How to Become a Literary Critic. New York: Beechhurst, 1947. "Sea and Sky: Herman Melville," pp. 80-96.

964 FRIEDMAN, Andrea Marian. "Driven by That Density Home: Herman Melville, Charles Olson, Robert Creeley, and the Problem of Knowledge in a World of Flux." Ph. D. diss., State University of New York (Buffalo), 1976. DA, 37 (1976), 2893A-2894A.

965 FRIEDMAN, Irene. "Melville's Billy Budd: 'A Sort of Upright Barbarian.'" Canadian Review of American Studies, 4 (1973), 87-95.

966 FRIEDMAN, Maurice. "The Modern Job: On Melville, Dostoevsky, and Kafka." Judaism, 12 (Fall, 1963), 436-455.

967 ________. Problematic Rebel: Melville, Dostoevsky, Kafka, Camus. New York: Random House, 1963. Reprinted Chicago: University of Chicago Press, 1970. Melville, pp. 49-148 and 437-441.

968 ________. "Bartleby and the Modern Exile," in Vincent, ed., Melville Annual, No. 1 (1965), pp. 64-81.

969 FRIEDRICH, Gerhard. In Pursuit of Moby-Dick: Melville's Image of Man. Wallingford, Pa.: Pendle Hill Pamphlets, 1958.

970 ________. "A Note on Quakerism and Moby-Dick: Hawthorne's 'The Gentle Boy' as a Possible Source." Quaker History, 54 (Autumn, 1965), 94-102.

971 ________. "The Melville Equation: His Truths of Fact and Fiction." Humanities Association Bulletin, 18 (Spring, 1967), 87-95.

972 FRIEL, Joseph C. "Ustinov's Film Billy-Budd, a Study in the Process of Adaptation: Novel to Play to Film." Literature/Film Quarterly, 4 (1976), 271-284.

973 FROST, Robert. "The Demiurge's Laugh," in Complete Poems of Robert Frost. New York: Holt, 1949. P. 35. Possible relation to chapter in Moby-Dick, omen of shrieking, seals, mermaids, etc.

974 FRYE, Northrop. "The Four Faces of Prose Fiction." Hudson Review, 2 (Winter, 1950), 582-595. Reprinted in Frye, Anatomy of Criticism. Princeton: Princeton University Press, 1957. Pp. 303-314.

975 FRYER, Judith J. "The Faces of Eve: A Study of Women in American Life and Literature in the Nineteenth Century." Ph. D. diss., Minnesota, 1972. DA, 34 (1973), 2558A.

976 ________. The Faces of Eve: Women in the Nineteenth Century American Novel. New York: Oxford University Press, 1976. "The Temptress: In Which the Ambiguities of the Dark Lady Are Compounded by the Appearance of the Pale Maiden: Melville's Isabel," pp. 47-54. "The American Princess: The Pale Maiden, Melville's Lucy," pp. 87-97. Both articles refer to Pierre.

977 FUKUMA, Kin-ichi. "'Billy Budd': The Testament of Acceptance?" Kyusha American Literature (Fukuoka, Japan), 3 (May, 1960), 9-14. In English.

978 FULCHER, James William. "The Mask Idea in Selected Fiction of Poe, Melville, and Twain." Ph.D. diss., Peabody, 1975. DA, 36 (1976), 6082A-6083A.

979 FULLER, Roy, ed. The Confidence-Man: His Masquerade. London: Lehmann, 1948; New York: Grove, 1949.

980 FULWILER, Toby. "The Death of the Handsome Sailor: A Study of Billy Budd and The Red Badge of Courage." Arizona Quarterly, 26 (1970), 101-112.

981 FURIA, Philip. "Hart Crane's 'At Melville's Tomb.'" Explicator, 33 (May, 1975), item 73.

982 ________. "'Is the Whited Monster': Lowell's Quaker Graveyard Revisited." Texas Studies in Literature and Language, 17 (1976), 837-854.

983 FURROW, Sharon. "The Terrible Made Visible: Melville, Salvator Rosa, and Piranesi." Emerson Society Quarterly, 19 (1973), 237-253.

984 FUSSELL, Edwin S. Frontier: American Literature and the American West. Princeton: Princeton University Press, 1965. "Herman Melville," pp. 232-326; "Indian Summer of the Literary West," pp. 327-396.

985 FUSSELL, Mary Everett Burton. "Billy-Budd: Melville's Happy Ending." Studies in Romanticism, 15 (1976), 43-57.

986 ________. "Last Testaments: Writers in Extremis." Ph.D. diss., University of California (San Diego), 1976. DA, 37 (1977), 5814A-5815A. Includes Billy-Budd and the late poetry.

987 GABRIEL, Ralph Henry. The Course of American Democratic Thought. New York: Ronald, 1940. "Melville, Critic of Mid-Nineteenth Century Beliefs," pp. 67-77.

988 GAILLARD, Theodore L., Jr. "Melville's Riddle for Our Time: 'Benito Cereno.'" English Journal, 61 (1972), 479-487.

989 GAINES, Kendra H. "A Consideration of an Additional Source for Melville's Moby-Dick." Extracts, 29 (1977), 6-12.

990 GALE, Robert L. "Evil and the American Short Story." Annali Istituto Universitario Orientale (Napoli, Sezione Germanica), 1 (1958), 183-202.

991 ________. "Bartleby--Melville's Father-in-Law." Annali Istituto..., 5 (1962), 57-72.

992 ________. "Redburn and Holden--Half Brothers, One Century Removed." Forum (Houston), 3 (1963), 32-36. Refers to Catcher in the Rye, by J. D. Salinger.

993 ________. "Melville's Moby-Dick, Chapters 91-93." Explicator, 22 (January, 1964), item 32.

994 ________. Plots and Characters in the Fiction and Narrative Poetry of Herman Melville. Hamden, Conn.: Archon, 1969.

995 GALE, Verna. "Melville's Conception of the Hero." M.A. thesis, Occidental (Los Angeles), 1949.

996 GALLAND, René. "Herman Melville et 'Moby-Dick.'" Revue Anglo-Américaine, 5 (October, 1927), 1-9. In French.

997 GALLOWAY, David D. "Herman Melville's Benito Cereno: An Anatomy." Texas Studies in Literature and Language, 9 (Summer, 1967), 239-252.

998 GAMBLE, Richard H. "Reflections of the Hawthorne-Melville Relationship in Pierre." American Literature, 47 (1975), 629-632.

999 GARDINER, Harold C., S. J., ed. American Classics Reconsidered: A Christian Appraisal. New York: Scribner, 1958. "Herman Melville: 1819-1891--Loyalty to the Heart," by Randall Stewart and Geoffrey Stone, pp. 210-228.

1000 GARDNER, John Fentress. "Bartleby: Art and Social Commitment." Philological Quarterly, 43 (January, 1964), 87-98.

1001 ________. Melville's Vision of America: A New Interpretation of Moby-Dick. New York: Myrin Institute, 1977. 47-page pamphlet.

1002 GARGANO, James W. "Melville's 'Jimmy Rose.'" Western Humanities Review, 16 (Summer, 1962), 276-280.

1003 GARLAND, Hamlin. Crumbling Idols (1894), ed. Robert E. Spiller. Gainesville, Fl.: Scholars' Facsimiles and Reprints, 1952. Melville, passim.

1004 GARNER, Stanton. "Melville and Thomas Campbell: The 'Deadly Space Between.'" English Language Notes, 14 (June, 1977), 289-290. Relates to Billy-Budd.

1005 ________. "Fraud as Fact in Herman Melville's Billy-Budd." San Jose Studies, 4 (May, 1978), 82-105.

1006 ________. "Melville in the Customhouse, 1881-1882: A Rustic Beauty Among the Highborn Dames of Court." Melville Society Extracts, 35 (1978), 12-15.

1007 ________. "A Vexillological Key to Melville's Attitude Toward Slavery," a paper on Benito Cereno, read at the winter meeting of the Melville Society, December, 1978.

1008 GARNETT, Richard S. "Mocha-Dick, or the White Whale of the Pacific." Times Literary Supplement, July 30, 1926. P. 509.

1009 ________. "Moby-Dick and Mocha Dick: A Literary Find." Blackwoods' Magazine, 226 (December, 1929), 841-858.

1010 GARRISON, Daniel H. "Melville's Doubloon and the Shield of Achilles." Nineteenth-Century Fiction, 26 (1971), 171-184.

1011 GARY, Lorena M. "Rich Colors and Ominous Shadows." South Atlantic Quarterly, 37 (January, 1938), 41-45.

1012 GASCHE, R. "The Scene of Writing: A Deferred Outset," in Weber, Samuel, and Henry Sussman, eds., Glyph I: Johns Hopkins Textual Studies. Baltimore: Johns Hopkins University Press, 1977.

1013 GASKINS, A. F. "Symbolic Nature of Claggart's Name." American Notes and Queries, 6 (1967), 56.

1014 GEGENHEIMER, Albert Frank, ed. Arizona Quarterly, 31 (1975). Special Melville issue.

1015 GEIGER, Don. "Demonism in Moby-Dick." Perspective, 6 (Spring, 1953), 111-124.

1016 ________. "Melville's Black God: Contrary Evidence in 'The Town-Ho's Story.'" American Literature, 25 (1954),

464-471. Reprinted in Stern, ed., Discussions of Moby-Dick (1960), pp. 93-97.

1017 GEISMAR, Maxwell, ed. Moby-Dick. London: Pocket Books, 1949. Abridged version.

1018 ________, ed. Billy Budd and Typee. New York: Washington Square, 1962.

1019 GEIST, Stanley. Herman Melville: The Tragic Vision and the Heroic Ideal. Cambridge: Harvard University Press, 1939. Based on Harvard Honors Thesis in English, No. 12.

1020 GEORGE, J. L. "Israel Potter: The Height of Patriotism." American Transcendental Quarterly, 7 (1970), 53-56.

1021 GERLACH, John. "Messianic Nationalism in the Early Works of Herman Melville: Against Perry Miller." Arizona Quarterly, 28 (1972), 5-26.

1022 GEROULD, Gordon Hall. The Patterns of English and American Fiction: A History. Boston: Little, Brown, 1942. "Interpreters: I. Hawthorne, Melville, and the Brontes," pp. 341-366.

1023 GERSTAECKER, Friedrich W. C. Narrative of a Journey Round the World. New York: Harper and Brothers, 1854. Excerpt reprinted in McCormick, ed., Life on a Whaler (1960), pp. 99-105.

1024 GETTMAN, Royal A., and Bruce Harkness. "Billy Budd: Foretopman," in Teachers' Manual for a Book of Stories. New York: Rinehart, 1955. Pp. 71-74.

1025 GIBBS, Charles K., Jr. "Myth and Creativity in Moby-Dick." Ph.D. diss., Massachusetts, 1973. DA, 34 (1974), 4200A.

1026 GIBBS, Robert J. "The Living Contour: The Whale Symbol in Melville and Pratt." Canadian Literature, 40 (1969), 17-25.

1027 GIBSON, William M. "Herman Melville's 'Bartleby' and 'Benito Cereno,'" in Hendrick, ed., The American Renaissance (1961), pp. 107-116.

1028 ________, ed. Moby-Dick. New York: Dell, 1959. Contains Introduction.

1029 GIDDINGS, T. H. "Melville, the Colt-Adams, and 'Bartleby.'" Studies in American Fiction, 2 (1974), 123-132.

1030 GIFFORD, G. E. "Melville in Baltimore." Maryland Historical Magazine, 51 (Spring, 1956), 245-246.

1031 GILENSON, Boris. "Melville in Russia: For the 150th Anniversary of His Birth." Soviet Literature, 9 (1969), 171-173.

1032 GILLESPIE, Gerald. "Rogues, Fools, and Satyrs: Ironic Ghosts in American Fiction," in Zyla, Wolodymyr T., and Wendell M. Aycock, eds., Proceedings of the Comparative Literature Symposium, Vol. V. Lubbock: Texas Tech University, 1972. Pp. 89-106.

1033 GILMAN, William H. "Melville's Liverpool Trip." Modern Language Notes, 60 (December, 1946), 543-547.

1034 ________. "Herman Melville's Early Life and Redburn." Ph.D. diss., Yale, 1947.

1035 ________. "A Note on Herman Melville in Honolulu." American Literature, 19 (May, 1947), 169.

1036 ________. Melville's Early Life and Redburn. New York: New York University Press, 1951.

1037 ________. "Review of Horsford's Edition of Melville's Journal ... to Europe." American Literature, 28 (March, 1956), 82-93.

1038 ________. "Rejoinder to Horsford's Rebuttal." American Literature, 28 (January, 1957), 520-523.

1039 ________. "Review of William B. Dillingham's An Artist in the Rigging." American Literature, 45 (1972), 120-121.

1040 GILMORE, Michael T. "Melville's Apocalypse: American Millennialism and Moby-Dick." Emerson Society Quarterly, 21 (1975), 154-161.

1041 ________. "Fathers and Sons in Moby-Dick." Extracts, 26 (1976), 2-3.

1042 ________. The Middle Way: Puritanism and Ideology in American Romantic Fiction. New Brunswick, N.J.: Rutgers University Press, 1977. Melville, passim.

1043 ________, ed. with Introduction. Twentieth-Century Interpretations of Moby-Dick: A Collection of Critical Essays. Englewood Cliffs, N.J.: Prentice-Hall, 1977.

1044 GIONO, Jean. "Pour saluer Melville." Nouvelle Revue Francaise, 26 (April 1, 1940), 433-458. In French.

1045 ________. Pour Saluer Melville. Paris, France: 1941. In French.

1046 GIORCELLI, Christina. "Le poesie 'italiane' de Herman Melville." Studi Americani (Rome), 14 (1968), 165-191. In Italian.

1047 GIOVANNINI, G. "Melville's Moby-Dick." Explicator, 5 (October, 1946), item 7.

1048 ________. "Melville's Pierre and Dante's Inferno." PMLA, 64 (March, 1949), 70-78.

1049 ________. "Melville and Dante." PMLA, 65 (March, 1950), 329. A defense against article by Chesley Mathews.

1050 ________. "The Hanging Scene in Billy-Budd." Modern Language Notes, 70 (November, 1955), 491-500. Reply to article by Harry Modean Campbell.

1051 GLASSER, William. "Moby-Dick." Sewanee Review, 77 (1969), 463-486.

1052 GLEASON, Philip. "Moby-Dick: Meditation for Democracy." The Personalist, 44 (1963), 499-517.

1053 GLEIM, William S. "Journal of Melville's Voyage in a Clipper Ship." New England Quarterly, 2 (June, 1929), 120-125.

1054 ________. "A Theory of Moby-Dick." New England Quarterly, 2 (June, 1929), 402-419.

1055 ________. The Meaning of Moby-Dick. New York: Brick Row Book Shop Printers, 1938.

1056 GLENN, Barbara. "Melville and the Sublime in Moby-Dick." American Literature, 48 (1976), 165-182.

1057 GLICK, Wendell. "Expediency and Absolute Morality in Billy-Budd." PMLA, 68 (March, 1953), 103-110.

1058 GLICKSBERG, Charles I. "Melville and the Negro Problem." Phylon, 2 (September, 1950), 207-215.

1059 GODARD, Alice L. "A Study of Melville's Social Criticism as Reflected in His Prose Writings." Ph.D. diss., Illinois, 1946.

1060 GOFORTH, David S. "Melville's Shorter Poems: The Substance and the Significance." Ph.D. diss., Indiana, 1967. DA, 29 (1969), 3097A.

1061 GOHDES, Clarence F. "Gossip About Melville in the South Seas." New England Quarterly, 10 (Spring, 1937), 526-531.

1062 ______. "Melville's Friend 'Toby.'" Modern Language Notes, 59 (January, 1944), 52-55.

1063 ______. American Literature in Nineteenth-Century England. New York: Columbia University Press, 1944. Melville, passim.

1064 GOLDFARB, Russell, and Clare R. "The Doubloon in Moby-Dick." Midwest Quarterly, 2 (April, 1961), 251-258.

1065 ______. Spiritualism and Nineteenth-Century Letters. Rutherford, N.J.: Fairleigh Dickinson University Press, 1978. Melville, pp. 146-147 and 175-179.

1066 GOLDMAN, A. "Melville's England," in Pullin, ed., Perspectives (1978), pp. 68-75. Critical reception.

1067 GOLDSMITH, Arnold L. "'The Discovery Scene' in Billy-Budd." Modern Drama, 3 (February, 1961), 339-342. Refers to play by Coxe.

1068 GOLEMBA, Henry L. "The Shape of Moby-Dick." Studies in the Novel, 5 (1973), 197-210.

1069 GOLLIN, Richard and Rita. "Justice in an Earlier Treatment of the Billy-Budd Theme." American Literature, 28 (January, 1957), 513-515.

1070 GOLLIN, Rita Kaplan. "Pierre's 'Metamorphosis of Dante's Inferno.'" American Literature, 39 (January, 1968), 542-545.

1071 ______. "The Intelligence Offices of Hawthorne and Melville." American Transcendental Quarterly, 26 supplement (1975), 44-47.

1072 ______. "The Forbidden Fruit of Typee." Modern Language Studies, 5 (1975), 31-34.

1073 ______. "The Quondam Sailor and Melville's Omoo." American Literature, 48 (1976), 75-79.

1074 GOSSE, Edmund W. "Herman Melville," in Silhouettes. London: Heinemann, 1925. Pp. 355-362. Discusses "Apple-Tree Table," and John Marr and Other Poems.

1075 GOSSOM, Deborah Decker. "Innocence and Inexperience in Melville's Fiction." Ph.D. diss., Indiana, 1976. DA, 37 (1976), 2179A-2180A.

1076 GOTO, Shoji. "Philosophy of the Fatalist: A Note on Pierre: Or the Ambiguities." Rikkyo Review (Japan), 24 (March, 1963), 53-65.

1077 GOTTLIEB, L. D. "Reflections on the Uses of Place: Darwin and Melville on the Galapagos." Bio-Science, 25 (1975), 172-175.

1078 GOULD, Jean. Young Mariner Melville. New York: Dodd, Mead, 1956. For young people.

1079 GRAHAM, Philip. "The Riddle of Melville's Mardi: A Reinterpretation." University of Texas Studies in English, 36 (1957), 93-99.

1080 GRANGER, Bruce Ingham. "The Gams in Moby-Dick." Western Humanities Review, 8 (Winter, 1953-1954), 41-47.

1081 GRAUMAN, Lawrence, Jr. "Suggestions on the Future of The Confidence Man." Papers on English Language and Literature, 1 (Summer, 1965), 241-249.

1082 GRAVES, Robert Dorset. "Polarity in the Shorter Fiction of Herman Melville." Ph.D. diss., Duke, 1966. DA, 27 (1966), 1821A-1822A.

1083 GRAY, Valerie Bonita. "Invisible Man's Literary Heritage: Benito Cereno and Moby-Dick." Ph.D. diss., Ohio State, 1976. DA, 37 (1977), 7129A.

GRDSELOFF, Dorothee see FINKELSTEIN, Dorothee

1084 GREEGER, George R. "The Symbolism of Whiteness in Melville's Prose Fiction." Jahrbuch für Amerikastudien (Frankfurt), 5 (1960), 147-163. In English.

1085 GREEN, Jesse D. "Diabolism, Pessimism, and Democracy: Notes on Melville and Conrad." Modern Fiction Studies, 8 (Autumn, 1962), 287-305.

1086 GREEN, Martin B. Re-Appraisals: Some Commonsense Readings in American Literature. New York: Norton, 1966. "Melville and the American Romance," pp. 87-112.

1087 GREENBERG, Robert M. "Chasing the Leviathan: Religious and Philosophic Uncertainty in Moby-Dick." Ph.D. diss., City University of New York, 1978. DA, 39 (1978), 1566A.

1088 GREENE, Maxine. "The Whale's Whiteness: On Meaning and Meaningless." Journal of Aesthetic Education, 2 (1968), 51-72.

1089 GREJDA, Edward S. "The Common Continent of Man: The Non-White Characters in the Fiction of Herman Melville." Ph.D. diss., Pittsburgh, 1968. DA, 30 (1969), 1566A.

1090 ______. The Common Continent of Man: Racial Equality in the Writings of Herman Melville. Port Washington, N.Y.: Kennikat, 1974.

1091 GRENANDER, M. E. "Sonnet V from Dylan Thomas' Altarwise by Owl-Light Sequence." Notes and Queries, 5 (June, 1958), 263.

1092 ______. "Benito Cereno and Legal Oppression: A Szaszian Interpretation." Journal of Libertarian Studies, 2 (1978), 337-342.

1093 GRENBERG, Bruce Leonard. "Thomas Carlyle and Herman Melville: Parallels, Obliques, and Perpendiculars." Ph.D. diss., University of North Carolina, 1963. DA, 24 (1964), 3323.

1094 GRIFFITH, Clark. "Emersonianism and Poeism: Some Versions of the Romantic Sensibility." Modern Language Quarterly, 22 (June, 1961), 125-134.

1095 ______. "Caves and Cave Dwellers: The Study of a Romantic Image." Journal of English and Germanic Philology, 62 (1963), 551-568.

1096 ______. The Long Shadow: Emily Dickinson's Tragic Poetry. Princeton: Princeton University Press, 1963. Melville, passim.

1097 GRIFFITH, Frank C. "Herman Melville and the Quest for God." Ph.D. diss., Iowa State University, 1952.

1098 GRIFFITHS, Darrell E. "Circles and Orphans." Books at Brown, 24 (1971), 68-81.

1099 GRIMM, Dorothy F. "Melville as Social Critic." Ph.D. diss., Pennsylvania, 1948.

1100 GRIMWOOD, A. A. "A Study of the Sources and Allegory of Melville's Mardi." Ph.D. diss., New York University, 1949.

1101 GROBMAN, Neil R. "The Tall-Tale Telling Events in Melville's Moby-Dick." Journal of the Folklore Institute, 12 (1975), 19-27.

1102 ______. "Melville's Use of Tall-Tale Humor." Southern Folklore Quarterly, 41 (1977), 183-194.

1103 GROSS, John J. "The Rehearsal of Ishmael: Melville's Redburn." Virginia Quarterly Review, 27 (Autumn, 1951), 581-600.

1104 ________. "Herman Melville and the Search for Community." Ph.D. diss., University of Iowa, 1955. DA, 15 (1955), 1619.

1105 ________. "Melville, Dostoevsky, and the People." Pacific Spectator, 10 (Spring, 1956), 160-170.

1106 ________. "Melville's The Confidence-Man: The Problem of Source and Meaning." Neuphilologische Mitteilungen (Helsinki), 60 (1959), 299-310. In English.

1107 ________. "The Faces of Plinlimmon and the 'Failures of the Fifties.'" Emerson Society Quarterly, 28 (1962), 6-9.

1108 GROSS, Seymour L. "Mungo Park and Ledyard in Melville's 'Benito Cereno.'" English Language Notes, 3 (December, 1965), 122-123.

1109 ________. "Hawthorne Versus Melville." Bucknell Review, 14 (December, 1966), 89-109.

1110 ________, ed. A Benito Cereno Handbook. Belmont, Calif.: Wadsworth, 1965. Reprinted criticism.

1111 GROSS, Theodore L. "Herman Melville and the Nature of Authority." Colorado Quarterly, 16 (Spring, 1968), 397-412. Reprinted in Gross, T. L., The Heroic Ideal in American Literature. New York: Free Press, 1971. Pp. 34-50.

1112 ________, and Stanley Werthheim. Hawthorne, Melville, Stephen Crane: A Critical Bibliography. New York: Free Press, 1971. Melville, pp. 101-201.

1113 GROSSINGER, Richard. "Melville's Whale: A Brief Guide to the Text." Io (Plainfield, Vt.), 22 (1976), 97-152. Available from Book People, Berkeley, California.

1114 GUERARD, Albert J., ed. with Introduction. Stories of the Double. Philadelphia: Lippincott, 1967. Includes "Bartleby," pp. 211-247. Contrasts in Literature series.

1115 GUETTI, James Lawrence, Jr. "The Failure of the Imagination: A Study of Melville, Conrad, and Faulkner." Ph.D. diss., Cornell, 1964. DA, 25 (1965), 4145-4146.

1116 ________. The Limits of Metaphor: A Study of Melville, Conrad, and Faulkner. Ithaca, N.Y.: Cornell University Press, 1967.

1117 GUIDO, John F. "Melville's Mardi: Bentley's Blunder." Papers of the Bibliographical Society of America, 62 (1968), 361-371.

1118 GULBENKEIN, Martha V. "A Study of Melville's Narrators from Typee to The Confidence-Man." Ph.D. diss., Brandeis, 1972. DA, 34 (1973), 315A.

1119 GUNN, Giles. "Matthiessen's Melville." Extracts, 17 (1974), 8-9.

1120 GUPTA, Raj Kumar. "Form and Style in Herman Melville's Pierre: Or the Ambiguities." Ph.D. diss., Pittsburgh University, 1964. DA, 26 (1965), 1631-1632.

1121 ________. "Imagery in Melville's Pierre." Kyushu American Literature (Fukuoka, Japan), 10 (1967), 41-49.

1122 ________. "Melville's Use of Non-Novelistic Conventions in Pierre." Emerson Society Quarterly, 48 (1967), 141-145.

1123 ________. "Pasteboard Masks: A Study of Symbolism in Pierre," in Mukherjee, S., and D. V. K. Raghavcharyulu, eds., Indian Essays in American Literature: Papers in Honor of Robert E. Spiller. Bombay, India: Popular Prakashan, 1969. Pp. 121-128.

1124 ________. "Hautboy and Plinlimmon: A Reinterpretation of Melville's 'The Fiddler.'" American Literature, 43 (1971), 437-442.

1125 ________. "'Bartleby': Melville's Critique of Reason." Indian Journal of American Studies (Hyderabad), 4 (1974), 66-71.

1126 GUTTMANN, Allen. "The Enduring Innocence of Captain Amasa Delano." Boston University Studies in English, 5 (Spring, 1961), 35-45.

1127 ________. "From Typee to Moby-Dick: Melville's Allusive Art." Modern Language Quarterly, 24 (1963), 237-244.

1128 HAAG, John. "Bartleby-ing for the Camera," in Vincent, ed., Melville Annual, No. 1 (1965), pp. 55-63.

1129 HAAVE, Ethel Mae. "Herman Melville's Pierre: A Critical Study." Ph.D. diss., Yale, 1948. DA, 30 (1969), 1527A-1528A.

1130 HABER, Richard. "Patience and Charity in The Encantadas' 'Chola Widow' Sketch and in 'Cock-A-Doodle-Doo!'" Massachusetts Studies in English, 3 (1972), 100-107.

1131 HABER, Tom Burns. "A Note on Melville's 'Benito-Cereno.'" Nineteenth-Century Fiction, 6 (September, 1951), 146-147.

1132 HABERSTROH, Charles Jr. "Melville's Fathers: A Study of the Father Substitutes in Melville's Fiction." Ph.D. diss., Pennsylvania State, 1971. DA, 32 (1972), 4564A.

1133 ________. "Redburn: The Psychological Pattern." Studies in American Fiction, 2 (1974), 133-144.

1134 ________. "Melville's Marriage and Mardi." Studies in the Novel, 9 (1977), 247-260.

1135 ________, ed. with Introduction. Timoleon. Folcroft, Pa.: Folcroft Library Editions, 1977.

1136 ________. "Melville's L'Homme Révolté." English Studies, 46 (1965), 390-402. In French.

1137 HAGOPIAN, John V., and Martin Dolch, eds. Insight I: Analyses of American Literature. Frankfurt am Main, Germany: Hirschgraben-Verlag, 1962. Melville, pp. 144-165.

1138 HAKUTANI, Yoshinobu. "Hawthorne and Melville's 'Benito Cereno.'" Hiroshima Studies in English Literature and Language, 10 (1963), 58-64.

1139 HALE, Charles. A Vocabulary of the Nukahira Language. Boston: Privately printed by the author, 1848.

1140 HALL, James B. "Moby-Dick: Parable of a Dying System." Western Review, 14 (Spring, 1950), 223-226.

1141 HALL, Joan Jaffe. "Some Problems of Structure in Herman Melville's Novels." Ph.D. diss., Stanford, 1961. DA, 22 (1962), 3663-3664.

1142 ________. "'Nick of the Woods': An Interpretation of the American Wilderness." American Literature, 35 (May, 1963), 173-182. Relates to The Confidence-Man and "Indian-Hating."

1143 ________. "The Historical Chapters of Billy-Budd." University of Kansas City Review, 30 (October, 1963), 35-40.

1144 ________. "Melville's Use of Interpolations." University of Kansas City Review, 33 (October, 1966), 51-59.

1145 HALL, Sallie J. "'Full Fathom Five': A Study of the Interpolated Poem in Melville's Billy-Budd." South Atlantic Bulletin, 42 (1977), 139-143.

1146 HALLIBURTON, David G. "The Grotesque in American Literature: Poe, Hawthorne, and Melville." Ph.D. diss., University of California (Riverside), 1966. DA, 27 (1967), 3840A-3841A.

1147 HALLMAN, Ralph J. Psychology of Literature: A Study of Alienation and Tragedy. New York: Philosophical Library, 1961. Melville, passim.

1148 HALVERSON, John. "The Shadow in Moby-Dick." American Quarterly, 15 (Fall, 1963), 436-446.

1149 HAMADA, Masajiro. "Two Utopian Types of American Literature: Typee and The Crater." Studies in English Literature (Tokyo), 40 (March, 1964), 199-214. Refers to novel by James Fenimore Cooper (1848), a Utopian social allegory.

1150 HAMALIAN, Leo. "'Art': A Poem by Herman Melville." Explicator, 8 (March, 1950), item 40.

1151 HAMMES, Kenneth W., Jr. "Melville, Dana, and Ames: Sources for Conrad's The Nigger of the Narcissus." Polish Literary Review, 19 (1974), 29-33.

1152 HAN, Pierre. "Innocence and Natural Depravity in Paradise Lost, Phèdre, and Billy Budd." Revue Belge de Philologie et d'Histoire, 49 (1971), 856-861.

1153 HAND, Harry E. "'And War Be Done': Battle-Pieces and Other Civil War Poetry of Herman Melville." Journal of Human Relations, 11 (Spring, 1963), 326-340.

1154 HANDS, Charles E. "The Comic Entrance to Moby-Dick." College Literature, 2 (1975), 182-191.

1155 HANDY, Edward Smith Craighill. "Native Culture in the Marquesas." Bernice P. Bishop Museum Bulletin, 9 (1923), no pagination given.

1156 ________. "Polynesian Religion." Bernice P. Bishop Museum Bulletin, 34 (1927), no pagination given.

1157 HANDY, Willowdean Chatterson. Tattooing in the Marquesas. Honolulu: Bishop Museum Publication, 1922.

1158 HANSON, Elizabeth Irene. "Melville and the Polynesian-Indian." Extracts, 17 (1974), 13-14.

1159 ________. "The Indian Metaphor in the American Renaissance." Ph.D. diss., University of Pennsylvania, 1977. DA, 38 (1977), 1388A.

1160 HARADA, Keiichi. "The Theme of Incest in The Sound and the Fury and in Pierre." American Literary Review (Tokyo), 14 (May, 1956), 1-7.

1161 ________. "Melville and Puritanism." Studies in English Literature (Tokyo), 32 (October, 1956), 1-20.

1162 HARASZTI, Zoltan. "Melville Defends Typee." Bulletin of Boston Public Library, 22 (June, 1947), 203-208. In the "More Books" column.

1163 HARDING, Walter. "A Note on the Title Moby-Dick." American Literature, 22 (January, 1951), 500-501.

1164 ________. "The Apple-Tree Table." Boston Public Library Quarterly, 8 (1956), 213-215.

1165 HARKNESS, Bruce. "Bibliography and the Novelistic Fallacy." Studies in Bibliography, 12 (1958), 59-73.

1166 HARRIS, Duncan S. "Melville and the Allegorical Tradition." Ph.D. diss., Brandeis, 1972. DA, 33 (1973), 6911A.

1167 HARRIS, Peter B. "Melville: The Language of the Visible Truth." Ph.D. diss., Indiana University, 1975. DA, 36 (1975), 888A.

1168 HARRIS, Susan Kumin. "Invisible Spheres: The Rhetorical Response to the Loss of Moral Certainty in Herman Melville and Mark Twain." Ph.D. diss., Cornell, 1977. DA, 38 (1978), 7332A-7333A.

1169 HART, James D. "Melville and Dana." American Literature, 9 (March, 1937), 49-55.

1170 ________. "A Note on Sherman Kent's 'Russian Christmas Before the Mast.'" American Literature, 14 (November, 1942), 294-298.

1171 HARTMAN, Jay H. "Volpone as a Possible Source for Melville's The Confidence-Man." Susquehanna University Studies, 7 (1965), 247-260.

1172 HARTWICK, Harry. The Foreground of American Fiction. New York: American Book Company, 1934. Melville, passim.

1173 HASKEL, Paxton, III. The Omnipresence of Herman Melville. New York: University Publishers, 1967. See William A. Henkin's review in Triquarterly, 10 (Fall, 1967), 220-232.

1174 HAUCK, Richard Boyd. "The Descent to Faith: Herman Melville," in Hauck, A Cheerful Nihilism: Confidence and 'The Absurd' in American Humorous Fiction. Bloomington: University of Indiana Press, 1971. Pp. 77-132.

1175 HAUN, Eugene. "Patriarch, Parent, and Prototype." Sewanee Review, 58 (October-December, 1950), 708-716.

1176 HAUSER, Helen Ann. "A Multi-Genre Analysis of Melville's Pierre: The Patterns Almost Followed." Ph.D. diss., University of Florida, 1975. DA, 36 (1976), 5296A-5297A.

1177 ________. "Spinozan Philosophy in Pierre." American Literature, 49 (1977), 49-56.

1178 HAVEN, Rev. Gilbert, and T. Russell. Father Taylor, the Sailor Preacher. Boston: Russell; San Francisco: Bancroft, 1872.

1179 HAVERSTICK, Iola S. "A Note on Poe and Pym in Melville's Omoo." Poe Newsletter, 2 (1969), 37.

1180 HAWTHORNE, Hildegarde. "Hawthorne and Melville." Literary Review of the New York Evening Post, 2 (February 4, 1922), 406.

1181 HAWTHORNE, Julian. Nathaniel Hawthorne and His Wife, 2 vols. Boston: Osgood, 1884. Melville, passim.

1182 ________. "When Herman Melville was 'Mr. Omoo.'" The Literary Digest of the International Book Review, 4 (1926), 561-564.

1183 HAYASHI, Nobuyuki. A Study of Herman Melville. Tokyo, Japan: Nanundo, 1958.

1184 HAYFORD, Harrison. "Two New Letters of Herman Melville." Journal of English Literary History, 11 (March, 1944), 76-83.

1185 ________. "Melville and Hawthorne: A Biographical and Critical Study." Ph.D. diss., Yale, 1945.

1186 ________. "The Significance of Melville's 'Agatha Letters.'" Journal of English Literary History, 13 (December, 1946), 299-310.

1187 ________. "Hawthorne, Melville, and the Sea." New England Quarterly, 19 (December, 1946), 435-452.

1188 ________. "Review of Newton Arvin's Herman Melville." Nineteenth-Century Fiction, 5 (September, 1950), 163-167.

1189 ________. "The Sailor Poet of White-Jacket." Boston Public Library Quarterly, 3 (July, 1951), 221-228.

1190 ________. "Melville's Freudian Slip." American Literature, 30 (1958), 366-368.

1191 ________. "Poe in The Confidence-Man." Nineteenth-Century Fiction, 14 (December, 1959), 207-218.

1192 ________. "Melville's *Usable* or *Visible* Truth." *Modern Language Notes*, 74 (December, 1959), 702-705.

1193 ________. "Contract: *Moby-Dick*." *Proof*, 1 (1971), 1-7.

1194 ________. "'Loomings': Yarns and Figures in the Fabric," in DeMott, Robert J., and S. Marovitz, eds., *Artful Thunder* (1975), pp. 119-137. Based upon a lecture given by Professor Hayford many times: "The Imagery of Melville's Prisoners." Book in progress.

1195 ________. "Unnecessary Duplicates: A Key to the Writing of *Moby-Dick*," in Pullin, ed., *Perspectives* (1978), pp. 128-161.

1196 ________, and Merrell Davis. "Herman Melville as Office-Seeker." *Modern Language Quarterly*, 10 (June and September, 1949), 168-183 and 377-388.

1197 ________, ed. *The Somers Mutiny Affair*. Englewood Cliffs, N.J.: Prentice-Hall, 1959. Contains good bibliography of primary source materials, including numerous references to *Billy-Budd*.

1198 ________, ed. "Reviews of *Moby-Dick*, 1851-1853," in Hayford and Parker, eds., *Moby-Dick* (1967), pp. 613-621.

1199 ________, and Merton Sealts, Jr., eds. *Billy-Budd, Sailor (An Inside Narrative)*. Chicago: University of Chicago Press, 1962. Reading text and genetic text.

1200 ________, and Hershel Parker, eds. *Moby-Dick*. New York: Norton, 1967. Norton Critical Edition.

1201 ________, and Walter Blair, eds. *Omoo*. New York: Hendricks House, 1975.

1202 ________, Hershel Parker, and G. Thomas Tanselle, eds. *Typee*. Historical Note by Leon Howard. Evanston and Chicago: Northwestern University Press and the Newberry Library, 1968. First volume of the Northwestern-Newberry edition of *The Writings of Herman Melville*.

1203 ________, eds. *Omoo*. Historical Note by Gordon Roper. Northwestern-Newberry edition, 1968.

1204 ________, eds. *Redburn*. Historical Note by Hershel Parker. Northwestern-Newberry edition, 1969.

1205 ________, eds. *Mardi*. Historical Note by Elizabeth S. Foster. Northwestern-Newberry edition, 1970.

1206 ________, eds. *White-Jacket*. Historical Note by Willard Thorp. Northwestern-Newberry edition, 1970.

1207 ________, eds. Pierre. Historical Note by Leon Howard. Northwestern-Newberry edition, 1971.

1208 HAYMAN, Allen. "Herman Melville's Theory of Prose Fiction: In Contrast with Contemporary Theories." Ph.D. diss., University of Illinois, 1961. DA, 21 (1961), 3782.

1209 ________. "The Real and the Original: Herman Melville's Theory of Prose Fiction." Modern Fiction Studies, 8 (August, 1962), 211-232.

1210 ________, ed. Modern Fiction Studies, 8 (August, 1962). Special Melville issue.

1211 HAYS, Peter T. "Slavery and Benito-Cereno: An Aristotelian View." Etudes anglaises, 23 (1970), 38-46.

1212 ________. "Mocha and Moby Dick." Extracts, 23 (1975), 9-10. Sources of Moby-Dick.

1213 HAYWARD, Becky Jon. "Nature Imagery in the Poetry of Herman Melville." Ph.D. diss., Duke, 1974. DA, 35 (1975), 6095A-6096A.

1214 HEAD, Brian F. "Camões and Melville." Revista Camoniana, 1 (1964), 36-77.

1215 HECKMAN, Sally L. "Moby-Dick: The Process of Understanding." Ph.D. diss., Rutgers, 1970. DA, 32 (1971), 3252A.

1216 HEFFERNAN, Thomas F. "Melville and Wordsworth." American Literature, 49 (1977), 338-351. Annotations in Melville's copy of Wordsworth.

1217 HEFFERNAN, William A. "Melville's Primitives: Queequeg and Fedallah." Lock Haven Bulletin, Series 2, No. 1 (November, 1964), 45-52.

1218 HEFLIN, Wilson L. "The Source of Ahab's Lordship Over the Level Lodestone." American Literature, 20 (November, 1948), 323-327.

1219 ________. "Melville's Third Whaler." Modern Language Notes, 64 (April, 1949), 241-245.

1220 ________. "A Man-of-War Button Divides Two Cousins." Boston Public Library Quarterly, 3 (January, 1951), 51-60.

1221 ________. "Herman Melville's Whaling Years." Ph.D. diss., Vanderbilt, 1952.

1222 _______. "Melville and Nantucket," in Hillway, ed., Centennial Essays (1953), pp. 165-179. Lecture read at the Melville Observance held in the Unitarian Church at Nantucket on August 15, 1951, and recorded in the Proceedings of the Nantucket Historical Association, 1951. Pp. 22-30.

1223 _______. "A Contemporary Resident of Eimoo Checks up in Omoo." Extracts, 15 (1973), 2-3. Summary of lecture given at the spring meeting, 1973, of the Melville Society.

1224 _______. "Two Notes on Billy-Budd." Extracts, 14 (1973), 8.

1225 _______. "New Light on Herman Melville's Cruise in the Charles and Henry. Historic Nantucket, 22 (1974), 6-27. Contains list of ship's library.

1226 _______. "A Biblical Source for 'The Whale Watch' in Moby-Dick." Extracts, 23 (1975), 13.

1227 _______. "Sources from the Whale-Fishery and 'The Town-Ho's Story,'" in De Mott and Marovitz, eds., Artful Thunder (1975), pp. 163-176.

1228 _______. "An Indignant Contemporary Editorial on White-Jacket." Extracts, 25 (1976), 8-9.

1229 _______. "Melville, Celestial Navigation, and Dead Reckoning." Extracts, 29 (1977), 3.

1230 HEILMAN, Robert. Magic in the Web: Action and Language in Othello. Lexington: University of Kentucky Press, 1956. Compares Iago and Claggart of Billy-Budd, pp. 37, 43, and passim.

1231 HEIMERT, Alan. "Moby-Dick and American Political Symbolism." American Quarterly, 15 (Winter, 1963), 498-534.

1232 HEITNER, John A. "Melville's Tragic Triad: A Study of His Tragic Visions." Ph.D. diss., University of Rochester, 1968. DA, 29 (1968), 229A-230A.

1233 HELLER, Louis. "Two Pequot Names in American Literature." American Speech, 36 (February, 1961), 54-57. Refers to Pequod and Uncas.

1234 HEMSTREET, Charles. Literary New York: Its Landmarks and Associations. New York: Putnam, 1903. Melville and Whitman, passim.

1235 HENCHEY, Richard F. "Herman Melville's Israel Potter, A Study in Survival." Ph.D. diss., University of Massachusetts, 1969. DA, 31 (1970), 1758A-1759A.

1236 HENDERSON, Harry B., III. "Melville: Rebellion, Tragedy, and Historical Judgment," in Henderson, Versions of the Past: The Historical Imagination in American Fiction. New York: Oxford University Press, 1974. Pp. 127-174.

1237 HENDRICK, George, ed. American Renaissance, The History of an Era: Essays and Interpretations. Frankfurt, Germany: Diesterweg, 1961. "Herman Melville's 'Bartleby' and 'Benito Cereno,'" by William M. Gibson, pp. 107-116.

1238 HENDRICKSON, John. "'Billy Budd': Affirmation of Absurdity." Re: Arts and Letters, 2 (Spring, 1969), 30-37.

1239 HENNELLY, Mark M., Jr. "Ishmael's Nightmare and the American Eve." American Imago, 30 (1973), 274-293.

1240 HENRY, Teuira. Ancient Tahiti. Honolulu: Based on material recorded by J. M. Orsmond, 1928.

1241 HERBERT, T. Walter, Jr. "Calvinism and Cosmic Evil in Moby-Dick." PMLA, 84 (1969), 1613-1619.

1242 _______. "Spiritual Exploration in Moby-Dick: A Study of Theological Background." Ph.D. diss., Princeton, 1969. DA, 31 (1970), 1278A.

1243 _______. "Homosexuality and Spiritual Aspiration in Moby-Dick." Canadian Review of American Studies, 6 (1975), 50-58.

1244 _______. Moby-Dick and Calvinism: A World Dismantled. New Brunswick, N.J.: Rutgers University Press, 1977.

1245 HERFORD, C. H. "Romanticism in the Modern World." Essays and Studies by Members of the English Association, 8 (1917), 107-134.

1246 HERNDON, Jerry A. "Parallels in Melville and Whitman." Walt Whitman Review, 24 (1978), 95-108.

1247 HERRING, Thelma. "The Escape of Sir William Heans: Hays' Debt to Hawthorne and Melville." Southerly (Sydney, Australia), 26 (1966), 75-82.

1248 HETHERINGTON, Hugh W. "The Reputation of Herman Melville in America." Ph.D. diss., University of Michigan, 1933.

1249 _______. "Early Reviews of Moby-Dick," in Hillway, ed., Centennial Essays (1953), pp. 89-122.

1250 _______. "A Tribute to the Late Hiram Melville." Modern Language Quarterly, 16 (December, 1955), 325-331.

1251 ________. Melville's Reviewers: British and American, 1846-1891. Chapel Hill: University of North Carolina Press, 1961.

1252 HEWITT, Elizabeth Chapman. "Irony, Protest, and Prophecy in Melville's First Six Books." Ph.D. diss., Tufts, 1975. DA, 36 (1975), 1505A.

1253 HIBLER, David J. "Drum-Taps and Battle-Pieces: Melville and Whitman on the Civil War." Personalist, 50 (1969), 130-147.

1254 HICKS, Granville. The Great Tradition: An Interpretation of America Since the Civil War. New York: Macmillan, 1933. "Heritage," pp. 1-31. Melville, passim.

1255 ________. "A Re-Reading of Moby-Dick," in Shapiro, ed., Twelve Original Essays on Great American Novels (1958), pp. 44-68.

1256 HIGGINS, Brian. "Mark Winsome and Egbert: 'In the Friendly Spirit,'" in Parker, ed., The Confidence-Man (1971), pp. 339-343.

1257 ________. "Plinlimmon and the Pamphlet Again." Studies in the Novel, 4 (1972), 27-38.

1258 ________. "The English Background of Melville's Pierre." Ph.D. diss., USC, 1972. DA, 33 (1973), 1726A.

1259 ________. Herman Melville: A Reference Guide. Boston: Hall, forthcoming as of 1974. No further announcement as of 1978.

1260 ________, and Hershel Parker. "The Flawed Grandeur of Melville's Pierre," in Pullin, ed., Perspectives (1978), pp. 162-196.

1261 HIGGINS, Joseph. The Whale Ship Book. New York: Rudder, 1927.

1262 HILLWAY, Tyrus. "Taji's Abdication in Herman Melville's Mardi." American Literature, 16 (November, 1944), 204-207.

1263 ________. "Herman Melville and Nineteenth-Century Science." Ph.D. diss., Yale, 1944. DA, 29 (1969), 3578A.

1264 ________. "A Note on Melville's Lecture in New Haven." Modern Language Notes, 60 (January, 1945), 55-57.

1265 ________. "Melville's Billy-Budd." Explicator, 4 (November, 1945), item 12.

1266 ________. "Taji's Quest for Certainty." *American Literature*, 18 (March, 1946), 27-34.

1267 ________. "Melville's Art: One Aspect." *Modern Language Notes*, 62 (November, 1947), 477-480.

1268 ________. "The Unknowns in Whale Lore." *American Notes and Queries*, 1st Series, 8 (August, 1948), 68-69. *American Notes and Queries: A Journal for the Curious* ran from 1941 to 1950; reorganized in 1962.

1269 ________. "Some Recent Articles Relating to Melville: January, 1947-September, 1948." *Melville Society Newsletter*, 4 (November 1, 1948), no pagination.

1270 ________. "Melville and the Spirit of Science." *South Atlantic Quarterly*, 48 (January, 1949), 77-88.

1271 ________. "Melville's Use of Two Pseudo-Sciences." *Modern Language Notes*, 64 (March, 1949), 145-150. Refers to phrenology and physiognomy.

1272 ________. "Pierre, The Fool of Virtue." *American Literature*, 21 (May, 1949), 201-211.

1273 ________. "Melville's Geological Knowledge." *American Literature*, 21 (May, 1949), 232-237.

1274 ________. *Melville and the Whale*. Illustrated brochure. Stonington, Conn.: Stonington, 1950.

1275 ________. "Melville as Critic of Science." *Modern Language Notes*, 65 (June, 1950), 411-414.

1276 ________. "Melville as Amateur Zoologist." *Modern Language Quarterly*, 12 (June, 1951), 159-164.

1277 ________. "Billy-Budd: Melville's Human Sacrifice." *Pacific Spectator*, 6 (Summer, 1952), 342-347.

1278 ________. "A Preface to *Moby-Dick*," in Hillway, ed., *Centennial Essays* (1953), pp. 22-29.

1279 ________. "Hollywood Hunts the White Whale." *Colorado Quarterly*, 5 (Winter, 1957), 298-305. Review of movie starring Gregory Peck.

1280 ________. *Herman Melville*. New York: Twayne; New Haven: College and University Press, 1963. United States Authors series.

1281 ________. "Herman Melville's Major Themes," in *Americana-Austriaca*, 58 (1966), 170-180. Edited by Klaus Lanzinger. Wien and Stuttgart, Germany: Braumuller, 1966.

1282 ________. "Two Books in Young Melville's Library." Bulletin of the New York Public Library, 71 (1967), 474-476.

1283 ________. "In Defense of Melville's 'Fleece.'" Extracts, 19 (1974), 10-11.

1284 ________. "Melville and the Young Revolutionaries," in Americana-Austriaca, 66 (1974), 43-58. Edited by Klaus Lanzinger. Wien and Stuttgart, Germany: Braumuller, 1974.

1285 ________. "Melville's Education in Science." Texas Studies in Literature and Language, 16 (Fall, 1974), 411-425.

1286 ________. "Quaker Language in Moby-Dick?" Extracts, 23 (1975), 11-12.

1287 ________, ed. Melville Society Newsletter, published irregularly, 1945-1960.

1288 ________, ed. Doctoral Dissertations on Herman Melville, 1932-1952. Greeley, Colo.: Published for the Melville Society, 1953.

1289 ________, ed. with Introduction. Mardi: A Voyage Thither. New Haven: College and University Press, 1973.

1290 ________, and Luther S. Mansfield, eds. Moby-Dick Centennial Essays, edited for the Melville Society. Dallas: Southern Methodist University Press, 1953.

1291 ________, and Hershel Parker, eds. A Directory of Melville Dissertations. Evanston, Ill.: Northwestern University Press for the Melville Society, 1962.

1292 HIND, Charles Leevis. "Herman Melville," in More Authors and I. London: John Lane, 1922. Pp. 223-228.

1293 HINER, James. "Only Catastrophe." Minnesota Review, 10 (1970), 82-89. Refers to Billy-Budd.

1294 HIRSCH, David H. "The Dilemma of the Liberal Intellectual: Melville's Ishmael." Texas Studies in Literature and Language, 5 (1963), 169-188.

1295 ________. "Melville's Ishmaelite." American Notes and Queries, 5 (April, 1967), 115-116.

1296 ________. "Verbal Reverberations and the Problem of Reality in Moby-Dick." Books at Brown, 24 (1971), 45-67.

1297 ________. "Hamlet, Moby-Dick, and Passional Thinking," in Evans, G. B., ed., Shakespeare: Aspects of Influence. Cambridge: Harvard University Press, 1976. Pp. 135-162.

1298 HITT, Ralph E. "Controversial Poetry of the Civil War Period--1830-1876." Ph.D. diss., Vanderbilt, 1955.

1299 ________. "Melville's Poems of Civil War Controversy." Studies in the Literary Imagination, 2 (1969), 57-68.

1300 HOAR, Victor Myers, Jr. "The Confidence Man in American Literature." Ph.D. diss., University of Illinois (Urbana), 1965. DA, 26 (1966), 2753-2754.

1301 HODGSON, John Alfred. "The World's Mysterious Doom: Melville and Shelley on the Failure of the Imagination." Ph.D. diss., Yale, 1972. DA, 35 (1975), 4431A-4432A.

1302 HOEFER, Jacqueline S. "After Moby-Dick: A Study of Melville's Later Novels." Ph.D. diss., Washington University, 1967. DA, 28 (1968), 2647A.

1303 HOELTJE, Hubert H. "Hawthorne, Melville, and 'Blackness.'" American Literature, 37 (March, 1965), 41-51.

1304 HOFFMAN, Daniel G. "Melville's Story of 'China Aster.'" American Literature, 22 (May, 1950), 137-149.

1305 ________. "Melville in the American Grain." Southern Folklore Quarterly, 14 (September, 1950), 185-191.

1306 ________. "Moby-Dick: Jonah's Whale or Job's?" Sewanee Review, 69 (Spring, 1961), 205-224.

1307 ________. "Loomings," in Hoffman, Form and Fable in American Fiction. New York: Oxford University Press, 1961. Pp. 219-232.

1308 ________. "Myth, Magic, and Metaphor in Moby-Dick," in Form and Fable (1961), pp. 233-278.

1309 ________. "The Confidence Man: His Masquerade," in Form and Fable (1961), pp. 279-313. Reprinted in Chase, ed., Melville: A Collection (1962), pp. 125-143.

1310 HOFFMAN, Frederick John. Freudianism and the Literary Mind. Baton Rouge: Louisiana State University Press, 1945 and 1957. Melville, passim.

1311 HOFFMAN, Leonard R. "Problems in Herman Melville: The Style from the Beginning Through Moby-Dick." Ph.D. diss., Stanford, 1954. DA, 14 (1954), 2346-2347.

1312 HOFFMAN, Michael J. "The Anti-Transcendentalism of Moby-Dick." Georgia Review, 23 (1969), 3-16. Reprinted in Hoffman, The Subversive Vision. Port Washington, N.Y.: Kennikat, 1972. Pp. 87-100.

1313 HOFFMANN, Charles G. "The Development of the Short Story in Hawthorne, Melville, and James." Ph.D. diss., Wisconsin, 1952.

1314 ______. "The Shorter Fiction of Herman Melville." South Atlantic Quarterly, 52 (July, 1953), 414-430.

1315 HOGAN, Robert. "The Amorous Whale: A Study in the Symbolism of D. H. Lawrence." Modern Fiction Studies, 5 (Spring, 1959), 39-46.

1316 HOHMAN, Elmo Paul. The American Whaleman. New York: Longmans, Green, 1928.

1317 HOLDEN, Sarah Halland. "Changes in the Novel: A Structuralist Comparison of Middlemarch, The Confidence-Man, and Absalom, Absalom!" Ph.D. diss., Rice, 1977. DA, 38 (1977), 1409A.

1318 HOLDEN, W. S. "Some Sources for Herman Melville's Israel Potter." M.A. thesis, Columbia, 1932.

1319 HOLDER, Alan. "Style and Tone in Melville's Pierre." Emerson Society Quarterly, 60 (1970), 76-86.

1320 HOLLAND, Laurence B. "Authority, Power, and Form: Some American Texts." Yearbook of English Studies, 8 (1978), 1-14. Includes Emerson, Hawthorne, Melville, and Clemens.

1321 HOLLIS, Sophie. "Moby-Dick, A Religious Interpretation." Catholic World, 163 (May, 1946), 158-162.

1322 HOLMAN, C. Hugh. "The Reconciliation of Ishmael: Moby-Dick and the Book of Job." South Atlantic Quarterly, 57 (Autumn, 1958), 477-490.

1323 HOLT, Henry. Garrulities of an Octogenarian Editor. Boston: Houghton Mifflin, 1923. Melville, passim.

1324 HOLTZ, Nancy Ann. "The Great Measures of Time: A Study of Cosmic Order in Nineteenth-Century American Thought." Ph.D. diss., University of Washington, 1977. DA, 38 (1977), 3500A-3501A.

1325 HOMANS, George C. "The Dark Angel: Tragedy of Herman Melville." New England Quarterly, 5 (October, 1932), 699-730.

1326 HOMBERGER, E. "Melville, Lt. Guert Gansevoort, and Authority: An Essay in Biography," in Pullin, ed., Perspectives (1978), pp. 255-274.

1327 HONIG, Edwin. "In Defense of Allegory." Kenyon Review, 20 (Winter, 1958), 1-19.

1328 ______. Dark Conceit: The Making of Allegory. Evanston, Ill.: Northwestern University Press, 1959. Melville, passim.

1329 HOOSON, Christopher John. "The City in the Nineteenth-Century American Novel." Ph.D. diss., Indiana University, 1975. DA, 36 (1975), 2821A.

1330 HORNER, Charles R. "Isaac Brown: Melville's 'Beadle-Faced Man.'" Extracts, 26 (1976), 11-13.

1331 HORSFORD, Howard C. "Journal of a Visit to Europe and the Levant: 1856-1857." Ph.D. diss., Princeton, 1951. DA, 15 (1955), 584-585.

1332 ______. "Evidence of Melville's Plans for a Sequel to The Confidence-Man." American Literature, 24 (March, 1952), 85-89.

1333 ______. "Herman Melville's Journal of a Visit to Europe and Levant, October 11, 1856-May 6, 1857." American Literature, 28 (January, 1957), 520-523.

1334 ______. "The Design of the Argument in Moby-Dick." Modern Fiction Studies, 8 (Autumn, 1962), 233-251.

1335 ______, ed. Journal of a Visit to Europe and the Levant: 1856-1857. Princeton: Princeton University Press, 1955. Reprinted Westport, Conn.: Greenwood, 1976.

1336 HOUGHTON, Donald E. "The Incredible Ending of Melville's Typee." Emerson Society Quarterly, 22 (1961), 28-31.

1337 HOUSE, Kay S. "Francesco Caracciolo, Fenimore Cooper, and Billy-Budd." Studi Americani, 19 (1976), 83-100.

1338 HOUSTON, Neal B. "Silent Apostles: Melville's Animus Against the Clergy." Research Studies, 34 (1966), 230-239.

1339 HOWARD, Frances K. "The Catalyst of Language: Melville's Symbol." English Journal, 57 (1968), 825-831.

1340 HOWARD, Leon. "Melville and Spenser--A Note on Criticism." Modern Language Notes, 46 (May, 1931), 291-292.

1341 ______. "A Predecessor of Moby-Dick." Modern Language Notes, 49 (May, 1934), 310-311. Refers to Joseph C. Hart's Miriam Coffin, a novel in 3 vols. (New York, 1834), and its similarity to Moby-Dick.

1342 ________. "Melville's Struggle with the Angel." Modern Language Quarterly, 1 (June, 1940), 195-206.

1343 ________. Herman Melville: A Biography. Berkeley: University of California Press; London: Cambridge University Press, 1951.

1344 ________. Literature and the American Tradition. Garden City, N.Y.: Doubleday, 1960. Whitman and Melville, pp. 169-183.

1345 ________. "The Case of the Missing Whaler." Manuscripts, 12 (1960), 3-9.

1346 ________. "Herman Melville," in Foerster and Falk, eds., Eight American Writers: An Anthology (1963), pp. 781-970.

1347 ________. Herman Melville. Minneapolis: University of Minnesota, 1961. University of Minnesota Pamphlets on American Authors series, 48 pp. Reprinted in Foster, ed., Six American Novelists (1968), pp. 82-117.

1348 ________. "Herman Melville," in Stegner, Wallace, ed., The American Novel: From James Fenimore Cooper to William Faulkner. New York: Basic, 1965. Pp. 25-34. Discusses Moby-Dick.

1349 ________. "The Mystery of Melville's Short Stories." Americana-Austriaca, 58 (1966), 204-216.

1350 ________. "Historical Note," in Hayford and Parker, eds., Typee. Northwestern-Newberry edition, 1968.

1351 ________. "Historical Note," in Hayford and Parker, eds., Pierre. Northwestern-Newberry edition, 1971.

1352 ________. "Clarel's Pilgrimage and the Calendar." Extracts, 16 (1973), 2-3.

1353 ________. "Melville and the American Tragic Hero," in Crawley, Thomas Edward, ed., Four Makers of the American Mind: Emerson, Thoreau, Whitman and Melville. Durham, N.C.: Duke University Press, 1976. Pp. 65-82.

1354 ________. "The Case of the Left-Out Letter," in Mysteries and Manuscripts. New York: Privately printed, 1976. Pp. 17-26. How Leon Howard became a Melville scholar.

1355 ________, ed. Moby-Dick. New York: Random House, 1950. Modern Library edition.

1356 HOWARTH, R. G. "Melville and Australia." Notes and Queries, 193 (May 1, 1948), 188.

1357 HOWE, Irving. "The Confidence-Man: A Review of the John Lehmann Edition." Tomorrow, 8 (May, 1949), 55-57.

1358 HOWE, M. A. DeWolf. "Tale of Tanglewood." Yale Review, 32 (December, 1942), 323-336.

1359 HOWES, Jeanne C. "Melville's Sensitive Years," in Vincent, ed., Melville and Hawthorne in the Berkshires (1968), pp. 22-41.

1360 ________. "Melville's Loom." Extracts, 30 (1977), 18-20.

1361 HOWINGTON, Don S. "Melville's 'The Encantadas': Imagery and Meaning." Studies in Literature of the Imagination, 2 (1969), 69-75.

1362 HOYLE, Norman E. "Herman Melville as a Magazinist." Ph.D. diss., Duke, 1960. DA, 21 (1961), 2295.

1363 HUBBELL, Jay B. Who Are the Major American Writers? Durham, N.C.: Duke University Press, 1972. Melville, pp. 57-63.

1364 HUBBEN, William. "Ahab, the Whaling Quaker." Religion in Life, 18 (Summer, 1949), 363-373.

1365 HUDSON, H. E. "Billy Budd: Adam or Christ?" The Crane Review, 7 (Winter, 1965), 62-67.

1366 HUDSON, H. H. "The Mystery of Herman Melville." Freeman, 3 (April 27, 1921), 156-157. Also in Current Opinion, 71 (October, 1921), 502-503.

1367 HUDSON, Vaughan. "Melville's Battle-Pieces and Whitman's Drum-Taps: A Comparison." Walt Whitman Review, 19 (1973), 81-92.

1368 HUDSON, W. H. "Snow and the Quality of Whiteness," in Idle Days in Patagonia. London: Dent, 1923. Pp. 110-117. Reprinted in The Best of W. H. Hudson, ed. by Odell Shepard. New York: Dutton, 1949. Pp. 35-42.

1369 HUGHES, Charles W. "Man Against Nature: Moby-Dick and 'The Bear.'" Ph.D. diss., Texas Tech, 1971. DA, 32 (1972), 5230A.

1370 HUGHES, R. G. "Melville and Shakespeare." Shakespeare Association Bulletin, 7 (July, 1932), 103-112.

1371 HUGILL, Stan, ed. Shanties from the Seven Seas. Illustrated. New York: Dutton, 1961.

1372 HULL, Raymona. "London and Melville's Israel Potter." Emerson Society Quarterly, 47 (1967), 78-81.

1373 ________. "After Moby-Dick: Melville's Apparent Failures." American Transcendental Quarterly, 7 (1970), 4.

1374 HULL, William. "Moby-Dick: An Interpretation." ETC: A Review of General Semantics, 5 (August, 1947), 8-21.

1375 HULTIN, Neil C. "Melville's Search for Meaning." Discourse, 7 (Autumn, 1964), 454-461.

1376 HUME, Robert D. "Gothic Versus Romantic: A Re-valuation of the Gothic Novel." PMLA, 84 (1969), 282-290.

1377 HUMMA, John B. "Melvillian Satire: Boomer and Bunger." American Transcendental Quarterly, 14 (1972), 10-11.

1378 ________. "Melville's Billy-Budd and Lawrence's 'The Prussian Officer': Old Adam and New." Essays in Literature (Western Illinois University), 1 (1974), 83-88.

1379 HUMPHREYS, Arthur Raleigh. "Herman Melville." John O' London's Week, 5 (July 6, 1961), 18-19.

1380 ________. Herman Melville. New York: Grove; Edinburgh: Oliver and Boyd, 1962.

1381 ________, ed. with notes and annotations of variant readings. White-Jacket. London: Oxford University Press, 1966.

1382 HUN, Henry. A Survey of the Activity of the Albany Academy. Albany, N.Y.: Privately printed for the Academy, 1934. Melville attended this school in 1830-1832.

1383 HUNGERFORD, Edward. "Poe and Phrenology." American Literature, 2 (November, 1930), 209-231.

1384 ________. "Walt Whitman and His Chart of Bumps." American Literature, 3 (January, 1931), 350-384.

1385 HUNSBERGER, Claude. "Bibliographical Compendium: Vectors in Recent Moby-Dick Criticism." College Literature, 2 (1975), 230-245.

1386 HUNT, Levi. A Voice from the Forecastle of a Whale Ship. Buffalo, N.Y.: Reese, 1848.

1387 HUNT, Livingston. "Herman Melville as a Naval Historian." Harvard Graduate Magazine, 39 (Summer, 1930), 22-30.

1388 HUNTRESS, Keith. "Melville's Use of a Source for White-Jacket." American Literature, 17 (March, 1945), 66-74.

1389 ________. "A Note on Melville's Redburn." New England Quarterly, 18 (June, 1945), 259-260.

1390 ________. "Melville, Henry Cheever, and 'The Lee Shore.'" New England Quarterly, 44 (September, 1971), 468-475.

1391 ________. "'Guinea' of White-Jacket and Chief Justice Shaw." American Literature, 43 (November, 1972), 639-641.

1392 HURLEY, Leonard Burwell. "The American Novel, 1830-1850." Ph.D. diss., North Carolina, 1932.

1393 HURT, James R. "Suddenly Last Summer: Williams and Melville." Modern Drama, 3 (February, 1961), 396-400. Discusses The Encantadas and Moby-Dick.

1394 HURTGEN, James R. "Herman Melville's Political Thought: An Examination of Billy-Budd, Sailor (An Inside Narrative)." Ph.D. diss., State University of New York (Buffalo), 1973. DA, 35 (1974), 1657A-1658A.

1395 HUSNI, Khahl. "The Whiteness of the Whale: A Survey of Interpretations, 1851-1970." College Language Association Journal, 20 (1976), 210-221.

1396 HUTCHENS, John K. "Field Report on Mr. Melville's New One." New York Herald Tribune Book Review, July 22, 1956.

1397 HUTCHINSON, William E. "A Definitive Edition of Moby-Dick." American Literature, 25 (November, 1953), 472-478. Review of Mansfield and Vincent edition (Hendricks House, 1952).

1398 HUTCHINSON, William Henry. "Demonology in Melville's Vocabulary of Evil." Ph.D. diss., Northwestern, 1966. DA, 27 (1966), 2132A-2133A.

1399 HYMAN, Stanley Edgar, and R. W. B. Lewis. "Two Views of the American Writer." Hudson Review, 2 (Winter, 1950), 600-619.

1400 ________. "Melville, the Scrivener." New Mexico Quarterly, 23 (Winter, 1953), 381-415. Reprinted in Hyman, The Promised End: Essays and Reviews, 1942-1962. Cleveland: World, 1963. Pp. 68-99.

1401 IDOL, John. "Ahab and the 'Siamese Connection.'" South-Central Bulletin, 34 (1974), 156-159.

1402 ILSON, Robert. "Benito Cereno: From Melville to Lowell." Salmagundi, 1 (1967), 78-86.

1403 INGE, M. Thomas. "Unamuno's Moby-Dick." Extracts, 16 (1973), 3-4.

1404 ________, ed. Bartleby the Inscrutable: A Collection of Commentary on Herman Melville's Tale "Bartleby the Scrivener." Hamden, Conn.: Shoe String, 1978.

1405 INGLIS, Bowman, et al., eds. Adventures in American Literature. New York: Harcourt, Brace, 1950. Melville, pp. 518-520. High school textbook.

1406 IO (Plainsfield, Vt.). Special Issue, 22 (1976). "An Olson-Melville Sourcebook, Vol. I: The New Found Land (North America)." Distributed by Book People, Berkeley, Calif., 1976.

1407 IO. Special Issue, 23 (1976). "An Olson-Melville Sourcebook, Vol. II: The Mediterranean (Eurasia)." Distributed by Book People, Berkeley, Calif., 1976.

1408 IRWIN, John T. "The Symbol of the Hieroglyphics in the American Renaissance." American Quarterly, 26 (1974), 103-126. Refers to Hawthorne, Melville, Emerson, Thoreau.

1409 ISANI, Mukhtar Ali. "Melville's Use of John and Awnsham Churchill's Collection of Voyages and Travels." Studies in the Novel, 4 (1972), 390-395.

1410 ________. "Zoroastrianism and the Fire Symbolism in Moby-Dick." American Literature, 44 (November, 1972).

1411 ________. "Melville and the 'Bloody Battle in Affghanistan.'" American Quarterly, 20 (1968), 645-649.

1412 ________. "The Naming of Fedallah in Moby-Dick." American Literature, 40 (1968), 380-385.

1413 ISHAG, Saada. "Herman Melville as an Existentialist: An Analysis of Typee, Mardi, and The Confidence Man." Emporia State Research Studies, 14 (December, 1965), 5-41, 60-62.

1414 ITOEUJI, Hiromi. "Another Aspect of Billy Budd." Kyushu American Literature (Fukuoka, Japan), 10 (1967), 29-40.

1415 IVES, Charles B. "Billy-Budd and the Articles of War." American Literature, 34 (March, 1962), 31-39.

1416 IVES, Charles E. Essays Before a Sonata. New York:

Knickerbocker, 1920. Edited by Howard Boatwright, and reprinted New York: Norton, 1961, 1964. Melville, passim.

1417 JACKSON, Arlene M. "Technique and Discovery in Melville's Encantadas." Studies in American Fiction, 1 (1973), 133-140.

1418 JACKSON, Holbrook. Romance and Reality: Essays and Studies. New York: Kennerly, 1912. "Southward Ho!" pp. 5-16.

1418a JACKSON, Kenny. "Israel Potter: Melville's 'Fourth of July' Story." College Language Association Journal, 6 (March, 1963), 194-204.

1419 JACKSON, Margaret Y. "Melville's Use of a Real Slave Mutiny in 'Benito Cereno.'" College Language Association Journal, 4 (December, 1960), 79-93.

1420 JACQUE, Valentina. "Moby-Dick in Russian." Soviet Literature, 6 (1962), 185-187.

1421 JAFFE, David. "Melville's Use of Some Sources in Mardi." M.A. thesis, Duke, 1936.

1422 ________. "Some Sources of Melville's Mardi." American Literature, 9 (March, 1937), 56-69.

1423 ________. "Some Origins of Moby-Dick: New Finds in an Old Source." American Literature, 29 (November, 1957), 263-277.

1424 ________. "The Captain Who Sat for a Portrait of Ahab." Boston University Studies in English, 4 (Spring, 1960), 1-22.

1425 ________. The Stormy Petrel and the Whale: Some Origins of Moby-Dick. Baltimore: Port City, 1976. Foreword by Jay Leyda. Illustrated.

1426 JAMES, C. L. R. Mariners, Renegades, and Castaways: The Story of Herman Melville and the World We Live In. New York: University Place Book Shop, privately printed for the author, 1953.

1427 JARRAD, Norman E. Melville Studies: A Tentative Bibliography. Melville Society Special Publication, December, 1959. 49-page chronological listing.

1428 ________. "Poems by Herman Melville: A Critical Edition of the Published Verse." Ph.D. diss., University of Texas (Austin), 1960. DA, 21 (1961), 2714-2715.

1429 ________, ed. Poems by Herman Melville: A Critical Edition of the Published Verse. Austin: University of Texas Press, 1960.

1430 JARVES, James Jackson. History of the Hawaiian or Sandwich Islands. London: Moxon, 1843.

1431 JASTER, Frank. "Melville's Cosmopolitan: The Experience of Life in The Confidence Man: His Masquerade." Southern Quarterly (University of Southern Mississippi), 8 (1970), 201-210.

1432 JAWORSKI, Philippe, ed. "Herman Melville: 'Bartleby.'" Delta English Studies, 6, pp. 5-129, and 7, pp. 7-202 (1978), special issue, in French and English. All articles are included here.

1433 ________. "Images de 'Bartleby.'" Delta English Studies, 6 (1978), 113-114. "Entretien avec Maurice Ronet," director of film adaptation, follows, pp. 115-129. Illustrated conversation.

1434 JEFFREY, David K. "Unreliable Narration in Melville's 'Jimmy Rose.'" Arizona Quarterly, 31 (1975), 69-72.

1435 JEFFREY, L. N. "A Concordance to the Biblical Allusions in Moby-Dick." Bulletin of Bibliography, 21 (May-August, 1956), 223-229.

1436 JERMAN, Bernard R. "'With Real Admiration': More Correspondence between Melville and Bentley." American Literature, 25 (November, 1953), 307-313.

1437 JESKE, Jeffrey M. "Macbeth, Ahab, and the Unconscious." American Transcendental Quarterly, 31 (1976), 8-12.

1438 JOHNSON, Arthur. "A Comparison (with Henry James) of Manners." New Republic, 20 (August 27, 1919), 113-115.

1439 JOHNSON, Jeanne. "The White Jacket." Thoth, 1 (Spring, 1959), 14-19.

1440 JOHNSON, Paul David. "American Innocence and Guilt: Black-White Destiny in Billy-Budd." Phylon, 36 (1975), 426-434.

1441 JOHNSON, Richard Colles. "An Attempt at a Union List of Editions of Melville, 1846-1891." American Book Collector, 19 (1970), 333-347.

1442 ______. "Melville in Anthologies." American Book Collector, 21 (1972), 7-8.

1443 JOHNSON, Theodore. "Textual Criticism and Error." American Notes and Queries, 11 (December, 1973), 102.

1444 JONES, Bartlett C. "American Frontier Humor in Melville's Typee." New York Folklore Quarterly, 15 (Winter, 1959), 283-288.

1445 JONES, Bufford. "Melville's Buccaneers and Crêbillon's Sofa." English Language Notes, 2 (1964), 122-126.

1446 ______. "Spenser and Shakespeare in The Encantadas, Sketch VI." Emerson Society Quarterly, 35 (1964), 68-73.

1447 JONES, Dan Burne. "Moby-Dick: The Un-used Kent Illustrations." Extracts, 30 (1977), 4-9. Illustrations.

1448 JONES, Joseph. "Ahab's 'Blood Quench': Theater or Metallurgy?" American Literature, 18 (March, 1946), 35-37.

1449 ______. "Humor in Moby-Dick." University of Texas Studies in English, 25 (March, 1946), 51-71.

1450 ______. "Melville: A 'Humorist' in 1890." American Notes and Queries, 8 (August, 1948), 68.

1451 JONES, Walter Dickinson. "A Critical Study of Herman Melville's Israel Potter." Ph.D. diss., University of Alabama, 1962. DA, 23 (1963), 4357-4358.

1452 JOSEPH, Vasanth. "Some Biblical Nuances in Moby-Dick." Osmania Journal of English Studies, 8 (1971), 69-77.

1453 JOSEPHS, Lois. "Teaching Moby-Dick: A Method and an Approach." English Journal, 56 (November, 1967), 1115-1119.

1454 JOSEPHSON, Matthew. "The Transfiguration of Herman Melville." Outlook, 150 (September 19, 1928), 809-811, 832, 836.

1455 ______. Portrait of the Artist as an American. New York: Harcourt, Brace, 1930. "Libertarians and Others," pp. 3-43; includes Melville, pp. 26-36.

1456 JOSWICK, Thomas Philip. "Typee: The Quest for Origin." Criticism, 17 (Fall, 1975), 335-354.

1457 ______. "The Unreturning Wanderer: Melville's Thematics of Origins." Ph.D. diss., State University of New York (Buffalo), 1975. DA, 36 (1976), 4492A.

1458 ______. "Figuring the Beginning: Melville's The Confidence-Man." Genre, 11 (1978), 389-409.

1459 ______. "The 'Incurable Disorder' in 'Bartleby the Scrivener.'" Delta English Studies, 6 (1978), 79-83.

1460 JUBAK, James. "The Influence of the Travel Narrative on Melville's Mardi." Genre, 9 (1976), 121-133.

1461 JUSTMAN, Stewart. "Repression and Self in 'Benito Cereno.'" Studies in Short Fiction, 15 (1978), 301-306.

1462 JUSTUS, James. "Beyond Gothicism: Wuthering Heights and an American Tradition." Tennessee Studies in Literature, 5 (1960), 25-33. Includes Hawthorne, Melville, and Faulkner.

1463 KAHN, Sholom J. "Herman Melville in Jerusalem: Excerpts from a Journal." Commentary, 23 (February, 1957), 167-172.

1464 KAMAN, John M. "The Lonely Hero in Hawthorne, Melville, Twain, and James." Ph.D. diss., Stanford, 1973. DA, 34 (1974), 5974A-5975A.

1465 KAPLAN, Harold. "Melville: One Royal Mantle of Humanity," in Kaplan, Democratic Humanism and American Literature. Chicago and London: University of Chicago Press, 1972. Pp. 159-197.

1466 KAPLAN, Sidney. "Herman Melville and the American National Sin." Ph.D. diss., Harvard, 1948.

1467 ______. "Omoo: Melville's and Boucicault's." American Notes and Queries, 10 (January, 1950), 150-151.

1468 ______. "The Moby-Dick in the Service of the Underground Railroad." Phylon, 12 (1951), 173-176.

1469 ______. "Can a Whale Sink a Ship? The Utica Daily Gazette vs. the New Bedford Whaleman's Shipping List." New York History, 32 (April, 1952), 159-163.

1470 ______. "Herman Melville and the Whaling Enderbys." American Literature, 24 (May, 1952), 224-229.

1471 ______. "Herman Melville and the American National Sin: The Meaning of Benito-Cereno." Journal of Negro History, 41 (October, 1956), 311-338, and 42 (January, 1957), 11-37. Reprinted in Gross, S. L., and J. E.

Hardy, eds., Images of the Negro in American Literature. Chicago: University of Chicago Press, 1966. Pp. 135-162.

1472 ________, ed. Herman Melville: Battle-Pieces and Aspects of War. Gainesville, Fla.: Scholars' Facsimiles and Reprints, 1960. Reprinted Amherst: University of Massachusetts Press, 1972.

1473 KARCHER, Carolyn Lury. "The Story of Charlemont: A Dramatization of Melville's Concepts of Fiction in The Confidence Man: His Masquerade." Nineteenth-Century Fiction, 21 (June, 1966), 73-84.

1474 ________. "The Spiritual Lesson of Melville's 'The Apple-Tree Table.'" American Quarterly, 23 (1971), 101-109.

1475 ________. "Melville's 'The Gees': A Forgotten Satire on Scientific Racism." American Quarterly, 27 (1975), 421-442.

1476 ________. "Melville and Racial Prejudice: A Re-Evaluation." Southern Review, 12 (April, 1976), 287-310.

1477 KASEGAWA, Koh. "Moby-Dick: A Tragedy of Madness." Thoughts Current in English Literature (Tokyo), 30 (Autumn, 1957), 63-88.

1478 ________. "Moby-Dick as a Symbolic Myth." Studies in English Literature (Tokyo), 36 (1960), 251-272.

1479 ________. "Emerson, Thoreau, Melville." Aoyama Journal of General Literature, 5 (November, 1964), 15-24.

1480 KATZ, Jonathan, ed. Gay American History. New York: Crowell, 1976. Melville, passim.

1481 KAUFMAN, Paul. "Defining Romanticism." Modern Language Notes, 40 (April, 1925), 193-204. Melville, passim.

1482 KAUL, A. N. The American Vision: Actual and Ideal Society in Nineteenth-Century Fiction. New Haven: Yale University Press, 1963. "Herman Melville: The New World Voyageur," pp. 214-279.

1483 KAUVER, Gerald B. "Chapter 54 of Moby-Dick." Arlington Quarterly, 2 (1970), 133-141. Refers to "The Town-Ho's Story."

1484 KAY, Donald. "Herman Melville's Literary Relationship with Evert Duyckinck." College Language Association Journal, 18 (March, 1975), 393-403.

1485 KAZIN, Alfred. On Native Grounds. New York: Reynal and Hitchcock, 1942. Reprinted, abridged, with a new Post-script, Garden City, N.Y.: Doubleday, Anchor, 1956. Melville, passim.

1486 ________. "The Inmost Leaf." New Republic, 111 (December, 18, 1944), 218-220.

1487 ________. "Ishmael in His Academic Heaven." New Yorker, 24 (February 12, 1949), 84, 87-89. Review of F. B. Freeman's edition of Billy-Budd (1948).

1488 ________. "On Melville as Scripture." Partisan Review, 17 (January, 1950), 67-75. Review of Chase's Herman Melville (1949). Reprinted in Kazin, The Inmost Leaf: A Selection of Essays. New York: Harcourt, Brace, 1955. Pp. 197-207.

1489 ________, Lawrance Thompson, and Lyman Bryson. "Moby-Dick," in Invitation to Learning Reader, 11 (1953), 205-211.

1490 ________. "Ishmael and Ahab." Atlantic Monthly, 198 (November, 1956), 81-85. Reprinted as Introduction, Moby-Dick, ed. Kazin (1956). Also reprinted in Beaver, H. L., ed., American Critical Essays: Twentieth Century. London: Oxford University Press, 1959. Pp. 332-347. Further reprints include Stern, ed., Discussions of Moby-Dick (1960), pp. 52-59; and Chase, ed., Melville: A Collection (1962), pp. 39-48.

1491 ________. "Moby-Dick," in Kazin, ed., The Open Form. New York: Harcourt, Brace, and World, 1961. Pp. 112-123.

1492 ________. "Melville, the New Yorker." New York Review of Books, 20 (1973), 3-8.

1493 ________, ed. with Introduction. Moby-Dick. New York and Boston: Houghton Mifflin, 1956. Riverside series.

1494 KEARNS, Edward A. "Omniscient Ambiguity: The Narrator of Moby-Dick and Billy-Budd." Emerson Society Quarterly, 58 (1970), 117-120.

1495 KEELER, Clinton. "Melville's Delano: Our Cheerful Axiologist." College Language Association Journal, 10 (September, 1966), 49-55.

1496 KEHLER, Harold. "On Naming White-Jacket." Extracts, 21 (1975), 4-5.

1497 KEHLER, Joel R. "Faulkner, Melville, and a Tale of Two

Carpenters." *Notes on Modern American Literature*, 1 (1977), item 22.

1498 KELLNER, Robert Scott. "Herman Melville: The Sketch of a Genre." *Massachusetts Studies in English*, 3 (1971), 22-26.

1499 ———. "Sex, Toads, and Scorpions: A Study of the Psychological Themes in Melville's *Pierre*." *Arizona Quarterly*, 31 (1975), 5-20.

1500 ———. "Whitman, Melville, and the Civil War: A Sharing of Mood and Metaphor." *American Notes and Queries*, 13 (1975), 102-105.

1501 ———. "Toads and Scorpions: Women and Sex in the Writings of Herman Melville." Ph.D. diss., University of Massachusetts, 1977. *DA*, 38 (1977), 2127A.

1502 KELLOGG, Remington. "Whales, Giants of the Sea." *National Geographic*, 67 (January, 1940), 35-90.

1503 KELLY, Michael J. "Claggart's 'Equivocal Words' and Lamb's 'Popular Fallacies.'" *Studies in Short Fiction*, 9 (1972), 183-186.

1504 KELLY, Robert Alan. "The Prophetic Figure in Herman Melville's Writing." Ph.D. diss., Louisiana State, 1976. *DA*, 37 (1976), 2872A. Studies *Mardi*, *Moby-Dick*, *Pierre*, *The Confidence-Man*, and *Billy-Budd*.

1505 ———. "The Failure of Prophecy in Melville's *Pierre*." *Christianity and Literature*, 27 (1978), 18-27.

1506 KEMPER, Kristie Ann. "The Search for a Political Theory in the Fiction of Herman Melville." Ph.D. diss., University of Tennessee, 1975. *DA*, 36 (1976), 4492A.

1507 KENDALL, Lyle H., Jr. "On the 'Whiteness of the Whale.'" *Notes and Queries*, 200 (June, 1955), 266.

1508a KENNEDY, Frederick James. "Herman Melville's Lecture in Montreal." *New England Quarterly*, 50 (1977).

1508b ———. "Dr. Samul Arth Jones and Herman Melville." *Extracts*, 32 (1977), 3-7.

1508c ———, and Joyce Deveau Kennedy. "Additions to *The Melville Log*." *Extracts*, 31 (1977), 4-8. Refers to work by Jay Leyda (1951).

1508d ———. "Elizabeth and Herman." *Melville Society Extracts*, 33 (1978), 4-12; and 34 (1978), 3-8.

1508e ________. "Herman Melville and Samuel Hay Savage, 1847-1857." Melville Society Extracts 35 (1978), 1-10. Contains photocopy of previously unpublished Melville letter.

1508f KENNEDY, Joyce Deveau and Frederick James Kennedy. "Pierre's Progeny: O'Neill and the Melville Revival." English Studies in Canada (Toronto), 3 (1977), 103-117.

1508g KENNEDY, Robert S. "The Theme of the Quest." English Record, 8 (Winter, 1957), 2-7.

1508h KENNEY, Alice P. The Gansevoorts of Albany: Dutch Patricians in the Upper Hudson Valley. Syracuse, N.Y.: Syracuse University Press, 1969.

1508i ________. "'Evidences of Regard': Three Generations of American Love Letters." Bulletin of the New York Public Library, 76 (1972), 92-119.

1508j ________. "Herman Melville and the Dutch Tradition." Bulletin of the New York Public Library, 79 (1976), 386-399.

1509 KENNEY, Blair G. "Melville's Billy-Budd: A Note on Captain Vere." American Notes and Queries, 9 (1971), 151-152.

1510 KENNY, Vincent S. "Herman Melville's Clarel." Ph.D. diss., New York University, 1965. DA, 27 (1966), 458A-459A.

1511 ________. "Clarel's Rejection of the Titans." American Transcendental Quarterly, 7 (1970), 76-81.

1512 ________. "Melville's Problem of Detachment and Engagement." American Transcendental Quarterly, 19 (1973), 30-37.

1513 ________. Herman Melville's Clarel: A Spiritual Autobiography. Hamden, Conn.: Shoe String, 1973.

1514 KENT, Rockwell. Illustrations for Moby-Dick. Chicago: Lakeside, 1930. 3 vols. limited edition; also published New York: Random House, 1930. 1-vol. trade edition.

1515 KERN, Alexander. "Melville's The Confidence Man: A Structure of Satire," in Brack, ed., American Humor (1977), 27-41.

1516 KERR, Howard. Mediums, and Spirit-Rappers, and Roaring Radicals: Spiritualism in American Literature, 1850-1900. Urbana: University of Illinois Press, 1972. "The Apple-Tree Table," pp. 43-54.

1517 KETTERER, David. "Some Co-ordinates in Billy-Budd." Journal of American Studies, 3 (1969), 221-237.

1518 ______. New Worlds for Old: The Apocalyptic Imagination, Science Fiction, and American Literature. Bloomington: Indiana University Press, 1973. "Melville's The Confidence Man and the Fiction of Science," pp. 267-295.

1519 ______. "Censorship and Symbolism in Typee." Melville Society Extracts, 34 (1978), 8.

1520 KEY, Howard C. "The Influence of Travel Literature upon Herman Melville's Fictional Technique." Ph.D. diss., Stanford, 1953.

1521 KEY, James Albert. "An Introduction to Melville's Bird Imagery." Ph.D. diss., Tulane, 1966. DA, 27 (1966), 1369A.

1522 ______. "Typee: A Bird's-Eye View." Publications of the Arkansas Philological Association, 1 (1975), 28-36.

1523 KEYSER, Elizabeth. "'Quite an Original': The Cosmopolitan in The Confidence-Man." Texas Studies in Literature and Language, 15 (1973), 279-300.

1524 KEYSSAR, Alexander. Melville's Israel Potter: Reflections on the American Dream. Cambridge: Harvard University Press, 1969.

1525 KIEFT, Ruth M. Vande. "'When Big Hearts Strike Together': The Concussion of Melville and Sir Thomas Browne." Papers on Language and Literature, 5 (1969), 39-50.

1526 KILBOURNE, W. G., Jr. "Montaigne and Captain Vere." American Literature, 33 (January, 1962), 514-517.

1527 KIMBALL, William J. "Charles Sumner's Contribution to Chapter 18 of Billy-Budd." South Atlantic Bulletin, 32 (1967), 13-14.

1528 ______. "The Melville of Battle-Pieces: A Kindred Spirit." Midwest Quarterly, 10 (July, 1969), 307-316.

1529 KIME, Wayne R. "'The Bell-Tower': Melville's Reply to a Review." Emerson Society Quarterly, 22 (1975), 28-38.

1530 ______. "The American Antecedents of James De Mille's A Strange Manuscript Found in a Copper Cylinder." Dalhousie Review, 55 (1975), 280-306.

1531 KIMMEY, John L. "Pierre and Robin: Melville's Debt to Hawthorne." Emerson Society Quarterly, 38 (1965), 90-92.

1532 KIMPEL, Sgt. Ben Drew. "Herman Melville's Thought After 1851." Ph.D. diss., University of North Carolina, 1942.

1533 ______. Two Notes on Herman Melville: "A Possible New Article by Melville?" and "'The Lightning-Rod Man.'" American Literature, 16 (March, 1944), 29-30, 30-32.

1534 KINNAMON, Jon M. "Billy-Budd: Political Philosophies in a Sea of Thought." Arizona Quarterly, 26 (1970), 164-172.

1535 KIRK, Carey H. "The Challenge of Involvement: A Response to Melville and Conrad." Ph.D. diss., Vanderbilt, 1971. DA, 33 (1972), 1731A.

1536 ______. "Moby-Dick: The Challenge of Response." Papers on Language and Literature, 13 (1977), 383-390.

1537 KIRKHAM, E. Bruce. "The Iron Crown of Lombardy in Moby-Dick." Emerson Society Quarterly, 58 (1970), 127-129.

1538 KIRKLAND, James W. "Animal Imagery in the Fiction of Herman Melville." Ph.D. diss., University of Tennessee, 1969. DA, 31 (1970), 1803A-1804A.

1539 KIRSCH, James. "The Enigma of Moby-Dick." Journal of Analytic Psychology (London), 3 (Summer, 1958), 131-148.

1540 KISSANE, James. "Imagery, Myth, and Melville's Pierre." American Literature, 26 (January, 1955), 564-572.

1541 KISSANE, Leedice. "Dangling Constructions in Melville's 'Bartleby.'" American Speech, 36 (October, 1961), 195-200.

1542 KITCH, John C. "Dark Laughter: A Study of the Pessimistic Tradition in American Humor." Ph.D. diss., Northwestern, 1964. Melville, pp. 83-160.

1543 KLIGERMAN, Charles. "The Psychology of Herman Melville." Psychoanalytic Review, 40 (April, 1953), 125-143.

1544 KLINE, Gary Dean. "Patterns of History in Herman Melville's Clarel." Ph.D. diss., University of Wisconsin, 1974. DA, 35 (1975), 7869A-7870A.

1545 KNAPP, Joseph G., S. J. "Tortured Torturer of Reluctant Rhymes: Melville's Clarel, an Interpretation of Post-Civil War America." Ph.D. diss., University of Minnesota, 1962. DA, 24 (1963), 2035.

1546 ______. "Melville's Clarel: Dynamic Synthesis." American Transcendental Quarterly, 7 (1970), 67-76.

1547 ______. Tortured Synthesis: The Meaning of Melville's Clarel. New York: Philosophical Library, 1971.

1548 KNAPP, L. M. "The Naval Scenes in Roderick Random." PMLA, 49 (June, 1934), 593-598. Novel by Tobias Smollett, 1748.

1549 KNAUF, David. "Notes on Mystery, Suspense, and Complicity: Lowell's Theatricalization of Melville's Benito-Cereno." Educational Theatre Journal, 27 (March, 1975), 40-55.

1550 KNIGHT, Grant Cochran. American Literature and Culture. New York: Ray Long and Richard R. Smith, 1932. Reprinted Chapel Hill: University of North Carolina Press, 1951. Herman Melville, pp. 214-221.

1551 KNIGHT, Karl F. "Melville's Variations of the Theme of Failure: 'Bartleby' and Billy-Budd." Arlington Quarterly, 2 (1969), 44-58.

1552 KNOX, George A. "Communication and Communion in Melville." Renascence, 9 (Autumn, 1956), 26-31.

1553 ______. "Lost Command: 'Benito Cereno' Reconsidered." The Personalist, 60 (Summer, 1959), 280-291.

1554 KOERNER, James D. "The Wake of the White Whale." Kansas Magazine, 4 (1954), 42-50.

1555 KOLVIG, Eric William. "Young Life's Old Routine: Patterns of Initiation in Herman Melville." Ph.D. diss., Yale, 1976. DA, 37 (1977), 4353A-4354A.

1556 KORKOWSKI, Eugene. "Melville and Des Pèriers: An Analogue for The Confidence-Man." American Transcendental Quarterly, 31 (1976), 14-19.

1557 KORNFELD, Milton H. "Bartleby and the Presentation of Self in Everyday Life." Arizona Quarterly, 31 (1975), 51-56.

1558 KOSINSKI, Mark Kermit. "American Culture as System: A Methodological Inquiry." Ph.D. diss., Bowling Green State, 1978. DA, 39 (1978), 3004A. Contains a section on Moby-Dick.

1559 KOSOK, Heinz. The Influence of the Gothic Novel on Melville. Hamburg, Germany: Gruyter, 1963. In German; has not been translated.

1560 ______. "Redburn's Image of Childhood." Emerson Society Quarterly, 39 (1965), 40-42.

1561 ______. "'A Sadder and a Wiser Boy': Herman Melville's

Redburn as a Novel of Initiation." Jahrbuch für Amerikastudien, 10 (1965), 126-152. In English.

1562 ________. "Ishmael's Audience in 'The Town-Ho's Story.'" Notes and Queries, 14 (1967), 54-56.

1563 KOTZIN, Miriam. "Putnam's Monthly and Herman Melville." Extracts, 24 (1975), 4-5.

1564 KOUNTOUPES, Gus George. "Method and Meaning in Melville's Short Stories." Ph.D. diss., University of Toledo, 1976. DA, 37 (1977), 4354A.

1565 KRAMER, Aaron. "The Prophetic Tradition in American Poetry, 1835-1900." Ph.D. diss., New York University, 1966. DA, 27 (1967), 3461A.

1566 ________. The Prophetic Tradition in American Poetry, 1835-1900. Rutherford, N.J.: Fairleigh Dickinson University Press, 1968. Melville, pp. 26-28 and passim.

1567 ________. Melville's Poetry: Toward the Enlarged Heart. Rutherford, N.J.: Fairleigh Dickinson University Press, 1972. Study of "Bridegroom Dick," "The Scout Toward Aldie," and "Marquis de Grandvin."

1568 KRAUSE, Sydney J., ed. Essays on Determinism in American Literature. Kent, Ohio: Kent State University Press, 1964. "Some Patterns from Melville's 'Loom of Time,'" by Luther S. Mansfield, pp. 19-35.

1569 KREUTER, Kent Kirby. "The Literary Response to Science, Technology, and Industrialism: Studies in the Thought of Hawthorne, Melville, Whitman, and Mark Twain." Ph.D. diss., University of Wisconsin (History), 1963. DA, 24 (1964), 2446.

1570 KRIEGEL, Leonard, ed. with Introduction. The Life and Remarkable Adventures of Israel Potter. New York: Corinth, 1962. Refers to work on which Melville based his novel.

1571 KRIEGER, Murray. The Tragic Vision. New York: Holt, Rinehart, and Winston, 1960. "Melville's 'Enthusiast': The Perversion of Innocence," pp. 195-209. Discusses Pierre.

1572 KRING, Walter D., and Jonathan S. Carey. "Two Discoveries Concerning Herman Melville." Pennsylvania Magazine of History and Biography, 87 (1975), 136-141. Letters concerning Melville's marriage.

1573 KRUSE, Joachim, ed. Illustrationen zu Melville's Moby-Dick.

Schleswig, Germany: Schleswiger Druckund Verlagshaus, 1976. Moby-Dick and whaling; text in German.

1574 KUHLMANN, Susan. "And Back to Melville," in Knave, Fool, and Genius: The Confidence Man as He Appears in Nineteenth Century Fiction. Chapel Hill: University of North Carolina Press, 1973. Pp. 104-122.

1575 KUKLICH, Bruce. "Myth and Symbol in American Studies." American Quarterly, 24 (1972), 435-450.

1576 KULKARNI, H. B. "Significance of Sacrifice in Moby-Dick," in Narasimhaiah, C. D., ed., Indian Response to American Literature. New Delhi: U.S. Educational Foundation, 1967. Pp. 29-37.

1577 ________. Moby-Dick, A Hindu Avatar: A Study of Hindu Myth and Thought in Moby-Dick. Logan: Utah State University Press, 1970. Monograph Series, No. 18.

1578 KUMMER, George. "Herman Melville and the Ohio Press." Ohio State Archeological and Historical Quarterly, 41 (January, 1936), 34-35. Lecture notices.

1579 KUNTZ, Joseph. Poetry Explication: A Checklist of Interpretation Since 1925. Chicago: Swallow, 1963. Melville listing, p. 181.

1580 KUTRIEH, Ahmad R. "Melville's The Confidence-Man: The Mode of High Parody." Ph.D. diss., Bowling Green State, 1973. DA, 34 (1974), 5182A.

1581 LACY, Patricia. "The Agatha Theme in Melville's Stories." University of Texas Studies in English, 35 (1956), 96-105.

1582 LAING, Alexander Kinnon. Seafaring America, ed. Joseph J. Thorndike. New York: American Heritage, 1974. Contains a wealth of illustrations. Melville, pp. 100, 159-160, and passim.

1583 LANE, Lauriat, Jr. "Dickens and Melville: Our Mutual Friends." Dalhousie Review, 51 (1971), 316-331.

1584 ________. "Melville and Dickens' American Notes." Extracts, 12 (1972), 3-4.

1585 ________. "Dickens and Melville: A Partial Comparison." Extracts, 23 (1975), 14.

1586 LANG, Hans-Joachim. "Melville's Dialog mit Captain Ringbolt." Jahrbuch für Amerikastudien, 14 (1969), 124-139. In German.

1587 ________. "Poe in Melville's 'Benito Cereno.'" English Studies Today, 5 (1973), 405-429.

1588 ________, and Benjamin Lease. "Melville's Cosmopolitan: Bayard Taylor in The Confidence-Man." American Studies: An International Newsletter, 22 (1977), 286-289.

1588a LANNON, Diedrê. "A Note on Melville's 'Benito Cereno.'" Massachusetts Studies in English, 2 (1970), 68-70.

1588b LANOIX, Annette. "Les Différents Types de discours ou les problèmes de l'énonciation dans 'Bartleby.'" Delta English Studies, 7 (1978), 191-202. In French.

1588c LANZINGER, Klaus. "Melville's Redburn: Old World Expectations and Disappointments," in Americana-Austriaca, 66 (1974), 67-76. Edited by Klaus Lanzinger. Wien and Stuttgart, Germany: Braumuller, 1974.

1588d LAPE, Denis A. "The Masks of Dionysus: An Application of Friedrich Nietzsche's Theory of Tragedy to the Works of Hawthorne and Melville." Ph.D. diss., University of Minnesota, 1971. DA, 32 (1972), 5188A.

1588e LAROQUE, François. "Bartleby l'idée fixe." Delta English Studies, 7 (1978), 143-153.

1588f LARRABEE, Stephen A. "Herman Melville's Early Years in Albany." New York History, 15 (April, 1934), 144-159.

1589 ________. "Melville Against the World." South Atlantic Quarterly, 34 (October, 1935), 410-418.

1590 LA RUE, Robert. "Whitman's Sea: Large Enough for Moby-Dick?" Walt Whitman Review, 7 (September, 1966), 51-59.

1591 LASH, Kenneth. "Captain Ahab and King Lear." New Mexico Quarterly, 19 (Winter, 1949), 438-455.

1592 LATHERS, Richard. The Reminiscences of Richard Lathers. New York: Grafton, 1907.

1593 LATHROP, Rose Hawthorne. Memories of Hawthorne. Boston: Osgood, 1897. Melville, passim.

1594 LAUBER, John. "Sultan of the Pequod: Ahab as Hero." Dalhousie Review, 58 (1978), 30-45.

1595 LAURENS, Gilbert. "Le Pharmakos au gingembre." Delta English Studies, 7 (1978), 111-126.

1596 LAWRENCE, D. H. *Studies in Classic American Literature.* New York: Seltzer, 1923. Reprinted New York: Doubleday, Anchor, 1953. "Moby-Dick, or the White Whale," pp. 156-174. Reprinted in Stern, ed., *Discussions* (1960), pp. 35-44.

1597 ———. "Herman Melville's *Typee* and *Omoo*," in Lawrence, *Studies* (1923), pp. 142-156.

1598 ———. "The Transcendental Element in American Literature: A Study of Some Unpublished D. H. Lawrence Manuscripts." *Modern Philology*, 60 (1962), 41-46.

1599 LAWSON, John Howard. *The Hidden Heritage.* New York: Citadel, 1950. Melville, pp. 427-432.

1600 LEAF, Munro. "*Moby-Dick* by Herman Melville." *American Magazine*, 131 (June, 1941), 58. For young people.

1601 LEARY, Lewis Gaston. *American Literature: A Study and Research Guide.* New York: St. Martin's, 1976. Melville, pp. 113-116.

1602 ———, ed. *Articles on American Literature: 1900-1950.* Durham, N.C.: Duke University Press, 1954. Melville, pp. 204-211.

1603 ———, ed. *Israel Potter: His Fifty Years of Exile.* New York: Sagamore, 1957.

1604 ———, ed. *American Literary Essays.* New York: Crowell, 1960. "Hawthorne and His Mosses," by Herman Melville, pp. 90-92.

1605 ———, ed. *The Teacher and American Literature.* Champaign, Ill.: National Council of Teachers of English, 1965. "Recent Scholarship on Hawthorne and Melville," by Arlin Turner, pp. 95-109.

1606 ———, ed. *Articles on American Literature: 1950-1967.* Durham, N.C.: Duke University Press, 1968. Melville, pp. 367-390.

1607 LEASE, Benjamin. "Melville's Gally Gallow." *American Speech*, 25 (October, 1950), 186.

1608 ———. "Melville and the Booksellers." *Melville Society Newsletter*, 7 (June, 1951), 2.

1609 ———. "The Chemistry of Genius: Melville and Anton Bruckner." *Personalist*, 48 (Spring, 1967), 224-241.

1610 ———. "Two Sides of a Tortoise: Darwin and Melville in the Pacific." *Personalist*, 49 (Fall, 1968), 531-539.

1611 LEAVIS, Queenie Dorothy. "Melville: The 1853-1856 Phase," in Pullin, ed., Perspectives (1978), pp. 197-228.

1612 LEBOWITZ, Alan L. "Herman Melville's Ahab: The Evolution and Extinction of the Hero." Ph.D. diss., Harvard, 1964.

1613 ________. Progress into Silence: A Study of Melville's Heroes. Bloomington: Indiana University Press, 1970.

1614 LEDBETTER, Jack W. "The Trial of Billy-Budd, Foretopman." American Bar Association Journal, 58 (1972), 614-619.

1615 LEDBETTER, Kenneth. "The Ambiguity of Billy-Budd." Texas Studies in Literature and Language, 4 (Spring, 1962), 130-134.

1616 LEDYARD, John, ed. A Journal of Captain Cook's Last Voyage. Hartford, Conn.: Printed and sold by Nathaniel Parker, "a few rods north of the court house," 1783. See biography of John Ledyard by Jared Sparks, c. 1834.

1617 LEE, A. Robert. "Moby-Dick: The Tale and the Telling," in Pullin, ed., Perspectives (1978), pp. 86-127.

1618 LEE, Dwight A. "Melville and George J. Adler." American Notes and Queries, 12 (1974), 138-141.

1619 LEE, Grace Farrell. "Pym and Moby-Dick: Essential Connections." American Transcendental Quarterly, 37 (1978), 73-86.

1620 LEESON, Ida. "Mutiny on the Lucy Ann." Philological Quarterly, 19 (October, 1940), 370-379. Whaler on which Melville sailed when leaving the Marquesas.

1621 LEFCOWITZ, Allan and Barbara. "Ahab's Other Leg: Notes on Melville's Symbolic Method." Emerson Society Quarterly, 47 (1967), 23-27.

1622 LEGGETT, William. "The Encounter--A Scene at Sea," in Seelye, ed., Arthur Gordon Pym,... (1967), pp. 291-304. William Leggett, 1801-1839, original publication in 1834.

1623 LEHMANN, John, ed. The Confidence-Man. London: Lehmann, 1948.

1624 LEISY, Ernest Edwin. American Literature. New York: Crowell, 1929. Melville, pp. 102-105.

1625 ________. "Fatalism in Moby-Dick," in Hillway, ed., Centennial Essays (1953), pp. 76-88.

1626 LEITER, Louis. "Queequeg's Coffin." Nineteenth-Century Fiction, 13 (December, 1958), 249-254.

1627 LEMON, Lee T. "Billy-Budd: The Plot Against the Story." Studies in Short Fiction, 2 (Fall, 1964), 32-43.

1628 LENSON, David R. "Examples of Modern Tragedy." Ph.D. diss., Princeton, 1971. DA, 32 (1972), 6433A-6434A.

1629 ______. "Tragedy in Prose Fiction: Moby-Dick," in Lenson, Achilles' Choice. Princeton: Princeton University Press, 1975. Pp. 40-64.

1630 LEONARD, J. Joseph. "Melville's Lima." Arizona Quarterly, 26 (1970), 100. An original poem.

1631 LEONARD, Sterling A., ed. Typee. New York: Harcourt, Brace, 1920.

1632 LEONE, Carmen J. "Melville's Style in Typee and Moby-Dick: A Linguistic Analysis." Ph.D. diss., Kent State, 1973. DA, 35 (1974), 3689A-3690A.

1633 LESSER, Simon O. Fiction and the Unconscious. Boston: Beacon, 1957. Melville, pp. 92-93 and passim.

1634 LESTER, James D. "Melville's The Piazza Tales: The Quest for Communication." Ph.D. diss., University of Oklahoma, 1970. DA, 31 (1971), 6015A-6016A.

1635 LEVERENZ, David. "Moby-Dick," in Crews, Frederick C., ed., Psychoanalysis and the Literary Process. Cambridge: Winthrop, 1970. Pp. 66-117.

1636 LEVIN, David. History as Romantic Art. Stanford, Calif.: Stanford University Press, 1959. Hawthorne and Melville, passim.

1637 LEVIN, Harry. "Don Quijote y Moby-Dick." Realidad, 2 (1947), 254-267. In Spanish.

1638 ______. "Don Quixote and Moby-Dick," in Flores, Angel, and M. J. Benardete, eds., Cervantes Across the Centuries. New York: Dryden, 1947. Pp. 217-226. Similar to item above.

1639 ______. "What Is Realism?" Comparative Literature, 3 (Summer, 1951), 196-197.

1640 ______. Contexts of Criticism. Cambridge: Harvard University Press, 1957. Melville, pp. 97-109, 203-206.

1641 ______. The Power of Blackness: Hawthorne, Poe, and

Melville. New York: Knopf, 1958. Reprinted New York: Vintage, 1960. Melville, pp. 165-237.

1642 LEVINE, Stuart. "Melville's 'Voyage Thither.'" Midwest Quarterly, 3 (Summer, 1962), 341-353.

1643 LE VOT, André. "Shakespeare et Melville: le Thème Impérial dans Moby-Dick." Etudes Anglaises, 17 (1964), 549-563. In French.

1644 LEVY, Harris. "Iowa Theater Lab's Moby-Dick." Drama Review, 19 (September, 1975), 63-67. Illustrated.

1645 LEVY, Leo B. "Hawthorne, Melville, and the Monitor." American Literature, 37 (March, 1965), 33-40.

1646 ______. "Criticism Chronicle: Hawthorne, Melville, and James." Southern Review (South Australia), 2 (Spring, 1966), 427-442.

1647 ______. "Hawthorne and the Idea of 'Bartleby.'" Emerson Society Quarterly, 47 (1967), 66-69.

1648 LEWIS, Charles Lee. Books of the Sea. Annapolis, Md.: U.S. Naval Institute, 1943. Melville, pp. 29-31 and passim.

1649 LEWIS, R. W. B. "Melville on Homer." American Literature, 22 (May, 1950), 166-177.

1650 ______. The American Adam: Innocence, Tragedy, and Tradition in the Nineteenth-Century. Chicago: University of Chicago Press, 1955. Reprinted Chicago: Phoenix, 1958. "Melville: The Apotheosis of Adam," pp. 127-155. Reprinted in Goldberg, G. J., and N. M. Goldberg, eds., The Modern Critical Spectrum. Englewood Cliffs, N.J.: Prentice-Hall, 1962. Pp. 321-341.

1651 ______. "Afterword to The Confidence Man." New York: Signet, 1964. Pp. 261-276.

1652 ______. Trials of the Word: Essays in American Literature and the Humanistic Tradition. New Haven: Yale University Press, 1965. "Days of Wrath and Laughter: Melville after Moby-Dick," pp. 36-76: "Tales and Poems," pp. 36-61; The Confidence Man, pp. 61-76. Similar to two items listed above (1963, 1964).

1653 ______, ed. with Introduction. Herman Melville: A Reader. New York: Dell, 1963.

1654 LEWISOHN, Ludwig. "The Weakness of Herman Melville." This Quarter, 3 (April-June, 1931), 610-617.

1655 ________. Expressionism in America. New York: Harpers, 1932. Revised and reissued as The Story of American Literature. New York: Harpers, 1937. Reprinted New York: Random House Modern Library, 1939. Melville, passim.

1656 LEYDA, Jay. "White Elephant vs White Whale." Town and Country, 101 (August, 1947), 68ff.

1657 ________. "The Army of the Potomac Entertains a Poet." Art and Action: Twice a Year, 16 (1948), 259-272.

1658 ________. "Ishmael Melville: Remarks on Board of Ship Amazon." Boston Public Library Quarterly, 1 (October, 1949), 119-134.

1659 ________. "An Albany Journal of Gansevoort Melville." Boston Public Library Quarterly, 2 (October, 1950), 327-347.

1660 ________. The Melville Log: A Documentary Life of Herman Melville, 2 vols. New York: Harcourt, Brace, 1951. Reprinted New York: Gordian, 1969. New reprint edition adds pp. 901-966.

1661 ________. "Another Friendly Critic for Melville." New England Quarterly, 27 (June, 1954), 243-249.

1662 ________. "Bartleby: Genesis of an Opera, 2," in Vincent, ed., Melville Annual, No. 1 (1965), pp. 42-44. See article by Aschaffenburg.

1663 ________. "Herman Melville, 1972," in Bruccoli, Mathew J., ed., The Chief Glory of Every People: Essays on Classical American Writers. Carbondale: Southern Illinois University Press, 1973. Pp. 161-171.

1664 ________, ed. The Complete Short Stories of Herman Melville. New York: Random House, 1949.

1665 ________, ed. The Portable Melville. New York: Viking Press, 1952.

1666 LEYRIS, Pierre, ed. and trans. Billy-Budd. Neuchatel and Paris: Attinger, 1935; Paris: Gallimard, 1937. In French.

1667 LIEBER, Todd Michael. "The Continuing Encounter: Studies of the American Romantic Hero." Ph.D. diss., Case Western Reserve, 1969. DA, 30 (1970), 3911A.

1668 ________. Endless Experiments. Columbus: Ohio State University Press, 1973. "Ishmael: The Hero in Flux," pp. 113-163.

1669 LIEBMAN, Sheldon W. "The 'Body and Soul' Metaphor in Moby-Dick." Emerson Society Quarterly, 50 supplement (1968), 29-34.

1670 LIMPRECHT, Nancy Silverman. "Repudiating the Self-Justifying Fiction: Charles Brockden Brown, Nathaniel Hawthorne, and Herman Melville as Anti-Romancers." Ph.D. diss., University of California (Berkeley), 1977. DA, 39 (1978), 886A.

1671 LINDEMAN, Jack. "Herman Melville's Civil War." Modern Age, 9 (1965), 387-398.

1672 ________. "Herman Melville's Reconstruction." Modern Age, 10 (1966), 168-172.

1673 LINDGREN, Charlotte. "Herman Melville and Atlantic Relations." History Today, 25 (1975), 663-670.

1674 ________. "The Lion and the Stag: Herman Melville Views the Irish." Antigonish Review, 26 (1976), 81-95.

1675 LINDON, Mathieu. "Descriptions d'un combat." Delta English Studies, 6 (1978), 5-27. Refers to "Bartleby."

1676 LISH, Terrence G. "Melville's Redburn: A Study in Dualism." English Language Notes, 5 (December, 1967), 113-120.

1677 ________. "Name Symbolism in Melville's Pierre, and a Selective Onomastic Glossary for His Prose." Ph.D. diss., University of Nevada, 1971. DA, 32 (1972), 4007A. Refers to a study of the origins and meanings of names.

1678 LITMAN, Vicki Halper. "The Cottage and the Temple: Melville's Symbolic Use of Architecture." American Quarterly, 21 (1969), 630-638.

1679 LITTLE, Thomas A. "Literary Allusions in the Writings of Herman Melville." Ph.D. diss., University of Nebraska, 1949.

1680 LLOYD, Francis V., Jr. "Melville's First Lectures." American Literature, 13 (January, 1942), 391-395.

1681 ________. "A Further Note on Herman Melville, Lecturer." Massachusetts Historical Society Bulletin, 20 (1964), 310-312.

1682 ________. "Melville's Moby-Dick." Explicator, 29 (1971), item 72.

1683 LOCKERBIE, D. B. "The Greatest Sermon in Fiction." Christianity Today, 8 (November 8, 1963), 9-12.

1684 LOFGREN, Hans Borje. "Democratic Skepticism: Literary-Historical Point of View in Cooper, Hawthorne, and Melville." Ph.D. diss., University of California (Santa Cruz). DA, 38 (1978), 6714A-6715A.

1685 LOGAN, John. "Psychological Motifs in Melville's Pierre." Minnesota Review, 7 (1967), 325-330.

1686 LONDON, Philip W. "The Military Necessity: Billy-Budd and Vigny." Comparative Literature, 14 (Spring, 1962), 174-186. Refers to French poet, novelist, 1797-1863.

1687 LONG, Raymond Ronald. "The Hidden Sun: A Study of the Influence of Shakespeare on the Creative Imagination of Herman Melville." Ph.D. diss., UCLA, 1965. DA, 26 (1966), 4634.

1688 LONG, William J. American Literature: A Study of the Men and Books That in the Earlier and Later Time Reflect American Spirit. Waltham, Mass.: Blaisdell, 1913. Melville, pp. 247 and passim.

1689 LONGENECKER, Marlene B. "The Landscape of Home: Wordsworth and Melville." Ph.D. diss., State University of New York (Buffalo), 1973. DA, 34 (1974), 5110A.

1690 ________. "Captain Vere and the Form of Truth." Studies in Short Fiction, 14 (1977), 337-343.

1691 LORANT, Laurie J. "Herman Melville and Race: Themes and Imagery." Ph.D. diss., New York University, 1972. DA, 34 (1973), 3349A.

1692 LOVE, Gladys E., and Lillian C. West. "Melville and His Public." American Notes and Queries, 2 (August, 1942), 67-71.

1693 LOVING, Jerome M. "Melville's Pardonable Sin." New England Quarterly, 47 (June, 1974), 262-278.

1694 LOWANCE, Mason I. "Veils and Illusions in 'Benito Cereno.'" Arizona Quarterly, 26 (1970), 113-126.

1695 LOWELL, Robert. Benito Cereno, a play based on the novel by Herman Melville, in Lowell, The Old Glory. New York: Farrar, Straus, and Giroux, 1964. Revised edition, 1968.

1696 LOWRY, Thomas C. F. "Melville's Moby-Dick, Chapter 31." Explicator, 16 (January, 1958), item 22. Refers to "Queen Mab" chapter.

1697 LUCAS, F. L. "Herman Melville." New Statesman, 18 (April 1, 1922), 730-731.

1698 ________. Authors: Dead and Living. London: Chatto and Windus, 1926; New York: Macmillan, 1926, reissued 1935. Melville, pp. 105-114.

1699 LUCAS, Thomas Edward. "Herman Melville as a Literary Theorist." Ph.D. diss., University of Denver, 1963. DA, 24 (1964), 2015.

1700 ________. "Herman Melville: The Purpose of the Novel." Texas Studies in Literature and Language, 13 (1972), 641-661.

1701 LUCETT, E. Rovings in the Pacific ... 1837-1849. London: Longmans, Brown, 1851.

1702 LUCID, Robert F. "The Influence of Two Years Before the Mast on Herman Melville." American Literature, 31 (November, 1959), 243-256.

1703 LUDWIG, Jack Berry, and W. Richard Poirier, eds. Instructor's Manual to Stories: British and American. Boston: Houghton Mifflin, 1953. Pp. 6-8. Refers to "Bartleby."

1704 LUEDERS, Edward G. "The Melville-Hawthorne Relationship in Pierre and The Blithedale Romance." Western Humanities Review, 4 (Autumn, 1950), 323-334.

1705 LUND, Charles C., II. "Beholding the Shadows of Fate: 'The Town-Ho's Story' in Moby-Dick." Ph.D. diss., Tufts, 1973. DA, 34 (1974), 5110A.

1706 LUNDKVIST, Artur. "Herman Melville." Bonniers Litterara Magasin (Stockholm), 11 (December, 1942), 773-786. In Swedish.

1707 LUNT, Dudley C. The Road to the Law. New York: Norton, 1965. Melville, pp. 14-15.

1708 LUTWACK, Leonard I. "Herman Melville and the Atlantic Monthly Critics." Huntington Library Quarterly, 13 (Spring, 1950), 414-416.

1709 ________. "Melville's Struggle with Style." Forum (Houston), 3 (Spring-Summer, 1962), 11-17.

1710 LYND, Robert. "Learned Sailorman," in Lynd, Books and Writers. London: Dent, 1922. Reprinted New York: Dent, 1952. Pp. 142-146.

1711 LYNDE, Richard D. "Melville's Success in 'The Happy Failure: A Story of the River Hudson.'" College Language Association Journal, 13 (1969), 119-130.

1712 LYNN, Kenneth S. Visions of America: Eleven Literary History Essays. Westport, Conn.: Greenwood, 1973. "Melville's 'Benito Cereno,'" pp. 26-42.

1713 ______, ed. The Comic Tradition in America. New York: Doubleday, 1958. Melville, pp. 259-261.

1714 MABBOTT, Thomas Ollive. "Inscription: For the Slain at Fredericksburgh." Notes and Queries, 149 (July 18, 1925), 42-43.

1715 ______. "A Letter from Herman Melville." Notes and Queries, 162 (February 27, 1932), 151-152. A reprint of and comment upon a letter from Melville to Dr. William Sprague.

1716 ______. "A Letter of Herman Melville." Notes and Queries, 176 (January 28, 1939), 60.

1717 ______. "A Source for the Conclusion of Moby-Dick." Notes and Queries, 181 (July 26, 1941), 47-48.

1718 ______. "Melville's Moby-Dick." Explicator, 8 (November, 1949), item 15.

1719 ______. "Melville's 'A Railroad Cutting near Alexandria in 1855.'" Explicator, 9 (June, 1951), item 55.

1720 McALEER, John J. "Poe and Gothic Elements in Moby-Dick." Emerson Society Quarterly, 27 (1962), 34.

1721 McCANN, Garth. "Circumstance and the Publication of Moby-Dick." Serif, 11 (1974), 58-60.

1722 McCARTHY, Harold T. "Israel R. Potter as a Source for Redburn." Emerson Society Quarterly, 59 (1970), 8-9. Refers to the anonymous pamphlet (1824) on which Melville later based his novel.

1723 ______. "Melville's Redburn and the City." Midwest Quarterly, 12 (1971), 395-410. Reprinted in McCarthy, The Expatriate Perspective: American Novelists and the Idea of America. Rutherford, N.J.: Fairleigh Dickinson University Press, 1974. Pp. 47-61.

1724 McCARTHY, Paul E. "Theme and Structure in the Novels of Herman Melville." Ph.D. diss., University of Texas (Austin), 1962. DA, 23 (1962), 237.

1725 ______. "The 'Soldier of Fortune' in Melville's The

Confidence Man." Emerson Society Quarterly, 33 (1963), 21-24.

1726 ________. "A Note on Teaching Moby-Dick." Emerson Society Quarterly, 35 (1964), 73-79.

1727 ________. "Character and Structure in Billy-Budd." Discourse, 9 (Spring, 1966), 201-217.

1728 ________. "Symbolic Elements in White-Jacket." Midwest Quarterly, 7 (July, 1966), 309-325.

1729 ________. "The Use of Tom Brown in Melville's White-Jacket." Emerson Society Quarterly, 47 (1967), 14-15.

1730 ________. "Melville's Use of Painting in Pierre." Discourse, 11 (1968), 490-505.

1731 ________. "The Extraordinary Man as Idealist in the Novels by Hawthorne and Melville." Emerson Society Quarterly, 54 (1969), 43-51. Reprinted in Cook, ed., Themes, Tones... (1968), pp. 43-51.

1732 ________. "Affirmative Elements in The Confidence Man." American Transcendental Quarterly, 7 (Summer, 1970), 56-61.

1733 ________. "City and Town in Melville's Fiction." Research Studies, 38 (1970), 214-229.

1734 ________. "Books on Melville in 1970." Studies in the Novel, 4 (1972), 98-111.

1735 ________. "Elements of Anatomy in Melville's Fiction." Studies in the Novel, 6 (1974), 38-61.

1736 ________. "Opposites Meet: Melville, Hemingway, and Heroes." Kansas Quarterly, 7 (1975), 40-54.

1737 ________. "Melville's Families: Facts, Figures, and Fates." South Dakota Review, 15 (1977), 73-93.

1738 ________. "Melville's Rascals on Land, Sea, and in the Air." Southern Quarterly, 16 (1978), 311-336.

1739 ________. "Six Views of Melville." Studies in the Novel, 10 (1978), 267-277. Review article.

1740 McCLARY, B. H. "Melville's Moby-Dick." Explicator, 21 (September, 1962), item 9.

1741 ________. "Melville, Twain, and the Legendary 'Tennessee Poet.'" Tennessee Folklore Society Bulletin, 29 (1963), 63-64.

1742 McCLOSKEY, J. C. "Moby-Dick and the Reviewers." Philological Quarterly, 25 (January, 1946), 20-31.

1743 McCOLGAN, Kristin Pruitt. "The World's Slow Stain: The Theme of Initiation in Selected American Novels." Ph. D. diss., University of North Carolina (Chapel Hill). DA, 36 (1975), 279A.

1744 McCORMICK, Edgar L., and Edward G. McGehee, eds. Life on a Whaler. Boston: Heath, 1960. Collection of primary materials on whaling.

1745 McCORQUODALE, Marjorie Kimball. "Melville's Pierre as Hawthorne." University of Texas Studies in English, 33 (1954), 97-102.

1746 McCORT, Thomas Michael. "Fate and Foreknowledge: Necessity and Prophecy in Melville's Fiction." Ph. D. diss., University of Michigan, 1977. DA, 38 (1977), 1391A-1392A.

1747 McCROSKERY, Margaret S. "Melville's Pierre: The Inner Voyage." Studies in the Humanities, 2 (1972), 1-9.

1748 McCULLAGH, James C. "More Smoke from Melville's Chimney." American Transcendental Quarterly, 17 (1973), 17-22.

1749 McCUTCHEON, Roger P. "The Technique of Melville's Israel Potter." South Atlantic Quarterly, 27 (April, 1928), 161-174.

1750 McDERMOTT, J. F. "The Spirit of the Times Reviews Moby-Dick." New England Quarterly, 30 (September, 1957), 392-395.

1751 MacDONALD, Allan. "A Sailor Among the Transcendentalists." New England Quarterly, 8 (September, 1935), 307-319.

1752 McDONALD, Dorothy Ritsuko. "The Captive King: The Persistence of Symbolic Memory in Herman Melville." Ph. D. diss., University of California (Berkeley), 1975. DA, 36 (1976), 4493A-4494A.

1753 McDONALD, Walter R. "Ishmael: The Function of a Comic Mask." CEA Critic, 37 (1975), 8-11.

1754 McELDERRY, Bruce R., Jr. "Three Earlier Treatments of the Billy-Budd Theme." American Literature, 27 (May, 1955), 251-257.

1755 ________. "The National Era Review of White-Jacket." Melville Society Newsletter, 15 (Winter, 1960), 2.

1756 McELROY, John Harmon. "Cannibalism in Melville's 'Benito Cereno.'" Essays in Literature, 1 (1974), 206-218.

1757 ________. "The Dating of the Action in Moby-Dick." Papers on Language and Literature, 13 (1977), 420-423.

1758 McENIRY, William Hugh. "The Young Melville: 1819-1852." Ph.D. diss., Vanderbilt, 1942.

1759 ________. "Some Contrapuntal Themes in Herman Melville," in Langford, Richard E., ed. Essays in Modern American Literature. Deland, Fla.: Stetson University Press, 1963. Pp. 14-25.

1760 McGRAVES, Donald E. "The Steering Gear of the Pequod." American Notes and Queries, 6 (May, 1946), 25.

1761 McHANEY, Thomas L. "The Textual Editions of Hawthorne and Melville." Studies in the Literary Imagination, 2 (1969), 27-41.

1762 ________. "The Confidence Man and Satan's Disguises in Paradise Lost." Nineteenth-Century Fiction, 30 (September, 1975), 200-206.

1763 McINTIRE, Mary Beth. "The Buried Life: A Study of The Blithedale Romance, The Confidence Man, and The Sacred Fount." Ph.D. diss., Rice, 1975. DA, 36 (1975), 2183A.

1764 McIVER, R. M., ed. Great Moral Dilemmas in Literature, Past and Present. New York: Harpers, 1956. "The Ceremony of Innocence," by William York Tindall, pp. 73-81. Refers to Billy-Budd.

1765 McKINNEY, Jill Louise. "Herman Melville and the Law." Ph.D. diss., University of Pennsylvania, 1975. DA, 36 (1976), 5299A-5300A.

1766 McLEAN, Albert F. "Spouter Inn and Whaleman's Chapel: The Cultural Matrices of Moby-Dick," in Vincent, ed., Melville and Hawthorne in the Berkshires (1968), pp. 98-108.

1767 MacMECHAN, Archibald McK. "The Best Sea Story Ever Written." Queen's Quarterly, 7 (October, 1899), 120-130. Reprinted in Humane Review, 7 (October, 1901), 242-252. Also reprinted in MacMechan, The Life of a Little College and Other Papers. Boston: Houghton Mifflin, 1914. Pp. 181-197.

1768 McMILLAN, Grant E. "Ishmael's Dilemma--The Significance of the Fiery Hunt." Centennial Review, 15 (1971), 204-217.

1769 ________. "Nature's Dark Side: Herman Melville and the Problem of Evil." Ph.D. diss., Syracuse University, 1973. DA, 35 (1974), 1055A.

1770 McNALLY, William. Evils and Abuses in the Naval and Merchant Service Exposed. Boston: Cassady and March, 1839.

1771 McNAMARA, Anne Marie. "Melville's Billy-Budd." Explicator, 21 (October, 1962), item 1.

1772 McNAMARA, Leo F. "Subject, Style, and Narrative Technique in 'Bartleby' and 'Wakefield.'" Michigan Academician, 3 (1971), 41-46.

1773 McNEILLY, Dorothy, V.B.D.R. "The Melvilles and Mrs. Ferris." Extracts, 28 (1976), 1-9. Letters.

1774 McQUITTY, Robert A. "A Rhetorical Approach to Melville's 'Bartleby,' 'Benito-Cereno,' and Billy-Budd." Ph.D. diss., Syracuse University, 1968. DA, 29 (1969), 4010A-4011A.

1775 MacSHANE, Frank. "Conrad on Melville." American Literature, 29 (January, 1958), 463-464.

1776 McSWEENEY, Kerry. "Melville, Dickinson, Whitman, and Psychoanalytic Criticism." Critical Quarterly, 19 (1977), 71-82. Review article.

1777 McWILLIAMS, John P., Jr. "'Drum-Taps' and Battle-Pieces: The Blossoms of War." American Quarterly, 23 (1971), 181-201.

1778 ________. "Rounding Cape Horn: Melville, Dana, and Literary Tradition." Extracts, 25 (1976), 3.

1779 McWILLIAMS, Wilson Carey. The Idea of Fraternity in America. Berkeley: University of California Press, 1973. Melville, pp. 328-371.

1780 MACY, John Albert. The Spirit of American Literature. New York: Boni and Liveright, 1908; New York: Doubleday, 1913. Melville, p. 16. Emerson, etc., have good representation.

1781 ________. The Story of the World's Literature. New York: Liveright, revised edition 1936. Illustrations by Onorio Ruotolo. See "American Fiction," pp. 519-540.

1782 ________, ed. American Writers on American Literature. New York: Liveright, 1931. "Melville," by Raymond Weaver, pp. 190-206.

1783 MACY, Obed. The History of Nantucket. Boston: Hilliard, Gray, 1835.

1784 MACY, William Hussey. There She Blows! The Whales We Caught and How We Did It. Boston: Lee and Shepard, 1899. Excerpt reprinted in McCormick, ed., Life on a Whaler (1960), pp. 53-61.

1785 MADSON, Arthur L. "Melville's Comic Progression." Wisconsin Studies in Literature, 1 (1964), 69-76.

1786 MAENO, Shigeru. A Melville Dictionary. Tokyo: Kaibunsha, 1976. In English.

1787 MAGAW, Malcolm Orrin. "Melville and the Christian Myth: The Imagery of Ambiguity." Ph.D. diss., Tulane, 1964. DA, 25 (1965), 4126.

1788 ________. "The Confidence Man and Christian Deity: Melville's Imagery of Ambiguity," in Reck, Rima D., ed., Explorations in Literature. Baton Rouge: Louisiana State University Press, 1966. Pp. 81-99.

1789 ________. "Apocalyptic Imagery in Melville's 'The Apple-Tree Table.'" Midwest Quarterly, 8 (July, 1967), 357-369.

1790 MAGOWAN, Robin. "Masque and Symbol in Melville's 'Benito Cereno.'" College English, 23 (February, 1962), 346-351.

1791 MAGRETTA, Joan Barbara Gorin. "The Iconography of Madness: A Study in Melville and Dostoevsky." Ph.D. diss., University of Michigan, 1976. DA, 37 (1976), 1533A.

1792 ________. "Radical Disunities: Models of Mind and Madness in Pierre and The Idiot." Studies in the Novel, 10 (1978), 234-250. Refers to novel by Dostoevsky.

1793 MAHONEY, Mother M. Denis. "Clarel: An Investigation of Spiritual Crises." Ph.D. diss., Catholic University, 1957.

1794 MAHONY, Catherine J. "Ixion's Wheel: Melville's Symbology of Time." Ph.D. diss., Auburn, 1973. DA, 34 (1974), 7196A.

1795 MAIER, Rosemarie A. "Melville's Personae in Moby-Dick." Ph.D. diss., University of Illinois (Urbana), 1972. DA, 33 (1973), 5685A.

1796 MAILLOUX, Steve, and Hershel Parker, eds. A Checklist of Melville Reviews. Melville Society Publication, 1975. 100 pp.

1797 MALBONE, Raymond G. "How Shall We Teach the New *Billy-Budd: Sailor?*" *College English*, 27 (March, 1966), 499-500.

1798 MALE, Roy R. "The Story of the Mysterious Stranger in American Fiction." *Criticism*, 3 (Fall, 1961), 281-294. Refers to *The Confidence-Man.*

1799 MALIN, Irving. "The Compulsive Design," in Madden, David, ed., *American Dreams, American Nightmares.* Carbondale: Southern Illinois University Press, 1970. Pp. 58-75. Discusses "The Bell-Tower."

1800 MANDEL, Ruth B. "Herman Melville and the Gothic Outlook." Ph.D. diss., University of Connecticut, 1969. *DA*, 30 (1970), 3015A-3016A.

1801 ______. "The Two Mystery Stories in 'Benito Cereno.'" *Texas Studies in Literature and Language*, 14 (1973), 631-642.

1802 MANDELL, Marvin. "Martyrs or Murderers? A Defense of Innocence." *Midwest Quarterly*, 18 (1977), 131-143. Discusses *Billy-Budd.*

1803 MANGOLD, Charlotte Weiss. "Herman Melville in German Criticism from 1900 to 1955." Ph.D. diss., University of Maryland, 1959. *DA*, 20 (1960), 4114.

1804 MANI, Lakshani. "The Apocalypse in Cooper, Hawthorne, and Melville." Ph.D. diss., McGill University (Montreal), 1972. *DA*, 34 (1973), 783A.

1805 MANLOVE, C. N. "An Organic Hesitancy: Theme and Style in *Billy-Budd,*" in Pullin, ed., *Perspectives* (1978), pp. 275-300.

1806 MANSFIELD, Luther S. "Herman Melville: Author and New Yorker, 1844-1851." Ph.D. diss., University of Chicago, 1936.

1807 ______. *Herman Melville: Author and New Yorker, 1844-1851.* Chicago: University of Chicago Press, 1938. Part of 1936 diss. Pamphlet. Entire diss. microfilmed by University of Chicago.

1808 ______. "Glimpses of Herman Melville's Life in Pittsfield, 1850-1851: Some Unpublished Letters of Evert A. Duyckinck." *American Literature*, 9 (March, 1937), 26-48.

1809 ______. "Melville's Comic Articles on Zachary Taylor." *American Literature*, 9 (January, 1938), 411-418.

1810 ________. "Symbolism and Biblical Allusions in Moby-Dick." Emerson Society Quarterly, 28 (1962), 20-23.

1811 ________. "Some Patterns from Melville's 'Loom of Time,'" in Krause, ed., Essays on Determinism (1964), pp. 19-35.

1812 ________. "The Emersonian Idiom and the Romantic Period in American Literature." Emerson Society Quarterly, 35 (1964), 23-28. Remarks on Melville.

1813 ________. "Melville and Hawthorne in the Berkshires," in Vincent, ed., Melville and Hawthorne in the Berkshires: A Symposium (1968), pp. 1-20.

1814 ________. "'Very Like a Whale': Herman Melville and Shakespeare," in Studies in Medieval, Renaissance, and American Literature, edited by Betsy Colquitt. Fort Worth: Texas Christian University Press, 1971. Pp. 143-156.

1815 ________, and Howard P. Vincent, eds. with Introduction and extensive annotation. Moby-Dick. New York: Hendricks House, 1952.

1816 MAQUET, Jean. "Sur Melville." Critique, 1 (August-September, 1946), 229-230. In French.

1817 MARCUS, Mordecai. "Melville's Bartleby as a Psychological Double." College English, 23 (February, 1962), 365-368.

1818 MARGOLIES, Edward. "Melville and the Blacks." College Language Association Journal, 18 (March, 1975), 364-373.

1819 MARGOLIES, J. A., ed. with Introduction by Christopher Morley. Strange and Fantastic Stories: An Anthology. New York: McGraw-Hill, 1946. "Bartleby, the Scrivener," pp. 530-567.

1820 MARINO, Bert G. "Melville and the Perfectionist Dilemma: A Study of Melville's Early Religious Thought." Ph.D. diss., Fordham, 1973. DA, 35 (1974), 3690A-3691A.

1821 MARKELS, Julian. "King Lear and Moby-Dick: The Cultural Connection." Massachusetts Review, 9 (1968), 169-176.

1822 ________. "Melville's Markings in Shakespeare's Plays." American Literature, 49 (1977), 34-48.

1823 MARKS, Barry A. "Retrospective Narrative in Nineteenth-Century American Fiction." College English, 31 (1970), 366-375. Studies Thoreau, Whitman, and Ishmael of Moby-Dick.

1824 MARKS, William S., III. "Melville, Opium, and Billy-Budd." Studies in American Fiction, 6 (1978), 33-45.

1825 MARLER, Robert F. "'Bartleby, the Scrivener' and the American Short Story." Genre, 6 (1973), 428-447.

1826 ________. "From Tale to Short Story: The Emergence of a New Genre in the 1850's." American Literature, 46 (1974), 153-169.

1827 MAROVITZ, Sanford E. "Old Man Ahab," in De Mott and Marovitz, eds., Artful Thunder (1975), pp. 139-161.

1828 ________. "Melville's Short Fiction of the 'Fifties.'" Melville Society Extracts, 33 (1978), 23-24.

1829 ________, and Masao Tsunematsu. "Melville Studies in Japan." Melville Society Extracts, 36 (1978), 1-6.

1830 MARSDEN, Walter. "Stories from the Deep." John O'London's Weekly, 60 (March 30, 1951), 181.

1831 MARSH, John L. "Verses in Celebration of the Life and Art of Herman Melville: A Checklist." Extracts, 14 (1973), 3-6.

1832 MARSHALL, H. P. "Herman Melville." London Mercury, 6 (November, 1924), 56-70.

1833 MARSHALL, Margaret Wiley. "A Footnote to Billy-Budd." Extracts, 30 (1977), 1-3. Remarks on the possible influence of Arichandra: The Martyr of Truth, an Indian drama, English translation 1863, London.

1834 MARSHALL, Thomas F. Three Voices of the American Tradition: Edgar A. Poe, Herman Melville, and Ernest Hemingway. Athens, Greece: 1956.

1835 MARTIN, Jay. Harvests of Change. Englewood Cliffs, N.J.: Prentice-Hall, 1967. Melville, passim.

1836 MARTIN, Lawrence H., Jr. "Melville and Christianity: The Late Poems." Massachusetts Studies in English, 2 (1969), 11-18.

1837 MARTIN, Robert K. "Crane's The Bridge, 'The Tunnel,' 11. 58-60." Explicator, 34 (1975), item 16.

1838 MARTIN, Terence. Teaching a Novel: Moby-Dick in the Classroom. New York: College Entrance Examination Board, 1965. Pp. 3-14.

1839 MARTINEAU, Barbara J. "Dramatized Narration in the Short

Fiction of Irving, Poe, and Melville." Ph.D. diss., Columbia, 1970. DA, 31 (1971), 4725A.

1840 MARTINEAU, Stephen Francis. "Opposition and Balance: A Characteristic of Structure in Hawthorne, Melville, and James." Ph.D. diss., Columbia, 1967. DA, 28 (1967), 1441A.

1841 MARTZ, Louis Lohr. Tragic Themes in Western Literature. New Haven: Yale University Press, 1955. Melville, passim.

1842 MARX, Leo. "Melville's Parable of the Walls." Sewanee Review, 61 (Autumn, 1953), 602-627. Refers to "Bartleby."

1843 ________. "The Machine in the Garden." New England Quarterly, 29 (March, 1956), 27-42. Melville, passim.

1844 ________. The Machine in the Garden: Technology and the Pastoral Ideal in America. New York: Oxford University Press, 1964. "Moby-Dick," pp. 277-319.

1845 ________. "'Noble Shit': The Uncivil Response of American Writers to Civil Religion in America." Massachusetts Review, 14 (1973), 709-739.

1846 ________. "American Writers and Civil Religion in America," in Richey, Russell E., and Donald G. Jones, eds., American Civil Religion. New York: Harper and Row, 1974. Pp. 222-251. Similar to 1973 article.

1847 ________. "Moby-Dick as an American Apocalypse." Extracts, 26 (1976), 3.

1848 MASON, Ronald Charles. "Melville and Hawthorne: A Study in Contrasts." The Wind and the Rain, 4 (Autumn, 1947), 93-100.

1849 ________. "Symbolism and Allegory in Melville." Penguin New Writing, 22 (1948), 28-35.

(Both articles above incorporated into Spirit Above the Dust, 1951)

1850 ________. Spirit Above the Dust. London: Lehmann, 1951. Second edition with a new Foreword by Howard P. Vincent. Mamaroneck, N.Y.: Appel, 1972.

1851 ________. "Implacable Sea: A Study of Melville's Poetry." Black Mountain Review, 1 (Summer, 1954), 41-44.

1852 MASTRIANO, Mary. "Melville's 'The Lightning-Rod Man.'" Studies in Short Fiction, 14 (1977), 29-33.

1853 MATHER, Frank Jewett, Jr. "Herman Melville." New York Review, 1 (August 9 and 16, 1919), 276-278 and 298-301. First overall survey of Melville's works.

1854 ______. "Herman Melville." Saturday Review of Literature, 5 (April 27, 1929), 945-946. Review of Lewis Mumford's Herman Melville (1929).

1855 ______. "Reminiscences of a Melvillian." Princeton Alumni Weekly, 38 (March 25, 1938), 555-556.

1856 MATHEWS, J. Chesley. "A Note on Melville and Dante." PMLA, 64 (December, 1949), 1238. See article by Giovannini, PMLA, 64 (March, 1949), 70-78, and Giovannini's reply to Mathews, PMLA, 65 (March, 1950), 329.

1857 ______. "Melville's Reading of Dante." Furman Studies, 6 (Fall, 1958), 1-8.

1858 MATHEWS, James W. "'Bartleby': Melville's Tragedy of Humours." Interpretations, 10 (1978), 41-48.

1859 MATHIEU, Bertrand. "'Plain Mechanic Power': Melville's Earliest Poems, Battle-Pieces and Aspects of the War." Essays in Arts and Sciences, 5 (1976), 113-128. Also published in Robillard, ed., Symposium (1976), pp. 113-128.

1860 MATLOCK, Jack. "Attica and Melville's Benito-Cereno." American Transcendental Quarterly, 26 (1975), 18-23.

1861 MATSUMOTO, M. "The Style of Moby-Dick." Anglica, 4 (January, 1961), 33-58.

1862 MATTHEWS, Dr. Leonard Harrison, et al., eds. The Whale, based on the drawings of Tre Tryckare. Sweden: Cagner, 1968. New text with drawings, New York: Crescent, 1974. Contains extensive bibliography on cetology and invaluable illustrations of the whale.

1863 MATTHIESSEN, Francis O. American Renaissance: Art and Expression in the Age of Emerson and Whitman. New York and London: Oxford University Press, 1941. "Melville," pp. 179-191 and 317-516.

1864 ______. "Melville as Poet," in Matthiessen, The Responsibilities of the Critic: Essays and Reviews. New York: Oxford University Press, 1952. Pp. 77-80. Essentially the same as Preface to Selected Poems (1944).

1865 ______. "Melville: L'urto delle forze." Delta, 2 (August, 1962), 1-9. In Italian.

1866 ______. "'Out of Unhandselled Savage Nature,'" in Goldberg, G. J., and N. M. Goldberg, eds., The Modern Critical Spectrum. Englewood Cliffs, N.J.: Prentice-Hall, 1962. Pp. 215-219. Excerpt from American Renaissance (1941), pp. 371-376.

1867 ________. "Billy-Budd, Foretopman," in Chase, Richard V., ed., Melville: A Collection (1962), pp. 156-168.

1868 ________, ed. Selected Poems of Herman Melville. Norfolk, Conn.: New Directions Press, 1944. A short Preface plus 22 pages of poems.

1869 MAUGHAM, W. Somerset. "Moby-Dick." Atlantic Monthly, 181 (June, 1948), 98-104.

1870 MAXWELL, Desmond E. S. "The Tragic Phase: Melville and Hawthorne," in Maxwell, American Fiction: The Intellectual Background. New York: Columbia University Press, 1963. Pp. 141-191.

1871 ________. Herman Melville. London: Routledge and Kegan Paul; New York: Humanities, 1968.

1872 MAXWELL, J. C. "Melville's Allusion to Pope." American Notes and Queries, 3 (September, 1964), 7.

1873 ________. "Melville and Milton." Notes and Queries, 12 (February, 1965), 60.

1874 ________. "Three Notes on Moby-Dick." Notes and Queries, 14 (February, 1967), 53.

1875 MAY, John Rollo. "The Possiblity of Renewal: The Ideal and the Real in Hawthorne, Melville, and Twain," in May, Toward a New Earth: Apocalypse in the American Novel. Notre Dame and London: University of Notre Dame Press, 1972. Pp. 42-91. Discusses The Confidence-Man.

1876 ________. Power and Innocence: A Search for the Sources of Violence. New York: Norton, 1972. Passages reprinted in Psychology Today, 6 (December, 1972), 53-58. Relates to Billy Budd and Allison Krause (one of the four students who died in the Kent State shooting incident).

1877 MAYOUX, Jean-Jacques. Melville. Paris, France: Editions du Seuèl, 1958. Translated from French by John Ashbery. New York: Grove, 1960.

1878 ________. "Mythe et symbole chez Herman Melville." Inventario, 15 (1960), 43-54. In French.

1879 MELDRUM, Barbara H. "Herman Melville's Mardi, Moby-

Dick, and Pierre: Tragedy in Recoil." Ph.D. diss., Claremont, 1964. DA, 28 (1967), 686A.

1880 ______. "Melville on War." Research Studies, 37 (1969), 130-138.

1881 ______. "The Artist in Melville's Mardi." Studies in the Novel, 1 (1969), 459-467.

1882 ______. "Structure in Moby-Dick: The Whale Killings and Ishmael's Quest." Emerson Society Quarterly, 21 (1975), 162-168.

1883 MELVILLE, Herman. The Works of Herman Melville. Standard edition, 16 vols. London: Constable, 1922-1924. Reprinted New York: Russell and Russell, 1963.

1884 ______. "Review of Cooper's The Sea Lions and The Red Rover." Literary World, 4 (April 28, 1849), 370; and 6 (March 16, 1850), 276-277.

1885 ______. "Hawthorne and His Mosses." Literary World, 7 (August 17 and 24, 1850), 125-127 and 145-147. Published "By a Virginian Spending His Summer [July] in Vermont," pseudo. Has been reprinted frequently, as in the following: Wilson, Edmund, ed., The Shock of Recognition (1943), pp. 187-204; Richardson, Lyon Norman, et al., eds., Heritage of American Literature, 2 vols. New York: Ginn, 1951. Vol. I, pp. 797-802; Brown, Clarence A., ed., Achievement of American Criticism. New York: Ronald, 1954. Pp. 289-301; Fiedler, ed., The Art of the Essay (1958), pp. 571-584; Miller, Perry, ed., The Golden Age of American Literature. New York: Braziller, 1959. Pp. 407-419; Leary, ed., American Literary Essays (1960), pp. 90-92. Excerpt; Trask, Georgianna Sampson, and Charles Burkhart, eds., Storytellers and Their Art. New York: Doubleday, 1963. Pp. 259-278; Hayford, ed., Moby-Dick (1967), pp. 535-551; and Cohen, B. Bernard, ed., The Recognition of Nathaniel Hawthorne. Ann Arbor: University of Michigan Press, 1969. Pp. 29-41.

1886 MELVILLE SOCIETY. Extracts: An Occasional Newsletter. Donald Yanella, editor, Department of English, Glassboro State College, Glassboro, N.J. 08028. $5 membership fee (1980). Melville Society organized in 1946; Extracts published since 1969; new format of Extracts initiated in 1978.

1887 MELVILLE SOCIETY. Melville Dissertations.

1888 MELVILLE SUPPLEMENT see Emerson Society Quarterly, 28 (Part 3, 1962).

1889 MENARD, Wilmon. "A Forgotten South Sea Paradise." Asia, 33 (September, 1933), 457-463; (October, 1933), 510.

1890 MENGELING, M. E. "Moby-Dick: The Fundamental Principles." Emerson Society Quarterly, 38 (1965), 74-87.

1891 ______. "Through 'The Encantadas': An Experienced Guide." American Transcendental Quarterly, 7 (1970), 37-43.

1892 MERRILL, Robert. "The Narrative Voice in Billy-Budd." Modern Language Quarterly, 34 (1973), 283-291.

1893 MESSENGER, William E. "Conrad and Melville Again." Conradiana, 2 (1970), 53-64.

1894 METCALF, Eleanor Melville (Melville's granddaughter). "A Pilgrim by Land and Sea." Horn Book, 3 (February, 1927), 3-11.

1895 ______. Herman Melville: Cycle and Epicycle. Cambridge: Harvard University Press, 1953.

1896 ______, ed. Melville's Journal of a Visit to London and the Continent, 1849-1850. Cambridge: Harvard University Press, 1948.

1897 METCALF, Paul (Melville's great-grandson). Genoa: A Telling of Wonders. Highland, N.C.: Williams, 1965. A novel based on Melville's life.

1898 ______. "Orca: Part Two," in De Mott and Marovitz, eds., Artful Thunder (1975), pp. 197-206. A play.

1899 ______. "Observations on the State of Melville Biography." Extracts, 27 (1976), 5-7.

1900 METZGER, Charles R. "Melville's Saints: Allusion in Benito Cereno." Emerson Society Quarterly, 58 (1970), 88-90.

1901 MEYER, Janice Jones. "'Bartleby the Scrivener': Performing the Narrator's Inner Conflict in Chamber Theatre." Communication Education (The Speech Teacher), 26 (1977), 348-351.

1902 MEYNELL, Viola. "Herman Melville: Moby-Dick." Dublin Review, 166 (January, 1920), 96-105.

1903 ______. "Great Story Teller." Living Age, 304 (March 20, 1920), 715-720.

1904 ______, ed. with Introduction. Moby-Dick. New York: Oxford University Press, 1920.

1905 MIDDLEBROOK, Jonathan. "The Piazza, the Blubber Boilers, and the Delirium." Extracts, 26 (1976), 2.

1906 MIDDLETON, John A. "Shark Talk: The Uses of Dialogue in Moby-Dick." Ph.D. diss., Indiana University, 1969. DA, 30 (1970), 4995A.

1907 ________. "A Source for 'Bartleby.'" Extracts, 15 (1973), 9.

1908 MILDER, Robert. "Melville's Intentions in Pierre." Studies in the Novel, 6 (Summer, 1974), 186-199.

1909 ________. "Melville and His Biographers." Emerson Society Quarterly, 22 (1976), 169-182. Review article.

1910 ________. "The Composition of Moby-Dick: A Review and a Prospect." Emerson Society Quarterly, 23 (1977), 203-216. Rebuttal of James Barbour's article (1975).

1911 ________. "'Knowing' Melville." Emerson Society Quarterly, 24 (1978), 96-117. Review article.

1912 MILFORD, H. S. "The Text of Typee." Times Literary Supplement, May 27, 1926. P. 355.

1913 MILLER, Arthur Hawks, Jr. "Melville Dissertations: An Annotated Directory." Extracts, 20 Supplement (1974), 1-11.

1914 ________. "Herman Melville: A New Biographical Profile." Ph.D. diss., Northwestern, 1973. DA, 34 (1973), 3419A. Published on demand; Ann Arbor: University Microfilms International, 1977.

1915 MILLER, Charles Wayne. An Armed America: Its Face in Fiction. New York: New York University Press, 1970. "Herman Melville and the Dissection of the Military World: A Warning to America," pp. 29-52.

1916 MILLER, Edwin Haviland. Herman Melville: A Biography. New York: Braziller, 1975.

1917 MILLER, F. DeWolfe. "Melville, Whitman, and the Forty Immortals," in English Essays in Honor of James Southall Wilson. Charlottesville: University of Virginia Press, 1951. Pp. 23-24. Refers to work by Benjamin de Casseres, Forty Immortals (1926).

1918 ________. "Another Chapter in the History of the Great White Whale," in Vincent, ed., Melville and Hawthorne in the Berkshires: A Symposium (1968), pp. 109-117.

1919 MILLER, James E., Jr. "Hawthorne and Melville: The Unpardonable Sin." PMLA, 70 (March, 1955), 91-111. Reprinted in Miller, Quests Surd and Absurd (1967), pp. 209-238.

1920 ________. "Billy-Budd: The Catastrophe of Innocence." Modern Language Notes, 73 (March, 1958), 168-176.

1921 ________. "The Many Masks of Mardi." Journal of English and Germanic Philology, 58 (July, 1959), 400-413.

1922 ________. "Redburn and White-Jacket: Initiation and Baptism." Nineteenth-Century Fiction, 13 (March, 1959), 273-293.

1923 ________. "The Achievement of Melville." University of Kansas City Review, 26 (August, 1959), 59-67.

1924 ________. "Melville's Quest in Life and Art." South Atlantic Quarterly, 58 (August, 1959), 587-602.

1925 ________. "Moby-Dick: The Grand Hooded Phantom." Annali Istituto Universitario Orientale (Napoli, Sezione Germanica), 2 (1959), 141-165.

1926 ________. "The Confidence Man: His Guises." PMLA, 74 (March, 1959), 102-111.

1927 ________. "The Complex Figure in Melville's Carpet." Arizona Quarterly, 15 (1959), 197-210.

1928 ________. "Melville's Search for Form." Bucknell Review, 8 (December, 1959), 260-276.

1929 ________. A Reader's Guide to Herman Melville. New York: Farrar, Straus, and Cudahy; London: Thames and Hudson, 1962.

1930 ________. Quests Surd and Absurd. Chicago: University of Chicago Press, 1967. "Hawthorne and Melville: No! in Thunder," pp. 186-208; "Hawthorne and Melville: The Unpardonable Sin (1955)," pp. 209-238.

1931 MILLER, Paul W. "Sun and Fire in Melville's Moby-Dick." Nineteenth-Century Fiction, 13 (September, 1958), 139-144.

1932 MILLER, Perry. "Melville and Transcendentalism." Virginia Quarterly Review, 29 (Autumn, 1953), 556-575. Reprinted in Miller, Nature's Nation (1967), pp. 184-196.

1933 ________. "Melville and Transcendentalism," in Hillway, ed., Centennial Essays (1953), pp. 123-152. Expanded version of article in Virginia Quarterly Review.

1934 ________. "The Romantic Dilemma in American Nationalism and the Concept of Nature." Harvard Theological Review, 48 (1955), 239-253.

1935 ________. The Raven and the Whale: The War of Words and Wits in the Era of Poe and Melville. New York: Harcourt, Brace, 1956. Melville, passim.

1936 ________. "The Common Law and Codification in Jacksonian America." Proceedings of the American Philosophical Society, 103 (1959), 463-468.

1937 ________. Nature's Nation. Cambridge: Harvard University Press, 1967. "Melville and Transcendentalism," pp. 184-196, and "An American Language," pp. 208-301. Posthumous publication.

1938 ________, ed. The Golden Age of American Literature. New York: Braziller, 1959. "Hawthorne and His Mosses," by Melville, pp. 407-419.

1939 MILLER, Ruth. "'But Laugh or Die': A Comparison of The Mysterious Stranger and Billy-Budd." Literary Half-Yearly (India), 11 (1970), 25-29.

1940 MILLGATE, Michael. "Melville and Marvell: A Note on Billy-Budd." English Studies, 49 (1968), 47-50.

1941 MILLHAUSER, M. "The Form of Moby-Dick." Journal of Aesthetics and Art Criticism, 13 (June, 1955), 527-532.

1942 MILLS, Gordon H. "The Significance of 'Arcturus' in Mardi." American Literature, 14 (May, 1942), 158-161.

1943 ________. "The Castaway in Moby-Dick." University of Texas Studies in English, 29 (1950), 231-248.

1944 ________. "American First Editions at Texas University: Herman Melville, 1819-1891." University of Texas Library Chronicle, 4 (Summer, 1951), 89-91.

1945 MILLS, Nicolaus C. "The Discovery of Nil in Pierre and Jude the Obscure." Texas Studies in Literature and Language, 12 (1970), 249-262.

1946 ________. "Herman Melville and Thomas Hardy," in Mills, American and English Fiction in the Nineteenth-Century: An Anti-genre Critique and Comparison. Bloomington: Indiana University Press, 1973. Pp. 74-91. Relates to Pierre.

1947 MILLSPAUGH, Clarence Arthur. "Herman Melville," a poem. Poetry, 51 (March, 1938), 317.

1948 MINER, Roy Waldo. "Marauders of the Sea." National Geographic Magazine, 68 (August, 1935), 185-207.

1949 ______. The Fabulous Forties: 1840-1850. New York: Putnam, 1924. Melville, passim.

1950 MINNIGERODE, Meade, ed. Some Personal Letters of Herman Melville and a Bibliography. New York: Brick Row Book Shop, 1922.

1951 MITCHELL, Charles. "Melville and the Spurious Truth of Legalism." Centennial Review, 12 (1968), 110-126.

1952 MITCHELL, Donald G. American Lands and Letters, 2 vols. New York: Scribner, 1899. Melville, Vol. II, p. 235 and passim.

1953 MITCHELL, Edward. "From Action to Essence: Some Notes on the Structure of Melville's The Confidence Man." American Literature, 40 (March, 1968), 27-37.

1954 MITCHELL, Robin Cave. "Omoo and the Development of Herman Melville's Narrative Technique." Ph.D. diss., University of Wisconsin, 1974. DA, 35 (1975), 4441A.

1955 MOBLEY, Janice Lee Edens. "Eating, Drinking, and Smoking in Melville's Fiction." Ph.D. diss., University of Tennessee, 1974. DA, 35 (1975), 5355A.

1956 MODERN FICTION STUDIES: Melville Special Number, 8 (Autumn, 1962). "Bibliography," by Maurice Beebe, Harrison Hayford, and Gordon Roper, pp. 312-346.

1957 MOGAN, Joseph J., Jr. "Pierre and Manfred: Melville's Study of the Byronic Hero." Papers on English Language and Literature, 1 (1965), 230-240.

1958 MOLDENHAUER, Joseph. "'Bartleby' and 'The Custom-House.'" Delta English Studies, 7 (1978), 21-62.

1959 MONTAGUE, Gene B. "Melville's Battle-Pieces." University of Texas Studies in English, 35 (1956), 106-115.

1960 MONTALE, Eugenio, ed. with Introduction. Herman Melville's Billy-Budd. Milan, Italy: Bompiani, 1942. In Italian. Introduction trans. by Barbara M. Arnett, and published, "An Introduction to Billy Budd: 1942." Sewanee Review, 68 (July-September, 1960), 419-422.

1961 MONTEIRO, George. "Melville and Keats." Emerson Society Quarterly, 31 (1963), 55.

1962 ______. "Elizabeth Shaw Melville as Censor." Emerson Society Quarterly, 62 (1971), 32-33.

1963 ________. "'Bartleby the Scrivener,' and Melville's Contemporary Reputation." Studies in Bibliography, 24 (1971), 195-196.

1964 ________. "Melville, 'Timothy Quicksand,' and the Dead-Letter Office." Studies in Short Fiction, 9 (1972), 198-201.

1965 ________. "Melville in Portuguese." Serif, 9 (1972), 23-24. Checklist of translations of Moby-Dick and a few other works by Melville.

1966 ________. "Mather's Melville Book." Studies in Bibliography, 25 (1972), 226-227.

1967 ________. "Reference to Typee and Pierre, 1884." Extracts, 15 (1973), 9.

1968 ________. "Melville's 'America.'" Explicator, 32 (May, 1974), item 72.

1969 ________. "Holmes on Melville." Extracts, 17 (1974), 10.

1970 ________. "Mrs. Melville and The New York Times." Extracts, 19 (1974), 11-12.

1971 ________. "Melville Reviews in The Independent." Papers of the Bibliographic Society of America, 68 (October, 1974), 434-439. Contains a new review of Battle-Pieces.

1972 ________. "'Far and Away the Most Original Genius That America Has Produced': Notations on The New York Times and Melville's Literary Reputation at the Turn of the Century." Resources for American Literary Study, 5 (Spring, 1975), 69-80.

1973 ________. "Half-Hour with Melville, 1887." Papers of the Bibliographic Society of America, 69 (July, 1975), 406-407.

1974 ________. "Herman Melville in the 1890's." Papers of the Bibliographic Society of America, 70 (August, 1976), 530-536.

1975 ________. "Clarel in the Catholic World." Extracts, 30 (1977), 11.

1976 ________. "More on Herman Melville in the 1890's." Extracts, 30 (1977), 12-14. Includes reprints of nineteenth-century notices.

1977 ________. "An Unnoticed Contemporary Review of Battle-Pieces." Extracts, 31 (1977), 11-12. Includes photocopy.

1978 ________. "'Not a Novel ... a Most Astounding Epic': Moby-Dick in 1900." Extracts, 32 (1977), 9. Includes reprint notice.

1979 ________. "Emanuel Félix's 'Leviathan': An Azorean Tribute to Melville." Melville Society Extracts, 33 (1978), 18-19.

1980 ________. "Clarel in the International Review." Melville Society Extracts, 34 (1978), 9.

1981 ________. "Poetry and Madness: Melville's Rediscovery of Camões in 1867." New England Quarterly, 51 (1978), 561-565.

1982 MONTGOMERY, John P. "The Creative Process and the Image of the Artist in Melville's Mardi." Ph.D. diss., Ohio University, 1972. DA, 33 (1973), 4356A-4357A.

1983 MOORE, Dennis J. "The Transformation of Billy-Budd: The Making of a Modern Myth." Ph.D. diss., Northwestern, 1970. DA, 31 (1971), 5417A.

1984 MOORE, Jack B. "Ahab and Bartleby: Energy and Indolence." Studies in Short Fiction, 1 (1963), 291-294.

1985 MOORE, John Brooks. "Introduction," to Pierre. Ed. Robert S. Forsythe with Preface by H. M. Tomlinson. New York: Dutton, 1929.

1986 MOORE, Maxine. "That Lonely Game: Melville's Mardi and the Almanac." Ph.D. diss., University of Kansas, 1972. DA, 34 (1973), 3350A-3351A.

1987 ________. "Melville's Pierre and Wordsworth: Intimations of Immortality." New Letters, 39 (1973), 89-107.

1988 ________. That Lonely Game: Melville's Mardi and the Almanac. Foreword by Hennig Cohen. Columbia: University of Missouri Press, 1975.

1989 MOORE, Richard Sinclair. "A New Review by Melville." American Literature, 47 (May, 1975), 265-270.

1990 ________. "Melville and Lyell's Second Voyage." Extracts, 21 (1975), 6-7.

1991 ________. "Owens' and Melville's Fossil Whale." American Transcendental Quarterly, 26 supplement (1975), 24.

1992 ________. "Burke, Melville, and the 'Power of Blackness.'" American Transcendental Quarterly, 29 (1976), 30-33.

1993 ______. "Melville's Aesthetics of Nature." Ph.D. diss., Duke, 1976. DA, 37 (1976), 3627A-3628A.

1994 MOORMAN, Charles. "Melville's Pierre and the Fortunate Fall." American Literature, 25 (March, 1953), 13-30.

1995 ______. "Melville's Pierre in the City." American Literature, 27 (January, 1956), 571-577.

1996 MORDELL, Albert. "Melville and White-Jacket." Saturday Review of Literature, 7 (July 4, 1931), 946.

1997 ______. "Frank T. Bullen and Herman Melville." Today's Japan, 6 (December, 1960), 77-83.

1998 MOREHEAD, Barbara. "Herman Melville's Use of the Narrator in Moby-Dick." Ph.D. diss., University of Chicago, 1950.

1999 MOREWOOD, Miss Agnes (Melville's grand-niece). "A Note on The Confidence Man." Melville Society Newsletter, November 10, 1947, no pagination.

2000 MORGAN, Sophia S. "The Death of a Myth: A Reading of Moby-Dick as Quixotic Literature." Ph.D. diss., University of Michigan, 1972. DA, 33 (1973), 5190A.

2001 MORIARTY, Jane Viva. "The American Novel in France, 1919-1939." Ph.D. diss., University of Wisconsin, 1954.

2002 MORISON, Samuel Eliot. Maritime History of Massachusetts, 1783-1860. Boston: Houghton Mifflin, 1921. Illustrated. Reprinted New York: Sentry paperback, 1961.

2003 ______. "How to Read Moby-Dick." Life, 40 (June 25, 1956), 57-68. Illustrated.

2004 ______, ed. "Melville's 'Agatha' Letter to Hawthorne." New England Quarterly, 2 (April, 1929), 296-307.

2005 MORPURGO, J. E. "Herman Melville and England." Month (London), 4 (September, 1950), 180-186.

2006 MORRIS, Lloyd R. The Rebellious Puritan: Portrait of Mr. Hawthorne. New York: Harcourt, Brace, 1927. Melville, passim.

2007 ______. "Melville: Promethean." The Open Court, 45 (September and October, 1931), 513-526, 621-635.

2008 MORRIS, Wright. Territory Ahead. New York: Harcourt, Brace, 1958. "High Seas: Herman Melville," pp. 67-77.

2009 _______. Earthly Delights; Unearthly Adornments. New York: Harper and Row, 1978. "Melville as Stylist," pp. 19-23.

2010 MORSBERGER, Robert E. "Melville's 'The Bell-Tower' and Benvenuto Cellini." American Literature, 44 (November, 1972), 459-462.

2011 MOSELEY, Caroline. "'Old Virginny' in Melville's 'The Paradise of Bachelors.'" Melville Society Extracts, 33 (1978), 13-15.

2012 MOSES, Carole Horsburgh. "Melville's Use of Spenser in 'The Piazza.'" College Language Association Journal, 20 (1976), 222-231.

2013 _______. "Like Race to Run: Melville's Use of Spenser." Ph.D. diss., State University of New York (Binghamton), 1978. DA, 38 (1978), 7335A.

2014 _______. "A Spenserian Echo in The Confidence-Man." Melville Society Extracts, 36 (1978), 16.

2015 MOSS, Sidney P. "'Cock-a-Doodle-Do!' and Some Legends in Melville Scholarship." American Literature, 40 (May, 1968), 192-210.

2016 _______. "Hawthorne and Melville: An Inquiry into Their Art and the Mystery of Their Friendship." Literary Monographs, 7 (1975), 47-84. Ed. by Eric Rothstein and Joseph Anthony Wittreich. Madison: University of Wisconsin Press.

2017 MOTTRAM, Eric. "Orpheus and Measured Forms: Law, Madness, and Reticence in Melville," in Pullin, ed., Perspectives (1978), pp. 229-254.

2018 MOWAT, Farley. A Whale for the Killing. Boston: Little, Brown, 1972. Reprinted Baltimore: Penguin, 1973.

2019 MOWDER, William. "Volition in Moby-Dick." Essays in Literature (University of Denver), 1 (1973), 18-30.

2020 MOWER, George R. "The Kentucky Tragedy: A Source for Pierre." Kentucky Folklore Record, 15 (1969), 1-2.

2021 MOYNIHAN, Robert D. "Irony in Moby-Dick." Essays in Arts and Sciences, 6 (1977), 55-67.

2022 MULQUEEN, James E. "Ishmael's Voyage: The Cycle of Everyman's Faith." Arizona Quarterly, 31 (1975), 57-68.

2023 MUMFORD, Lewis. "The New Men of Letters: A Review of

John Freeman's Herman Melville." New Republic, 48 (September 29, 1926), 166-167.

2024 ______. The Golden Day. New York: Boni and Liveright, 1926. "Twilight: Melville," pp. 142-153.

2025 ______. "The Significance of Herman Melville." New Republic, 56 (October 10, 1928), 212-214.

2026 ______. "The Young Olympian." Saturday Review of Literature, 5 (December 15, 1928), 514-515.

2027 ______. "The Writing of Moby-Dick." American Mercury, 15 (December, 1928), 482-490. Reprinted in Withim, R. A., ed., Essays of Today. Boston: Houghton Mifflin, 1931. Pp. 281-288. Deals with the influence of Hawthorne on Melville.

2028 ______. Herman Melville: A Study of His Life and Vision. New York: Literary Guild of America, 1929. Revised edition, New York: Harcourt, Brace, and World, 1963.

2029 ______. "Melville: Moby-Dick," excerpt from Herman Melville (1929), in Mumford, Interpretations and Forecasts, 1922-1972. New York: Harcourt, Brace, and Jovanovitch, 1973. Pp. 51-63.

2030 MUNSON, Gorham. Style and Form in American Prose. Garden City, N.Y.: Doubleday, Doran, 1929. Reprinted Port Washington, N.Y.: Kennikat, 1969. "Prose for Fiction: Herman Melville," pp. 135-149.

2031 MURPHY, Robert Cushman. "Floating Gold." Journal of the American Museum of Natural History, 33 (1933). See "In Quest of Floating Gold," illustrated. Literary Digest, 116 (September 23, 1933), 18.

2032 MURRAY, Henry A. "Personality and Creative Imagination," in English Institute Essays, 1942. New York: Columbia University Press, 1943. Pp. 139-142.

2033 ______. "'In Nomine Diaboli.'" New England Quarterly, 24 (December, 1951), 435-452. Reprinted in Hillway, ed., Centennial Essays (1953), pp. 3-21; also in Chase, ed., Melville: A Collection (1962), pp. 62-74.

2034 ______. "Bartleby and I," in Vincent, ed., Melville Annual, No. 1 (1965), pp. 3-24.

2035 ______. "Dead to the World: The Passions of Herman Melville," in Shneidman, ed., Essays in Self-Destruction (1967), pp. 7-29.

2036 ________, ed. with Introduction and Annotation. Pierre. New York: Hendricks House, 1949.

2037 MURRY, John Middleton. The Problem of Style. London: Oxford University Press, 1922. Reprinted London: Oxford Paperbacks, 1960. See "The English Bible; and The Grand Style," pp. 110-129.

2038 ________. "Herman Melville's Silence." Times Literary Supplement, July 10, 1924. Pp. 433-439. Reprinted in Murry, Discoveries. London: Cape, 1929 and 1940. Pp. 257-263. Also reprinted as "The End of Herman Melville," in Murry, John Clare and Other Studies. London: Neville, 1950. Pp. 209-212.

2039 ________. "Quo Warranto?" Adelphi, 2 (August, 1924), 194.

2040 ________. Son of Woman: The Story of D. H. Lawrence. London: Cape; New York: Smith, 1931. Melville, pp. 265-272.

2041 MUSHABAC, Jane. "Humor in Melville." Ph.D. diss., City University of New York, 1977. DA, 38 (1977), 266A.

2042 MYERS, Henry Alonzo. "Captain Ahab's Discovery: The Tragic Meaning of Moby-Dick." New England Quarterly, 15 (March, 1942), 15-34. Reprinted in Myers, Tragedy: A View of Life. Ithaca, N.Y.: Cornell University Press, 1956. Pp. 57-77.

2043 ________. Are Men Equal? An Inquiry into the Meaning of American Democracy. New York: Putnam, 1945. Reprinted Ithaca, N.Y.: Great Seal, 1955. Melville, pp. 51-56 and passim.

2044 MYERS, Margaret. "Mark Twain and Melville." Mark Twain Journal, 14 (1968), 5-8.

2045 MYERSON, Joel, ed. with text. "Comstock's White Whale and Moby-Dick." American Transcendental Quarterly, 29 (1976), 8-27. Consists of discussion and facsimile reprinting of Comstock's Voyage to the Pacific (1838).

2046 ________, ed. Studies in the American Renaissance: 1977. Boston: Twayne, 1978. Melville, passim.

2047 ________, ed. Studies in the American Renaissance: 1978. Boston: Twayne, 1978. Melville, passim.

2048 ________, ed. Studies in the American Renaissance: 1979. Boston: Twayne, 1979. Melville, passim.

2049 ________, and Arthur H. Miller. Melville Dissertations: An

Annotated Directory. Melville Society Publication, 1972. See also Hillway and Parker, Dissertations Directory (1962); Miller, A. H., for 1974 listing; and Woodress, Dissertations: 1891-1966.

2050 NADEAU, Robert L. "Melville's Sailor in the Sixties," in Peary, Gerald, and Roger Shatzin, eds., The Classic American Novel and the Movies. New York: Ungar, 1977. Pp. 124-131. Also contains an article about the movie "Moby-Dick," by Brandon French, pp. 52-61.

2051 NARITA, Shigehesa. "Melville on Arnold." Studies in English Literature (Tokyo), English number (1966), 41-53.

2052 NARUSE, Takeshi. "Bartleby's Denial: On the Meaning of 'Prefer Not To.'" Expository Times (Edinburgh), 1 (February, 1962), 50-60.

2053 NARVESON, Robert. "The Name 'Claggart' in Billy-Budd." American Speech, 43 (1972), 229-232.

2054 NASCIMENTO, Daniel C. "Melville's Berkshire World: The Pastoral Influence upon His Life and Works." Ph.D. diss., University of Maryland, 1971. DA, 32 (1972), 5193A.

2055 NASH, J. V. "Herman Melville: 'Ishmael' of American Literature." The Open Court, 40 (December, 1926), 734-XX.

2056 NATHANSON, Leonard. "Melville's Billy-Budd, Chapter 1." Explicator, 22 (1964), item 75.

2057 NAULT, Clifford A., Jr. "Herman Melville's Two-Stranded Novel: An Interpretation of Moby-Dick as an Enactment of Father Mapple's Sermon and the Lesser Prophecies, with an Essay on Herman Melville Interpretation." Ph.D. diss., Wayne State, 1960. DA, 22 (1961), 1979-1980.

2058 NECHAS, James W. "Synonymy, Repetition, and Restatement in the Vocabulary of Herman Melville's Moby-Dick." Ph.D. diss., University of Pennsylvania, 1973. DA, 34 (1974), 5196A.

2059 ________. "Ambiguity of Word and Whale: The Negative Affix in Moby-Dick." College Literature, 2 (1975), 198-225.

2060 NEFF, Winifred. "Satirical Use of a 'Silly Reference' in Israel Potter." American Transcendental Quarterly, 7 (1970), 51-53.

2061 NEIDER, Charles, ed. Short Novels of the Masters. New York: Rinehart, 1948. Introduction to "Benito Cereno," pp. 7-11.

2062 NELSON, Carl. "The Ironic Allusive Texture of Lord Jim: Coleridge, Crane, Milton, and Melville." Conradiana, 4 (1972), 47-59.

2063 NELSON, Gerald L. "Narrator as Character in Melville's Redburn." Ph.D. diss., University of Nebraska, 1971. DA, 33 (1972), 2901A.

2064 NELSON, Lowry. "Night Thoughts on the Gothic Novel." Yale Review, 52 (December, 1962), 236-257.

2065 NELSON, Raymond J. "The Art of Herman Melville: The Author of Pierre." Yale Review, 59 (1970), 197-214.

2066 NESAULE, Valda. "The Christ Figure and the Idea of Sacrifice in Herman Melville's Billy-Budd, in Graham Greene's The Potting Shed, and in Feodor Dostoevsky's 'The Dream of a Ridiculous Man.'" Ph.D. diss., Indiana University, 1975. DA, 36 (1976), 5284A.

2067 NEWBERY, Ilse Sofie Magdalene. "The Unity of Herman Melville's Piazza Tales." Ph.D. diss., University of British Columbia (Vancouver), 1964. DA, 26 (1966), 4668.

2068 _______. "'The Encantadas': Melville's Inferno." American Literature, 38 (March, 1966), 49-68.

2069 NEWMAN, R. G. "An Early Berkshire Appraisal of Moby-Dick." American Quarterly, 9 (Fall, 1957), 365-366.

2070 NICHOL, Charles. "The Iconography of Evil and Ideal in 'Benito Cereno.'" American Transcendental Quarterly, 7 (1970), 25-31.

2071 NICHOL, John W. "Melville's 'Soiled Fish of the Sea.'" American Literature, 21 (November, 1949), 338-339. Relates to White-Jacket.

2072 _______. "Melville and the Midwest." PMLA, 66 (September, 1951), 613-625.

2073 NICHOLS, Martha Frances. "Sun Imagery in the Novels of Herman Melville." Ph.D. diss., Tulane, 1968. DA, 29 (1968), 1904A.

2074 NILON, Charles H. "Some Aspects of the Treatment of Negro Characters by Five Representative American Novelists." Ph.D. diss., University of Wisconsin, 1952. DA, 12 (1952), 232. Study includes Cooper, Melville, Albion W. Tourgée, Ellen Glasgow, and Faulkner.

2075 _______. Bibliography of Bibliographies in American Literature. New York: Bowker, 1970. Melville, pp. 123-126. Includes primary and secondary materials.

2076 NNOLIM, Charles E. Melville's "Benito-Cereno": A Study in Meaning of Name Symbolism. New York: New Voices, 1974.

2077 NOBLE, David W. "The Jeremiahs: James Fenimore Cooper, Nathaniel Hawthorne, and Herman Melville," in Noble, The Eternal Adam and the New World Garden. New York: Braziller, 1968. Pp. 1-47.

2078 NOEL, Daniel C. "'The Portent Unwound': Religious and Psychological Development in the Imagery of Herman Melville, 1819-1854." Ph.D. diss., Drew, 1967. DA, 28 (1967), 1791A.

2079 _______. "Figures of Transition: Moby-Dick as Radical Theology." Cross Currents, 20 (1970), 201-220.

2080 NOONE, John B., Jr. "Billy-Budd: Two Concepts of Nature." American Literature, 29 (November, 1957), 249-262.

2081 NORMAN, Liane. "Bartleby and the Reader." New England Quarterly, 44 (1971), 22-39.

2082 NORRIS, William. "Abbott Lawrence in The Confidence-Man: American Success or American Failure." American Studies (University of Kansas), 17 (1976), 25-38.

2083 NORTHRUP, C. S. "Herman Melville," in Stanton, Theodore, ed., A Manuel of American Literature. New York: Putnam, 1909. Pp. 164-165.

2084 NOTOYA, Ginsaku. "Angry God and Silent God--On the Symbolical Meaning of Moby-Dick." Critica, 6 (Spring, 1962), 2-18.

2085 OAKLAND, John. "Romanticism in Melville's 'Bartleby' and Pierre." Moderna Sprak (Stockholm), 70 (1976), 209-219.

2086 OATES, Joyce Carol. "Melville and the Manichean Illusion." Texas Studies in Literature and Language, 4 (1962), 117-129.

2087 _______. "Melville and the Tragedy of Nihilism," in Oates, The Edge of Impossibility: Tragic Forms in Literature. New York: Vanguard, 1972. Pp. 59-83.

2088 O'BRIEN, Ellen Joan. "The Histrionic Vision: Dramatic and Theatrical Forms in the Novels of Herman Melville." Ph.D. diss., Yale, 1976. *DA*, 38 (1977), 266A.

2089 O'BRIEN, Fitz-James (unsigned article). "Our Young Authors--Melville." *Putnam's Monthly Magazine*, 1 (February, 1853), 155-164. Reprinted in Branch, ed., Melville: *The Critical Heritage* (1974), pp. 323-329.

2090 ______ (unsigned article). "Our Authors and Authorship: Melville and Curtis." *Putnam's Monthly Magazine*, 9 (April, 1857), 384-393. Reprinted in Branch, ed., *Melville: The Critical Heritage* (1974), pp. 361-368. Refers to George William Curtis, known for books of travel, etc.

2091 O'BRIEN, Frederick. *White Shadows in the South Seas.* New York: Century, 1919.

2092 O'BRIEN, Matthew. "'The Maddest Folly of the Campaign': A Diarist and a Poet Confront Kennesaw Mountain." *Civil War History*, 23 (1977), 241-250. On a poem in *Battle-Pieces*.

2093 OBUCHOWSKI, Peter A. "*Billy-Budd* and the Failure of Art." *Studies in Short Fiction*, 15 (1978), 445-452.

2094 O'CONNOR, William Van. "Melville and the Nature of Hope." *University of Kansas City Review*, 22 (Winter, 1955), 123-130.

2095 ______. "Plotinus Plinlimmon and the Principle of Name-Giving," in O'Connor, *The Grotesque: An American Genre and Other Essays.* Carbondale: Southern Illinois University Press, 1962. Pp. 92-97.

2096 O'DANIEL, Therman Benjamin. "A Study of Melville's Journals, Lectures, and Letters." Ph.D. diss., University of Ottaway (Canada), 1955.

2097 ______. "An Interpretation of the Relation of the Chapter Entitled 'The Symphony' to *Moby-Dick* as a Whole." *College Language Association Journal*, 2 (September, 1958), 55-57.

2098 ______. "Herman Melville as a Writer of Journals." *College Language Association Journal*, 4 (December, 1960), 94-105.

2099 O'DONNELL, Charles Robert. "The Mind of the Artist: Cooper, Thoreau, Hawthorne, and Melville." Ph.D. diss., Syracuse University, 1956. *DA*, 17 (1957), 1752.

2100 O'DONNELL, Thomas F. "Where Is Grand Old Pierre?" *Extracts*, 28 (1976), 16-18.

2101 OGATA, Toshihito. "On Moby-Dick." Joshidai Bungaku, 14 (March, 1962), 35-55. In English.

2102 OGLESBY, Carl. "Melville, or Water Consciousness and Its Madness: A Fragment from a Work-in-Progress." Tri-Quarterly, 23-24 (1972), 123-141. Also printed in White, George Abbott, and Charles Newman, eds., Literature in Revolution. New York: Holt, Rinehart, and Winston, 1972. Pp. 123-141.

2103 OKAMOTO, Hidoo. "Billy-Budd, Foretopman as Melville's Testament of Acceptance." Studies in English Literature (Japan), 25 (1959), 225-243.

2104 OKAMOTO, Katsumi. "The End of Melville--As Seen Through Billy-Budd." Geibun (Kinki University), 2 (May, 1962), 1-20.

2105 OLDSEY, Bernard, ed. College Literature, 2 (1975), 155-245. Special issue, Third Quarter, devoted entirely to Moby-Dick.

2106 OLIVER, Egbert Samuel. "Herman Melville and the Idea of Progress." Ph.D. diss., University of Washington (Seattle), 1940.

2107 _______. "Melville's Goneril and Fanny Kemble." New England Quarterly, 18 (December, 1945), 489-500.

2108 _______. "A Second Look at 'Bartleby.'" College English, 6 (May, 1945), 431-439.

2109 _______. "Melville's Picture of Emerson and Thoreau in The Confidence-Man." College English, 8 (November, 1946), 61-72.

2110 _______. "'Cock-A-Doodle-Do!' and Transcendental Hocus-Pocus." New England Quarterly, 21 (June, 1948), 204-216.

2111 _______. "Herman Melville's 'The Lightning-Rod Man.'" The Philadelphia Forum, 35 (June, 1956), 4-5, 17.

2112 _______. "Melville's 'Tartarus.'" Emerson Society Quarterly, 28 (1962), 23-25.

2113 _______, ed. The Piazza Tales. New York: Hendricks House, 1948.

2114 OLMSTED, Francis Allyn. Incidents of a Whaling Voyage. New York: Appleton, 1841. Reprinted New York: Bell, 1969. New Introduction by W. Storrs Lee.

2115 OLSON, Charles. "Lear and Moby-Dick." Twice-A-Year, 1 (Fall-Winter, 1938), 165-189.

2116 ______. "David Young, David Old." Western Review, 14 (1949), 63.

2117 ______. Call Me Ishmael. New York: Reynal and Hitchcock, 1947. Reprinted New York: Grove, 1958. Also reprinted San Francisco: City Lights, 1966.

2118 ______. "Melville et Shakespeare ou le dêcouverte de Moby-Dick." Temps Modernes, 7 (October, 1951), 647-676. In French.

2119 ______. "Materials and Weights of Herman Melville." New Republic, 137 (September 8 and 15, 1952), 20-21, 11-21.

2120 ______. "Equal, That Is, to the Real Itself." Chicago Review, 12 (1958), 98-104. Review of Milton Stern, Fine Hammered Steel (1957).

2121 OMANS, Stuart E. "The Variations on a Masked Leader: A Study on the Literary Relationship of Ralph W. Ellison and Herman Melville." South Atlantic Bulletin, 40 (1975), 15-23.

2122 OPITZ, E. A. "Herman Melville: An American Seer." Contemporary Review, 2 (December, 1946), 348-353.

2123 ORIANS, G. Harrison. "The Indian-Hater in Early American Fiction." Journal of American History, 27 (1933), 33-44.

2124 ______. "Censure of Fiction in American Romances and Magazines." PMLA, 52 (March, 1937), 195-214.

2125 ORMOND, Jeanne Dowd. "The Knave with a Hundred Faces: The Guises of Hermes in Nashe, Fielding, Melville, and Mann." Ph.D. diss., University of California (Irvine), 1974. DA, 35 (1975), 7320A-7321A.

2126 ORTEGO, Philip D. "The Existential Roots in Billy-Budd." Connecticut Review, 4 (1970), 80-87.

2127 ORTH, Ralph H. "An Early Review of The Confidence Man." Emerson Society Quarterly, 43 (1966), 48.

2128 ORWELL, George. "Review of Herman Melville by Lewis Mumford," in Orwell, Collected Essays, Journalism, and Letters, 4 vols. New York: Harcourt, Brace, 1968. Vol. I, pp. 19-21. Orwell, pseud. for Eric Arthur Blair.

2129 OSBORNE, Frances Thomas. "Herman Melville Through a Child's Eyes." Bulletin of the New York Public Library, 69 (December, 1965), 655-660.

2130 OSBOURN, R. V. "The White Whale and the Absolute." Essays in Criticism, 6 (April, 1956), 160-170.

2131 OWLETT, F. C. "Herman Melville, 1819-1891: A Centenary Tribute." Bookman (London), 56 (August, 1919), 164-167.

2132 P., B. A. "Ageless and Edible." American Notes and Queries, 7 (December, 1947), 141.

2133 PACE, Janyce Akard. "Elements of Prophecy in the Prose Fiction of Herman Melville." Ph.D. diss., Oklahoma State, 1974. DA, 36 (1976), 7424A.

2134 PACKARD, Hyland. "Mardi: The Role of Hyperbole in Melville's Search for Expression." American Literature, 49 (1977), 241-253.

2135 PACKARD, Robert Joslin. "A Study of Melville's Clarel." Ph.D. diss., Columbia, 1963. DA, 24 (1963), 2018-2019.

2136 PAEZ, Ramiro. "Moby-Dick, la historia de la persecución de la ballena blanca." Atenea, 152 (1963), 149-155. In Spanish.

2137 PAFFORD, Ward, and Floyd C. Watkins. "'Benito Cereno': A Note in Rebuttal." Nineteenth-Century Fiction, 7 (June, 1952), 68-70.

2138 PALMER, V. W. "Tales of Ancient Whales." Nature Magazine, 35 (April, 1942), 213-214, 221.

2139 PALTSITS, Victor H. "Herman Melville's Background and New Light on the Publication of Typee," in Bookmen's Holiday, ed. by Paltsits, et al. New York: New York Public Library Press, 1943. Pp. 248-268.

2140 ________, ed. "Family Correspondence of Herman Melville." Bulletin of the New York Public Library, 33 (July and August, 1929), 507-525, 575-625. Also published as book. New York: New York Public Library Press, 1929.

2141 PALUSKA, Duane A. "The Dead Letter Office: A Study of Melville's Fiction, 1852-1857, with a Checklist of Writings Related to Melville's Tales, Israel Potter, and The Confidence Man." Ph.D. diss., Brandeis, 1970. DA, 31 (1970), 2934A.

2142 PANNWITT, Barbara, ed. The Art of Short Fiction. Boston: Ginn, 1964. Melville, pp. 244-246.

2143 PARKE, John. "Seven Moby-Dicks." New England Quarterly,

28 (September, 1955), 319-338. Reprinted in Feidelson and Brodtkorb, eds., Interpretations (1959), pp. 84-101. Also in Stern, ed., Discussions (1960), pp. 66-76.

2144 PARKER, Hershel C. "The Metaphysics of Indian-Hating." Nineteenth-Century Fiction, 18 (September, 1963), 165-173.

2145 ________. "Melville's Salesman Story." Studies in Short Fiction, 1 (Winter, 1964), 154-158. Refers to "The Lightning-Rod Man."

2146 ________. "Herman Melville and Politics: A Scrutiny of the Political Milieux of Herman Melville's Life and Works." Ph.D. diss., Northwestern, 1963. DA, 24 (1964), 5390-5391.

2147 ________. "Gansevoort Melville's Role in the Campaign of 1844." New York Historical Society Quarterly, 49 (April, 1965), 143-173.

2148 ________. "New Cross-Lights on Melville in the 1870's." Emerson Society Quarterly, 39 (1965), 24-25.

2149 ________. "Species of 'Soiled Fish.'" Certified Editions of American Authors Newsletter, 1 (1968), 11-12.

2150 ________. "Historical Note," in Hayford, et al., eds., Redburn. Evanston and Chicago: Northwestern-Newberry, 1969. Pp. 315-352.

2151 ________. "Three Melville Reviews in the London Weekly Chronicle." American Literature, 41 (1970), 584-589.

2152 ________. "Melville's Satire of Emerson and Thoreau: An Evaluation of the Evidence." American Transcendental Quarterly, 7 (1970), 61-67. See also ATQ, 9 (1971), 70.

2153 ________. "A Re-examination of Melville's Reviewers by Hugh W. Hetherington, 1961." American Literature, 42 (1970), 226-232.

2154 ________. "The Story of China Aster: A Tentative Explication," in Parker, ed., The Confidence Man (1971), pp. 353-356.

2155 ________. "Melville and the Concept of 'Author's Final Intentions.'" Proof, 1 (1971), 156-168.

2156 ________. "Historical Note," in Hayford, et al., eds., Pierre. Evanston and Chicago: Northwestern-Newberry, 1971. Pp. 379-392.

2157 ______. "'Benito Cereno' and Cloister-Life: A Re-Scrutiny of a 'Source.'" Studies in Short Fiction, 9 (1972), 221-232. Refers to Cloister-Life of the Emperor Charles the Fifth, by William Stirling (London, 1853).

2158 ______. "Five Reviews Not in Moby-Dick as Doubloon." English Language Notes, 9 (1972), 182-185.

2159 ______. "Trafficking in Melville." Modern Language Quarterly, 33 (1972), 54-66. Review of five books published in 1970.

2160 ______. "Further Notices of Pierre." Extracts, 12 (October, 1972), 4-5.

2161 ______. "Melville," in American Literary Scholarship: A Review of Current Scholarship. 1972, pp. 40-58; 1973, pp. 65-84; 1974, pp. 43-59; 1975, pp. 59-82; 1976, pp. 47-59; and 1977, pp. 49-62.

2162 ______. "The Confidence-Man and the Use of Evidence in Compositional Studies: A Rejoinder." Nineteenth-Century Fiction, 28 (1973), 119-124.

2163 ______. "Regularizing Accidentals: The Latest Form of Infidelity." Proof, 3 (1973), 1-20.

2164 ______. "Practical Editions: Herman Melville's Moby-Dick." Proof, 3 (1973), 371-378. Refers to classroom texts.

2165 ______. "Quite an Original." Extracts, 16 (1973), 9-10. Review-essay on Harold Beaver's edition of Moby-Dick (1972).

2166 ______. "Dead Letters and Melville's 'Bartleby.'" Resources for American Literary Study, 4 (1974), 90-99.

2167 ______. "A Review of Moby-Dick." English Language Notes, 9 (1974), 182-185. Reprinted from The Independent, (1851).

2168 ______. "Evidence for 'Late Insertions' in Melville's Works." Studies in the Novel, 7 (1975), 407-424.

2169 ______. "Being Professional in Working on Moby-Dick." College Literature, 2 (1975), 192-197.

2170 ______. "Why Pierre Went Wrong." Studies in the Novel, 8 (1976), 7-23.

2171 ______. "The Ambiguous Portrait of Vine in Melville's Clarel." Extracts, 26 (1976), 4-5.

2172 ________. "Contract: Pierre by Herman Melville." Proof, 5 (1977), 27-44.

2173 ________. "Conjectural Emendations: An Illustration from the Topography of Pierre's Mind." Literary Research Newsletter, 3 (1978), 62-66.

2174 ________, ed. "Gansevoort Melville's 1846 London Journal." Bulletin of the New York Public Library, 69 (1965), 633-654; and 70 (1965), 36-49, 113-131. Also published as book. New York: New York Public Library, 1965.

2175 ________, ed. The Recognition of Herman Melville: Selected Criticism Since 1846. Ann Arbor: University of Michigan Press, 1967.

2176 ________, ed. The Confidence Man: His Masquerade. New York: Norton, 1971. Norton Critical Edition.

2177 ________, ed. Shorter Works of Hawthorne and Melville. Columbus, Ohio: Merrill, 1972.

2178 ________, and Bruce Bebb. "The CEAA: An Interim Assessment." Papers of the Bibliographic Society of America, 68 (1974), 129-148.

2179 ________, and Henry Binder. "Exigencies of Composition and Publication: Billy-Budd, Sailor and Pudd'nhead Wilson." Nineteenth-Century Fiction, 33 (1978), 131-143.

2180 ________, and Harrison Hayford, eds. Moby-Dick. New York: Norton, 1967. Norton Critical Edition.

2181 ________, and Harrison Hayford, eds. Moby-Dick as Doubloon: Essays and Extracts (1851-1970). New York: Norton, 1970. Reprinted criticism. Annotated bibliography, 1921-1969, pp. 367-388.

2182 PARKES, Henry Bamford. The American Experience. New York: Knopf, 1947. Melville, pp. 201-205.

2183 ________. "Poe, Hawthorne, Melville: An Essay in Sociological Criticism." Partisan Review, 16 (February, 1949), 157-165.

2184 PARKS, Aileen Wells. "Leviathan: An Essay in Interpretation." Sewanee Review, 47 (March, 1939), 130-132.

2185 PARRINGTON, Vernon Louis. Main Currents in American Thought, 3 vols. New York: Harcourt, Brace, 1927-1930. Melville, Vol. II, pp. 258-267.

2186 PARRY, E. A. "When Literature Went to Sea." Bookman,

75 (June, 1932), 243-248. Relates to Cooper, Dana, Melville.

2187 PASTON, George. At John Murray's: Records of a Literary Circle, 1843-1892. London: Murray; New York: Dutton, 1932. Melville, pp. 51-52 and passim.

2188 PATRICK, Walton R. "Melville's 'Bartleby' and the Doctrine of Necessity." American Literature, 41 (1969), 39-54.

2189 PATTEE, Fred Lewis. Side-Lights on American Literature. New York: Century, 1922. Melville, passim.

2190 _______. The Development of the American Short Story: An Historical Survey. New York and London: Harper, 1923. Reprinted New York: Biblo and Tannen, 1966. Hawthorne, pp. 91-115; Melville, pp. 116-128.

2191 _______. "Herman Melville." American Mercury, 10 (January, 1927), 33-43.

2192 _______. The New American Literature, 1890-1930. New York: Century, 1930. Melville, pp. 359-384.

2193 _______. The First Century of American Literature, 1770-1870. New York: Appleton-Century, 1935. Melville, passim.

2194 _______. The Feminine Fifties. New York: Appleton-Century, 1940. "Melville and Whitman," pp. 28-49.

2195 PATTERSON, F. M. "The San Dominick's Anchor." American Notes and Queries, 3 (October, 1964), 19-20. Refers to "Benito Cereno."

2196 PAUL, Sherman. "Melville's 'The Town-Ho's Story.'" American Literature, 21 (May, 1949), 212-222. Reprinted in Stern, ed., Discussions (1960), pp. 87-92.

2197 _______. "Morgan Neville, Melville, and the Folk Hero." Notes and Queries, 194 (June 25, 1949), 278.

2198 _______. "Hawthorne's Ahab." Notes and Queries, 196 (June 9, 1951), 255-257.

2199 _______, ed. Moby-Dick. New York: Dutton, 1950.

2200 PAVESE, Cesare. "Herman Melville: The Literary Whaler." La Cultura, 11 (January-March, 1932), 83-93. In Italian. Translated and published in English, Sewanee Review, 68 (Summer, 1960), 407-418.

2201 PAYNE, John. "Herman Melville," a poem, in Vigil and

Vision: New Sonnets. London: Villon Society, 1903. P. 62. Reprinted in Parker, ed., Recognition (1967), p. 148.

2202 PEARCE, Howard D. "The Narrator of 'Norfolk Isle and the Chola Widow.'" Studies in Short Fiction, 3 (Fall, 1965), 56-62.

2203 PEARCE, Roy Harvey. "Melville's Indian-Hater: A Note on the Meaning of The Confidence-Man." PMLA, 67 (December, 1962), 942-948.

2204 ________. "The Metaphysics of Indian-Hating: Leatherstocking Unmasked," in Pearce, Historicism Once More. Princeton: Princeton University Press, 1969. Pp. 109-136.

2205 PEARSON, Edmund. Queer Books. New York: Doubleday, Doran, 1928. Melville not discussed; see chapter "From Sudden Death," pp. 215-231, on crime and hangings.

2206 PEARSON, Norman Holmes. "Billy-Budd: The King's Yarn." American Quarterly, 3 (Summer, 1951), 99-114.

2207 PEARY, Gerald, and Roger Shatzin, eds. The Classic American Novel and the Movies. New York: Ungar, 1977. Includes study of The Scarlet Letter, The House of the Seven Gables, Moby-Dick, and Billy-Budd.

2208 PECKHAM, Morse. "Toward a Theory of Romanticism." PMLA, 66 (1951), 5-23.

2209 ________. "Toward a Theory of Romanticism: II. Reconsiderations." Studies in Romanticism, 1 (1961), 1-8.

2210 ________. "Hawthorne and Melville as European Authors," in Vincent, ed., Melville and Hawthorne in the Berkshires (1968), pp. 42-62. Reprinted in Peckham, The Triumph of Romanticism. Columbia: University of South Carolina Press, 1970.

2211 PELTZ, William L. L. The Top Flight at Number One Lafayette Street. Albany, N.Y.: Printed for the author, 1939.

2212 PERCIVAL, M. O. A Reading of Moby-Dick. Chicago: University of Chicago Press, 1950.

2213 PERKINS, George. "Death by Spontaneous Combustion in Marryat, Melville, Dickens, Zola, and Others." Dickensian, 60 (1964), 57-63.

2214 PERRINE, Laurence. "The Nature of Proof in the Interpretation of Poetry." English Journal, 51 (September, 1962), 393-398. Melville, passim.

2215 PERRY, Robert L. "Billy-Budd: Melville's Paradise Lost." Midwest Quarterly, 10 (1969), 173-185.

2216 PERSONS, Stow. Free Religion: An American Faith. New Haven: Yale University Press, 1947. Emerson and Melville, passim. See chapter "The Religion of Humanity," pp. 99-129.

2217 _______. American Minds: A History of Ideas. New York: Holt, Rinehart, and Winston, 1958. Melville and Moby-Dick, pp. 202, 213.

2218 PETERS, R. L. "Melville's Moby-Dick." Explicator, 16 (April, 1958), item 44.

2219 PETERSON, Audrey C. "Brain-Fever in Nineteenth-Century Literature: Fact and Fiction." Victorian Studies, 19 (1976), 445-464.

2220 PETERSON, Sandra M. "The View from the Gallows: The Criminal Confession in American Literature." Ph.D. diss., Northwestern, 1971. DA, 33 (1972), 2947A.

2221 PETRULLO, Helen B. "The Neurotic Hero of Typee." American Imago, 12 (1955), 317-323.

2222 PHELPS, Donald. "The Holy Family in Pierre." Prose, 5 (1972), 99-113.

2223 PHELPS, Leland R. "Moby-Dick in Germany." Comparative Literature, 10 (Fall, 1958), 349-355.

2224 _______. "The Reaction to 'Benito Cereno' and Billy-Budd in Germany." Symposium, 13 (Fall, 1959), 294-299.

2225 _______. A Preliminary Checklist of Foreign Language Materials on the Life and Works of Herman Melville. Melville Society Special Publication, April, 1960.

2226 _______. A Preliminary Checklist of the Works of Herman Melville in Translation. Melville Society Special Publication, April, 1961.

2227 PHILBRICK, Thomas L. "Another Source for White-Jacket." American Literature, 29 (January, 1958), 431-439.

2228 _______. "Melville's 'Best Authorities.'" Nineteenth-Century Fiction, 15 (September, 1960), 171-179. Relates to White-Jacket.

2229 _______. James Fenimore Cooper and the Development of American Sea Fiction. Cambridge: Harvard University Press, 1961. Includes Melville.

2230 PHILLIPS, Barry. "'The Good Captain': A Reading of 'Benito Cereno.'" Texas Studies in Literature and Language, 4 (Summer, 1962), 188-197. Excerpt reprinted in Gross, ed., Benito Cereno Handbook (1965), pp. 111-115.

2231 PHILLIPS, John A. "Melville Meets Hawthorne: How a Champagne Picnic on Monument Mountain Led to a Profound Revision of Moby-Dick and Disenchantment." American Heritage, 27 (1975), 16-21, 87-90.

2232 PICKERING, James H. "Melville's 'Ducking' Duyckinck." Bulletin of the New York Public Library, 70 (1966), 551-552.

2233 PILKINGTON, William T. "Melville's 'Benito Cereno': Source and Technique." Studies in Short Fiction, 2 (Spring, 1965), 247-255.

2234 ________. "'Benito Cereno' and the 'Valor-Ruined Man' of Moby-Dick." Texas Studies in Literature and Language, 7 (Summer, 1965), 201-207.

2235 ________. "'Benito Cereno' and the American National Character." Discourse, 8 (Winter, 1965), 49-63.

2236 PINKER, Michael Joseph. "The Iconography of Madness, or the Sterne Voyage of the Pequod: The Tale of a Tub in American Literature." Ph.D. diss., University of Michigan, 1976. DA, 37 (1976), 1533A. Sterne's influence on Melville.

2237 PINSKER, Sanford. "'Bartleby the Scrivener': Language as Wall." College Literature, 2 (1975), 17-27.

2238 PIRANO, F. "Moby-Dick di Herman Melville." Convivium, 15 (1943), 209-243. In Italian.

2239 PITT, A. Stuart. "Moody Ahab and His Heaven Insulting Purpose." Historic Nantucket, 4 (October, 1956), 23-27.

2240 ________. "'A Semi-Romance of the Sea': Miriam Coffin as Precursor of Moby-Dick." Historic Nantucket, 19 (October, 1972), 15-30. Refers to Miriam Coffin: Or, The Whale Fishermen, the first American novel on whaling, by Joseph C. Hart (1834).

2241 PITZ, H. C. "A Painter of Themes--Gil Wilson." American Artist, 21 (April, 1957), 30-35. Includes drawings of Moby-Dick and Leaves of Grass.

2242 PLOMER, William, ed. Herman Melville: Selected Poems. London: Hogarth, 1943.

2243 ________, ed. with Introduction. Billy-Budd: Foretopman. London: Lehmann, 1947.

2244 ________, ed. White-Jacket, or The World in a Man-Of-War. New York: Grove, 1952.

2245 PLUMSTEAD, Arthur W. "Herman Melville's Concern with Time." Ph.D. diss., University of Rochester, 1960.

2246 ________. "'Bartleby': Melville's Venture into a New Genre," in Vincent, Howard P., ed., Melville Annual, No. 1 (1965), pp. 82-93.

2247 POCHMANN, Henry A. German Culture in America: Philosophical and Literary Influences, 1600-1900. Madison: University of Wisconsin Press, 1950. Melville, pp. 436-440 and 755-760.

2248 ________. "Review of Heinz Kosok's Influence of the Gothic Novel on Melville." American Literature, 36 (1964), 224-225. Book is in German; has not been translated.

2249 ________, and Gay Wilson Allen. Introduction to Masters of American Literature. Carbondale: Southern Illinois University Press, 1969. Based on material in Pochmann and Allen, eds., Masters of American Literature, 2 vols. (1949). Melville, pp. 102-107.

2250 POENICKE, Klaus. "A View from the Piazza: Herman Melville and the Legacy of the European Sublime." Comparative Literature Studies, 4 (1967), 267-281.

2251 POGGI, Valentina. "Pierre: Il 'Kraken' di Melville." Studi Americani, 10 (1964), 71-100. In Italian.

2252 POIRIER, Richard. A World Elsewhere: The Place of Style in American Literature. New York: Oxford University Press, 1966. Melville, passim.

2253 POLK, James. "Melville and the Idea of the City." University of Toronto Quarterly, 41 (1972), 277-292. Discusses from Typee to Clarel.

2254 POLLARD, Carole Ann. "Melville's Hall of Mirrors: Reflective Imagery in Pierre." Ph.D. diss., Kent State, 1975. DA, 36 (1975), 3717A-3718A.

2255 POLLIN, Burton R. "Additional Unrecorded Reviews of Melville's Books." Journal of American Studies, 9 (April, 1975), 55-68.

2256 ________. "An Unnoticed Contemporary Review of Moby-Dick." Extracts, 22 (1975), 3-4.

2257 ________. "Unreported American Reviews of Melville, 1849-1855." Extracts, 23 (1975), 7-8.

2258 POMMER, Henry F. "Melville as Critic of Christianity." Friends' Intellegencer, 102 (February 24, 1945), 121-123.

2259 ________. "Milton's Influence on Herman Melville." Ph.D. diss., Yale, 1946.

2260 ________. "Melville's 'The Gesture' and the Schoolbook Verses." American Notes and Queries, 6 (January, 1947), 150-151.

2261 ________. "Herman Melville and the Wake of the Essex." American Literature, 20 (November, 1948), 290-304.

2262 ________. Milton and Melville. Pittsburgh: University of Pittsburgh Press, 1950.

2263 POPS, Martin Leonard. "Herman Melville," in Herzberg, Max J., ed., The Reader's Encyclopedia of American Literature. New York: Crowell, 1962. Pp. 723-728.

2264 ________. "The Winding Quest: A Study of Herman Melville." Ph.D. diss., Columbia, 1965. DA, 28 (1968), 4141A.

2265 ________. The Melville Archetype. Kent, Ohio: Kent State University Press, 1970.

2266 ________. "Melville: To Him, Olson." Modern Poetry Studies, 2 (1971), 61-96.

2267 ________. "Melville: To Him, Olson." Olson issue of Boundary, 2 (1974), 55-84. Revision of 1971 article.

2268 PORTE, Joel. The Romance in America: Studies in Cooper, Poe, Hawthorne, Melville, and James. Middletown, Conn.: Wesleyan University Press, 1969. Melville, pp. 152-192.

2269 PORTNAY, Howard N. "Emerson, Melville, and 'The Poet.'" Junction (Brooklyn College), 1 (1973), 172-175.

2270 POSTMAN, Neil. "Teaching Novel and Film: Moby-Dick." English Record, 14 (October, 1963), 41-44.

2271 POTTER, David. "Reviews of Moby-Dick." Journal of Rutgers University Library, 3 (June, 1940), 62-65. Concludes that Moby-Dick was a moderate success.

2272 ________. "The Brodhead Diaries: 1846-1849." Journal of Rutgers University Library, 11 (December, 1947), 21-27.

2273 POULET, Georges. "Timelessness and Romanticism." Journal of the History of Ideas, 15 (1954), 3-22.

2274 ______. Studies in Human Time, translated from French by Elliott Coleman. Baltimore: Johns Hopkins University Press, 1956. Melville, pp. 337-341.

2275 POWELL, Lawrence Clark. "The Alchemy of Books." American Library Association Bulletin, 46 (1952), 266-272.

2276 ______. "My Melville," in Islands of Books. Los Angeles: Ward Ritchie, 1952. Pp. 68-74.

2277 ______. "Of Whales and Grass," in Books in My Baggage. Cleveland: World, 1960. Pp. 49-55.

2278 POWERS, William. "Bulkington as Henry Chatillon." Western American Literature, 3 (1968), 153-155.

2279 POWYS, John Cowper. "Melville and Poe," in Enjoyment of Literature. New York: Simon and Schuster, 1938. Pp. 379-405.

2280 PRIDEAUX, Tom. "Duel of Saints and Sinners: A Review of the movie 'Billy-Budd.'" Life, December 12, 1952. Pp. 128-132.

2281 PRIESTLEY, J. B. Literature and Western Man. New York: Harper and Brothers, 1960. "The Novelists," pp. 222-273.

2282 PRINCETON UNIVERSITY LIBRARY CHRONICLE. Special Melville Issue, 13 (Winter, 1952), 63-118. See listing under Rice, Howard C.

2283 PRITCHETT, V. S. "Without the Whale." New Statesman, 55 (January, 1958), 504-505.

2284 PROCTOR, Page S., Jr. "A Source for the Flogging Incident in White-Jacket." American Literature, 22 (May, 1950), 176-182.

2285 PRY, Elmer R., Jr. "That 'Grand, Ungodly, God-like Man': Ahab's Metaphoric Character." Style, 6 (1972), 159-177.

2286 PRYSE, Marjorie L. "The Marked Character in American Fiction: Essays in Social and Metaphysical Isolation." Ph.D. diss., University of California (Santa Cruz), 1973. DA, 35 (1974), 1119A-1120A.

2287 PRZEMECKA, Irena. "Herman Melville's and Robert Lowell's 'Benito Cereno': Tale into Drama." Zagadnienia Rodzajów Literackich, 14 (1971), 5762.

2288 PUETT, Amy Elizabeth. "Melville's Wife: A Study of Elizabeth Shaw Melville." Ph.D. diss., Northwestern, 1969. DA, 30 (1970), 2666A-2667A.

2289 PUK, Francine Shapiro. "The Sovereign Nature of 'The Bell Tower.'" Extracts, 27 (1976), 14-15.

2290 ______. "'Bartleby the Scrivener': A Study in Self-Reliance." Delta English Studies, 7 (1978), 7-20.

2291 PULLIN, Faith. "Typee: The Failure of Eden," in Pullin, ed., Perspectives (1978), pp. 1-28.

2292 ______, ed. New Perspectives on Melville. Edinburgh: University of Edinburgh Press; Kent: Kent State University Press, 1978.

2293 PURCELL, James M. "Melville's Contributions to English." PMLA, 56 (September, 1941), 797-808. Accounts for 180 words used by Melville.

2294 PUTNAM, George A., ed. A Memoir of George Palmer Putnam. New York: Putnam, 1902. Refers to founder of publishing firm.

2295 PUTNAM, John B. "Whaling and Whalecraft," in Hayford, Harrison, ed., Moby-Dick (1967), pp. 509-517.

2296 PUTNAM, Wallace. Moby-Dick Seen Again: Diary of an Artist Reading Melville's Book. New York: Blue Moon, 1975.

2297 PUTZEL, Max. "The Source and Symbols of Melville's 'Benito Cereno.'" American Literature, 34 (May, 1962), 191-206.

2298 QUENNELL, Peter. "The Author of Moby-Dick." New Statesman (London), 33 (August 24, 1929), 604. Comments on Chapter 42, "The Whiteness of the Whale."

2299 QUINN, Arthur Hobson. "The Creator of Moby-Dick." Yale Review, 12 (October, 1922), 205-209.

2300 ______. American Fiction: An Historical and Critical Survey. New York: Appleton-Century, 1936. "Herman Melville and the Exotic Romance," pp. 149-158.

2301 ______, ed. The Literature of the American People: An Historical and Critical Survey. New York: Appleton-Century-Crofts, 1915. Reissued 1951. "The Establishment of a National Literature," by Quinn, pp. 175-568; includes Melville.

2302 QUINN, Patrick F. "Poe's Imaginary Voyage." Hudson Review, 4 (Winter, 1952), 562-585.

2303 QUIRK, Thomas Vaughan. "Saint Paul's Types of the Faithful and Melville's Confidence Man." Nineteenth-Century Fiction, 28 (March, 1974), 472-477.

2304 ________. "The Confidence Man: Melville's Problem of Faith." Ph.D. diss., University of New Mexico, 1977. DA, 38 (1977), 3503A.

2305 RACHAL, John. "Melville on Vere: A Revealing Letter?" American Notes and Queries, 15 (1976), 36-38.

2306 RAHV, Philip. "The Dark Lady of Salem." Partisan Review, 8 (September-October, 1941), 362-381. Principally about Hawthorne; Melville passim.

2307 ________. "Melville and His Critics." Partisan Review, 17 (Fall, 1950), 732-735. Reprinted in Rahv, Image and Idea: Twenty Essays on Literary Themes. Norfolk, Conn.: New Directions, 1957. Pp. 182-187.

2308 ________, ed. Discovery of Europe: The Story of American Experience in the Old World. Boston: Houghton Mifflin, 1947. Melville, pp. 128-138: "What Redburn Saw in Launcelott's-Hey," Chapter 37 of Redburn.

2309 ________, ed. Literature in America: An Anthology of Literary Criticism. New York: Meridian, 1957. "The Whale," chapter from Herman Melville (1950), by Newton Arvin, pp. 168-188.

2310 RALEIGH, John Henry. "The Novel and the City: England and America in the Nineteenth-Century." Victorian Studies, 11 (1968), 291-328.

2311 RALPH, George. "History and Prophecy in Benito-Cereno." Educational Theatre Journal, 22 (1970), 155-160.

2312 RAMAKRISHNA, P. "Moral Ambiguity in Herman Melville's 'Benito Cereno,'" in Criticism and Research. Benares, India: Benares Hindu University Press, 1966. Pp. 136-145.

2313 RAMPERSAD, Arnold. Melville's "Israel Potter": A Pilgrimage and Progress. Bowling Green, Ohio: Bowling Green State University Popular Press, 1969.

2314 RAMSEY, Paul. "God's Grace and Man's Guilt." Journal of Religion, 31 (January, 1951), 21-37.

2315 RAMSEY, William McCrea. "The Confidence-Man: Melville and the Reader." Ph.D. diss., University of North Carolina (Chapel Hill), 1977. DA, 38 (1978), 7336A-7337A.

2316 RANDALL, David A., and John T. Winterich. "One Hundred Good Novels: Herman Melville, Moby-Dick." Publishers' Weekly, 137 (January 20, 1940), 255-257.

2317 RANDALL, John H., III. "Bartleby vs. Wall Street: New York in the 1850's." Bulletin of the New York Public Library, 78 (1975), 138-144.

2318 RANISZESKI, Edward L. "The Significance of the Christian Ethic in Herman Melville's Pierre; Or The Ambiguities." Ph.D. diss., Bowling Green State, 1972. DA, 34 (1973), 738A.

2319 RASCO, Laven. "The Biographies of Herman Melville: A Study in Twentieth-Century Biography." Ph.D. diss., Northwestern, 1956. DA, 17 (1957), 357.

2320 RATHBUN, John W. "Billy-Budd and the Limits of Perception." Nineteenth-Century Fiction, 20 (June, 1965), 19-34.

2321 RAWLINGS, Carl D. "Prophecy in the Novel." Ph.D. diss., University of Washington, 1972. DA, 34 (1973), 2575A-2576A.

2322 RAY, Gordon Norton, ed. with Foreword, and C. Walker Barrett, Introduction. The American Writer in England. Charlottesville: University Press of Virginia, 1969.

2323 RAY, Richard E. "'Benito Cereno': Babo as Leader." American Transcendental Quarterly, 7 (1970), 31-37.

2324 READ, Sir Herbert. English Prose Style. London: Bell, 1953. Melville, pp. 198-200 and passim.

2325 RECK, Tom S. "Melville's Last Sea Poetry: John Marr and Other Sailors." Forum (Houston), 12 (1974), 17-22.

2326 REDMAN, Ben Ray. "New Editions." Saturday Review of Literature, 32 (November 26, 1949), 28. Review of Grove Press edition of The Confidence-Man, ed. by Roy Fuller.

2327 REED, Arthur L. "Social, Political, and Religious Thought in Herman Melville's Mardi." M.A. thesis, Yale, 1942.

2328 REED, Henry. "Books in General: 'Billy-Budd.'" New Statesman and Nation (London), 35 (May 31, 1947), 397.

2329 ———. "Moby-Dick: A Play for Radio." London: BBC, 1947.

2330 REED, Walter L. "Meditation on the Hero: Narrative Form in Carlyle, Kierkegaard, and Melville." Ph.D. diss., Yale, 1969. DA, 31 (1970), 1288A.

2331 ———. "Melville: The Extended Hero and Expanded Meditation," in Reed, Meditations on the Hero: A Study of the Romantic Hero in Nineteenth-Century Fiction. New Haven: Yale University Press, 1974. Pp. 138-186.

2332 ———. "The Measured Forms of Captain Vere." Modern Fiction Studies, 23 (1977), 227-235.

2333 REES, John Owen, Jr. "Spenserian Analogues in Moby-Dick." Emerson Society Quarterly, 18 (1972), 174-178.

2334 REES, Robert A. "Melville's Alma and the Book of Mormon." Emerson Society Quarterly, 43 (1966), 41-46.

2335 REEVES, Paschal. "'The Deaf-Mute' Confidence Man: Melville's Imposter in Action." Modern Language Notes, 75 (January, 1960), 18-20.

2336 REGAN, Charles Lionel. "Melville's Horned Women." English Language Notes, 5 (1967), 34-39.

2337 ———. "The Dilemma of Melville's Horned Women." American Notes and Queries, 12 (1974), 133-134.

2338 REICH, Charles A. "The Tragedy of Justice in Billy-Budd." Yale Review, 56 (Spring, 1967), 368-389.

2339 REID, Benjamin L. "Old Melville's Fable." Massachusetts Review, 9 (Summer, 1968), 529-546. Discusses Moby-Dick and Billy-Budd. Reprinted in Reid, Tragic Occasions (1971), pp. 137-162.

2340 ———. "Leviathan Is the Text," in Reid, Tragic Occasions: Essays on Several Forms. Port Washington, N.Y.: Kennikat, 1971. Pp. 95-135.

2341 REINERT, Otto. "Bartleby the Inscrutable: Notes on a Melville Motif." Americana-Norvegica (Oslo), 1 (1966), 180-205. Edited by Sigmund Skard and Henry H. Wasser.

2342 ———. "'Secret Mines and Dubious Side': The World of Billy-Budd." Americana-Norvegica (Oslo), 4 (1973), 183-192. Edited by Brita Seyerstad.

2343 REISS, John P., Jr. "Problems of the Family Novel: Cooper, Hawthorne, and Melville." Ph.D. diss., University of Wisconsin, 1968. DA, 30 (1969), 1178A-1179A.

2344 REIST, John S., Jr. "Surd Evil and Suffering Love." Universitas, 2 (1964), 81-90. In Spanish.

2345 RENVOISE, Jean-Paul. "Billy-Budd: opêra de Benjamin Britten." Etudes anglaises, 18 (1965), 367-382.

2346 REQUA, Kenneth A. "The Pilgrim's Problems: Melville's Clarel." Ball State University Forum, 16 (1975), 16-20.

2347 RESINK, G. J. "Samburan Encantada." English Studies, 47 (February, 1966), 35-44. Also published in Conradiana, 1 (1968), 37-44.

2348 REYNOLDS, J. N. "Mocha Dick: Or the White Whale of the Pacific." The Knickerbocker, New York Monthly Magazine, 13 (May, 1839), 377-392. Reprinted in Harrison and Parker, eds., Moby-Dick (1967), pp. 571-590.

2349 REYNOLDS, Larry John. "A Study of Herman Melville's Views of Man." Ph.D. diss., Duke, 1974. DA, 35 (1975), 7267A-7268A.

2350 _______. "Vine and Clarel." Extracts, 23 (1975), 11.

2351 _______. "Anti-Democratic Emphasis in White-Jacket." American Literature, 48 (1976), 13-28.

2352 _______. "Melville's Use of 'Young Goodman Brown.'" American Transcendental Quarterly, 31 (1976), 12-14.

2353 _______. "The Pattern of Violence." Melville Society Extracts, 33 (1978), 19-21.

2354 REYNOLDS, Michael S. "The Prototype for Melville's Confidence-Man." PMLA, 86 (1971), 1009-1013.

2355 RICE, Howard C., Jr., et al. "Moby-Dick by Herman Melville: A Century of an American Classic--Catalogue of an Exhibition at Princeton University Library, October 15--December 15, 1951." Princeton University Library Chronicle, 13 (Winter, 1952), 63-118.

2356 RICE, Julian C. "Moby-Dick and Shakespearean Tragedy." Centennial Review, 14 (1970), 444-468.

2357 _______. "The Ship as Cosmic Symbol in Moby-Dick and 'Benito Cereno.'" Centennial Review, 16 (1972), 138-154.

2358 _______. "Claggart and the Satanic Type." American Transcendental Quarterly, 26 (1975), 37-40.

2359 RICE, Nancy Hall. "Beauty and the Beast and the Little Boy: Clues about the Origins of Sexism and Racism from Folklore and Literature: Chaucer's 'The Prioress's Tale,' Melville's 'Benito Cereno,' and Hawthorne's 'Rappaccini's Daughter.'" Ph. D. diss., University of Massachusetts, 1975. DA, 36 (1975), 875A.

2360 RICHARDSON, Nancy Lee. "Herman Melville's Attitude Toward America." Ph. D. diss., University of Delaware, 1977. DA, 38 (1977), 2129A.

2361 RICHARDSON, R. D. "Melville," in Myth and Literature in the American Renaissance. Bloomington: Indiana University Press, 1978. Pp. 195-233.

2362 RICHIE, Donald. "Herman Melville." Studies of Current English (Tokyo), 10 (November, 1955), 33-40.

2363 RICKS, Beatrice, and Joseph D. Adams. Herman Melville: A Reference Bibliography, 1900-1972, with Selected Nineteenth-Century Materials. Boston: Hall, 1973.

2364 RIDEOUT, Walter B. "Instructor's Manual" for The Experience of Prose. New York: Crowell, 1960. "Benito Cereno," pp. 15-16.

2365 RIDGE, George Ross, and Davy S. Ridge. "A Bird and a Motto: Source for 'Benito Cereno.'" Mississippi Quarterly, 12 (Winter, 1959-1960), 22-29.

2366 RIEGEL, O. W. "The Anatomy of Melville's Fame." American Literature, 3 (May, 1931), 195-203.

2367 RIPLEY, George (published anonymously). "Review of Moby-Dick." Harper's New Monthly Magazine, 4 (December, 1851), 137. Reprinted in Hayford and Parker, eds., Moby-Dick (1967), pp. 616-617.

2368 RISING GENERATION, THE (Japan). Special Melville issue, 1969.

2369 RITCHIE, M. C. "Herman Melville." Queen's Quarterly, 37 (January, 1930), 36-61.

2370 RITTERBUSCH, Dale E. "A Concealed Melville Couplet." Extracts, 16 (1973), 11.

2371 ROBBINS, J. Albert, ed. American Literary Manuscripts: A Checklist of Holdings in Academic, Historical, and Public Libraries, Museums, and Authors' Homes in the United States. Athens: University of Georgia Press, 1960. Reissued, 1977.

2372 ROBERTS, David A. "Structure and Meaning in Melville's 'The Encantadas.'" Emerson Society Quarterly, 22 (1976), 234-244.

2373 ROBERTS, Morley. "The Sea in Fiction." Queen's Quarterly, 37 (January, 1930), 18-35.

2374 ROBERTSON, J. G., ed. "Romanticism: A Symposium." PMLA, 55 (March, 1940), 1-20.

2375 ROBERTSON, R. B. Of Whales and Men. New York: Knopf, 1954.

2376 ROBILLARD, Douglas. "Theme and Structure in Melville's John Marr and Other Sailors." English Language Notes, 6 (1969), 187-192.

2377 ________. "'I Laud the Inhuman Sea': Melville as Poet in the 1880's," in Robillard, ed., Symposium (1976), pp. 193-206.

2378 ________. "Monroe Edwards and Melville's Bartleby." English Language Notes, 15 (1978), 291-294.

2379 ________, ed. "Symposium: Melville the Poet." Essays in Arts and Sciences, 5 (special issue, 1976), 83-206.

2380 ________, ed. Poems of Herman Melville. New Haven: College and University Press, 1976.

2381 ROCHE, Arthur J., III. "A Literary Gentleman in New York: Evert A. Duyckinck's Relationship with Nathaniel Hawthorne, Herman Melville, Edgar Allan Poe and William Gilmore Simms." Ph.D. diss., Duke, 1973. DA, 34 (1974), 4282A.

2382 ROCKWELL, Frederick S. "De Quincey and the Ending of Moby-Dick." Nineteenth-Century Fiction, 9 (December, 1954), 161-168.

2383 ROGERS, Jane E. "The Transcendental Quest in Emerson and Melville." Ph.D. diss., Pittsburgh, 1973. DA, 35 (1974), 1632A.

2384 ROGERS, Robert. "The 'Ineludible Gripe' of Billy-Budd." Literature and Psychology, 14 (Winter, 1964), 9-22.

2385 ________. A Psychological Study of the Double in Literature. Detroit: Wayne State University Press, 1970. Melville, pp. 67-70, 133-137, and passim.

2386 ROHEIM, Geza. "The Dragon and the Hero." American Imago, 1 (March and June, 1940), 40-69, 61-94.

2387 ROHRBERGER, Mary. "Point of View in 'Benito Cereno': Machinations and Deceptions." College English, 27 (April, 1965), 541-546.

2388 ROPER, Gordon. "Melville's Use of Autobiographical Material in Redburn." M.A. thesis, University of Chicago, 1938.

2389 ________. "An Index to Herman Melville's Mardi, Moby-Dick, Pierre, and Billy-Budd." Ph.D. diss., University of Chicago, 1944.

2390 ________. "Melville's Moby-Dick, 1851-1951." Dalhousie Review, 31 (August, 1951), 167-179.

2391 ________. "Before Moby-Dick." University of Chicago Magazine, 48 (October, 1955), 4-9.

2392 ________. "On Teaching Moby-Dick." Emerson Society Quarterly, 28 (1962), 2-4.

2393 ________. "Historical Note," in Hayford, et al., eds., Omoo (1968), pp. 319-344.

2394 ________, et al., eds. Melville Supplement. Emerson Society Quarterly, 28 (1962), 2-30.

2395 ROPPEN, Georg. "Melville's Sea: Shoreless, Indefinite as God." Americana-Norvegica (Oslo), 4 (1973), 137-181.

2396 ROSE, Edward J. "Melville, Emerson, and the Sphinx." New England Quarterly, 36 (June, 1963), 249-258.

2397 ________. "The Queenly Personality: Walpole, Melville, and Mother." Literature and Psychology, 15 (1965), 216-229.

2398 ________. "Annihilation and Ambiguity: Moby-Dick and 'The Town Ho's Story.'" New England Quarterly, 45 (1972), 541-558.

2399 ROSE, William, ed. "Symposium on Romanticism." Journal of History of Ideas, 2 (1941), 257-338.

2400 ROSEN, Bruce. "Typee and Omoo: Melville's Literary Apprenticeship." Ph.D. diss., New York University, 1965. DA, 27 (1966), 461A-462A.

2401 ROSEN, Roma. "Herman Melville's Uses of Shakespeare's Plays." Ph.D. diss., Northwestern, 1962. DA, 23 (1963), 3356.

2402 ROSENBACH, A. S. W., Introduction. Moby-Dick. New York: Doubleday, 1928. Edited by Carl Maltby Benson.

2403 ROSENBERG, Samuel. "Come Out Herman Melville, Wherever You Are! (The Man Who Turned to Stone)," in Rosenberg, The Come As You Are Masquerade Party (1970). Reprinted Baltimore: Penguin, 1972, as The Confessions of a Trivialist.

2404 ROSENBERRY, Edward Hoffman. "The Comic Spirit in the Art of Herman Melville." Ph. D. diss., University of Pennsylvania, 1953.

2405 ________. Melville and the Comic Spirit. Cambridge: Harvard University Press, 1955.

2406 ________. "Queequeg's Coffin-Canoe: Made in Typee." American Literature, 30 (January, 1959), 529-530.

2407 ________. "Awash in Melvilliana." New England Quarterly, 33 (December, 1960), 525-528.

2408 ________. "Melville's Ship of Fools." PMLA, 75 (December, 1960), 604-608.

2409 ________. "Israel Potter, Benjamin Franklin, and the Doctrine of Self-Reliance." Emerson Society Quarterly, 28 (1962), 27-29.

2410 ________. "The Problem of Billy-Budd." PMLA, 80 (December, 1965), 489-498.

2411 ________. "Melville and His 'Mosses.'" American Transcendental Quarterly, 7 (1970), 47-51. Discusses "I and My Chimney" and "The Apple-Tree Table."

2412 ________. "Moby-Dick: Epic Romance." College Literature, 2 (1975), 155-170.

2413 ________. Melville: An Author Guide. London and Boston: Routledge and Kegan Paul, 1978.

2414 ROSENBURG, Jerome H. "A World Apart: Comparative Studies in American and Australian Literary Development of the Nineteenth-Century." Ph. D. diss., University of Texas (Austin), 1971. DA, 32 (1972), 6390A-6391A.

2415 ROSENFELD, William. "The Divided Burden: Common Elements in the Search for a Religious Synthesis in the Works of Theodore Parker, Horace Bushnell, Nathaniel Hawthorne, and Herman Melville." Ph. D. diss., University of Minnesota, 1961. DA, 22 (1962), 4019.

2416 ________. "Uncertain Faith: Queequeg's Coffin and Melville's Use of the Bible." Texas Studies in Literature and Language, 7 (Winter, 1966), 317-327.

2417 ROSENFIELD, Claire. "The Shadow Within: The Conscious and Unconscious Use of the Double." Daedalus, Spring, 1967. Reprinted in Guerard, ed., Stories of the Double (1967), pp. 311-331.

2418 ROSENHEIM, Frederick. "Flight from Home." American Imago, 1 (December, 1940), 1-30.

2419 ROSENTHAL, Bernard. "Nature's Slighting Hand: The Idea of Nature in American Writing, 1820-1860." Ph.D. diss., University of Illinois, 1968. DA, 29 (1969), 2226A.

2420 ______. "Melville, Marryat, and the Evil-Eyed Villain." Nineteenth-Century Fiction, 25 (1970), 221-224.

2421 ______. "Elegy for Jack Chase." Studies in Romanticism, 10 (1971), 213-229.

2422 ______. "Melville's Island: Benito-Cereno." Studies in Short Fiction, 11 (Winter, 1974), 1-9.

2423 ROSENTHAL, M. L., and A. J. M. Smith. Exploring Poetry. New York: Macmillan, 1955. Melville, pp. 372-375. Discusses "Billy in the Darbies."

2424 ROSS, Donald J. "Who's Talking? How Characters Become Narrators in Fiction." Modern Language Notes, 91 (1976), 1222-1242. Includes Melville.

2425 ROSS, Ernest C. "The Development of the English Sea Novel." Ph.D. diss., University of Virginia, 1924.

2426 ______. The English Sea Novel. Ann Arbor, Mich.: Edwards Brothers, 1926.

2427 ROSS, Morton L. "Captain Truck and Captain Boomer." American Literature, 37 (November, 1965), 316. Refers to Cooper's Homeward Bound (1838) and Chapter 100 of Moby-Dick.

2428 ______. "Moby-Dick as an Education." Studies in the Novel, 6 (Spring, 1974), 62-75.

2429 ROTHFORK, John. "The Sailing of the Pequod: An Existential Voyage." Arizona Quarterly, 28 (1972), 55-60.

2430 ROTHSCHILD, Herbert, Jr. "The Language of Mesmerism in 'The Quarter-Deck' Scene of Moby-Dick." English Studies, 53 (1972), 235-238.

2431 ROUDAUT, Jean. "A propos de 'Bartleby': Compilation." Delta English Studies, 6 (1978), 37-42. In French.

2432 ROUDIEZ, Léon S. "Strangers in Melville and Camus." French Review, 31 (January, 1958), 217-226.

2433 ______. "Camus and Moby-Dick." Symposium, 15 (Spring, 1961), 30-40.

2434 ROUNDY, Nancy Louise. "The Right Whale's Head and the Sperm Whale's Head: A Tension in Herman Melville's Works." Ph.D. diss., University of Iowa, 1976. DA, 37 (1976), 2878A-2879A.

2435 ________. "Fancies, Reflections, and Things: The Imagination as Perception in 'The Piazza.'" College Language Association Journal, 20 (1977), 539-546.

2436 ________. "Present Shadows: Epistemology in Melville's 'Benito Cereno.'" Arizona Quarterly, 34 (1978), 344-350.

2437 ROUNTREE, Thomas J., ed. Critics on Melville. Coral Gables, Fla.: University of Miami Press, 1972.

2438 ROURKE, Constance. American Humor: A Study of the National Character. New York: Harcourt, Brace, and World, 1931. Reprinted New York: Doubleday, 1953. Melville, Chapter VI, pp. 191-200 and passim.

2439 ROUSE, H. Blair. "Democracy, American Literature, and Mr. Fast." English Journal, 36 (1947), 321-323. See article by Howard Fast (1947).

2440 ROUSSEAUX, André. "Mardi." Figaro Litteraire, 5 (December 9, 1950), 2. In French.

2441 ________. "A travers l'oeuvre de Melville." Figaro Litteraire, 6 (August 11, 1951), 2. In French.

2442 ROUTH, H. V. Towards the Twentieth Century. New York and London: Macmillan, 1937. Melville, passim.

2443 ROWLAND, Beryl. "Melville's Bachelors and Maids: Interpretation Through Symbol and Metaphor." American Literature, 41 (1969), 389-405.

2444 ________. "Melville's Waterloo in 'Rich Man's Crumbs.'" Nineteenth-Century Fiction, 25 (1970), 216-221.

2445 ________. "Sitting Up with a Corpse: Malthus According to Melville in 'Poor Man's Pudding and Rich Man's Crumbs.'" Journal of American Studies, 6 (1972), 69-83.

2446 ________. "Grace Church and Melville's Story of 'The Two Temples.'" Nineteenth-Century Fiction, 28 (1973), 339-346.

2447 ________. "Melville Answers the Theologians: The Ladder of Charity in 'The Two Temples.'" Mosaic, 7 (1974), 1-13.

2448 ROZENBERG-SACKS, Hélène. "The Entranced Consciousness: A Phenomenological Study of Melville's Clarel." Ph.D. diss., Sorbonne, Paris, December, 1972.

2449 ________. "Allegory and Nominal Identity in Melville's Poem Clarel." Literary Onomastics Studies, 1 (1974), 40-46.

2450 ________. "Huis-clos dans 'Bartleby.'" Delta English Studies, 6 (1978), 29-35. In French.

2451 RUBIN, Joseph Jay. "Melville's Reputation, 1847." Notes and Queries, 176 (April 29, 1939), 298.

2452 RUBIN, Louis D., Jr. The Teller in the Tale. Seattle: University of Washington Press, 1967.

2453 RUBINSTEIN, Annette T. "Henry James, American Novelist, or: Isabel Archer, Emerson's Granddaughter," in Rudich, Norman, ed., Weapons of Criticism: Marxism in America and the Literary Tradition. Palo Alto, Calif.: Ramparts, 1976. Pp. 311-326.

2454 RUCKER, Mary E. "Melville's Israel Potter: A Pilgrimage and Progress, a review of book by Arnold Rampersad." Arizona Quarterly, 26 (Summer, 1970), 182-183.

2455 RUKEYSER, Muriel. Willard Gibbs. Garden City, N.Y.: Doubleday, Doran, 1942. Melville, pp. 353-357. Refers to professor of mathematics and physics at Yale, 1871-1903.

2456 ________. The Life of Poetry. New York: Wyn, 1949. Melville, pp. 25-26, 68-73.

2457 RULAND, Richard. The Rediscovery of American Literature. Cambridge: Harvard University Press, 1967. Melville, pp. 238-250, 256-282, and passim.

2458 ________. "Melville and the Fortunate Fall: Typee as Eden." Nineteenth-Century Fiction, 23 (December, 1968), 312-323.

2459 RUNDEN, John P. "Imagery in Herman Melville's Shorter Fiction: 1853-1856." Ph.D. diss., University of Indiana, 1952.

2460 ________, ed. Melville's Benito Cereno: Text for Guided Research. Boston: Heath, 1965.

2461 RUSSELL, Frank Alden (Ted Malone, pseud.). American Pilgrimage. New York: Dodd, Mead, 1942. Republished as Should Old Acquaintance. Haddonfield, N.J.: Bookmark, 1943. Melville, pp. 119-133.

2462 RUSSELL, Jack. "Israel Potter and 'Song of Myself.'" American Literature, 40 (March, 1968), 72-77.

2463 RUSSELL, W. Clark. "A Claim for American Literature." North American Review, 154 (1892), 138-149.

2464 ________, ed. with Preface. Typee. London: John Lane, 1904.

2465 RUST, Richard Dilworth. "Vision in Moby-Dick." Emerson Society Quarterly, 33 (1963), 73-75.

2466 ________. "Dollars Damn Me: Money in Moby-Dick," in Schubert, Karl, and Ursula Muller-Richter, eds., Geschichte und Gesellschaft in der amerikanischen Literatur. Heidelberg, Germany: Quelle and Meyer, 1975. Pp. 49-54. Essay by Rust in English.

2467 RYAN, Robert Charles. "Weeds and Wildings... Reading Text and Genetic Text from Mss. Left Unpublished." Ph.D. diss., Northwestern, 1967. DA, 28 (1967), 2262A.

2468 ________. "Review of Several Melville Books Published in 1970." Studies in Romanticism, 10 (1971), 230-240.

2469 RYAN, Steven T. "The Gothic Formula of 'Bartleby.'" Arizona Quarterly, 34 (1978), 311-316.

2470 RYSTEN, Felix S. A. "False Prophets in Fiction: Camus, Dostoevsky, Melville, and Others." Ph.D. diss., USC, 1968. DA, 29 (1969), 3586A-3587A.

2471 ________. "Melville's Moby-Dick," in Rysten, False Prophets in the Fiction of Camus, Dostoevsky, Melville and Others. Coral Gables, Fla.: University of Miami Press, 1972. Melville, pp. 92-111.

2472 SACHS, Viola. The Myth of America: Essays in the Structures of the Literary Imagination. The Hague: Mouton, 1974. Preface by Daniel Aaron.

2473 SACKMAN, Douglas. "The Original of Melville's 'Apple-Tree Table.'" American Literature, 11 (January, 1940), 448-451.

2474 SADER, Marion, ed. Comprehensive Index to Little Magazines: 1890-1970, 8 vols. Millwood, N.Y.: Kraus Thompson, 1976. Melville, Vol. 5, pp. 3014-3018. Lists reviews and articles; especially good for listings of reviews.

2475 SADLEIR, Michael. Excursions in Victorian Bibliography. London: Chaundy and Cox, 1922. Melville, pp. 217-234.

2476 ________. "Bibliography of the First Editions of the Prose Works of Herman Melville," in Collected Works of Herman Melville, 16 vols. London: Constable, 1922-1924. Vol. 12, pp. 337-358.

2477 ST. ARMAND, Barton Levi. "Curtis's 'Bartleby': An Unrecorded Melville Reference." Papers of the Bibliographic Society of America, 71 (1977), 219-220. Refers to George William Curtis, editor and lecturer, reform advocate, etc., 1824-1892.

2478 SALE, Arthur. "Captain Vere's Reasons." Cambridge Journal, 5 (October, 1951), 3-18.

2479 ________. "The Glass Ship: A Recurrent Image in Melville." Modern Language Quarterly, 17 (June, 1956), 118-127.

2480 SALT, Henry Stephens. "Herman Melville: Imperial Cockneydom." Scottish Art Review, 2 (June-December, 1889), 186-190.

2481 ________. "Melville." Universal Review, 4 (May, 1889), 78.

2482 ________. "Marquesan Melville." Gentleman's Magazine, 272 (March, 1892), 248-257.

2483 SALVIDGE, Stanley. "Herman Melville and Liverpool." Spectator, 139 (July 16, 1927), 88-89.

2484 SALZBERG, Joel. "The Artist Manqué: Tower Symbolism in Melville and Crane." American Transcendental Quarterly, 29 (1976), 55-61.

2485 SAMPSON, Joan P. "The Ambiguity of Ambergris in Moby-Dick." College Literature, 2 (1975), 226-228.

2486 SANDBERG, Alvin. "Erotic Patterns in 'The Paradise of Bachelors and the Tartarus of Maids.'" Literature and Psychology, 18 (1968), 2-8.

2487 ________. "The Quest for Love and the Quest for Revenge in Herman Melville." Ph.D. diss., City University of New York, 1970. DA, 31 (1971), 6568A.

2488 SANDER, Lucille A. "Melville's Symbolism of the Pipe." Emerson Society Quarterly, 59 (1970), 4-7.

2489 SANDERLIN, Reed. "A Re-examination of the Role of the Lawyer-Narrator in Melville's 'Bartleby.'" Interpretations, 10 (1978), 49-55.

2490 SANDERS, Paul S., ed. The Book of Job: A Collection of Critical Essays. Englewood Cliffs, N.J.: Prentice-Hall, 1968. Melville, passim.

2491 SANDERS, William. "Emerson and Melville: The Oversoul and the Underworld." Junction (Brooklyn College), 2 (1973), 25-29.

2492 SANFORD, John. View from This Wilderness. Foreword by Paul Mariani. Santa Barbara, Calif.: Capra, 1977. Melville, pp. 83-84.

2493 SAROTTE, Georges-Michel. Like a Brother, Like a Lover: Male Homosexuality in the American Novel and Theater from Herman Melville to James Baldwin. Translated from French by Richard Miller. Garden City, N.Y.: Doubleday, Anchor, 1978.

2494 SARTRE, Jean-Paul. "Moby-Dick." Adam International Review, 343-344 (1970), 86-87. London publication in French and English.

2495 SATTELMEYER, Robert. "The Origin of Harry Bolton in Redburn." American Transcendental Quarterly, 31 (1976), 23-25.

2496 ________, and James Barbour. "A Possible Source and Model for 'The Story of China Aster' in Melville's The Confidence-Man." American Literature, 48 (1977), 577-583. "Edgar Preston" in China Aster, or Youth's Book of Varieties (1847).

2497 ________, and James Barbour. "The Sources and Genesis of Melville's 'Norfolk Tale and the Chola Widow.'" American Literature, 50 (1978), 398-417.

2498 SATTERFIELD, John. "Perth: An Organic Digression in Moby-Dick." Modern Language Notes, 74 (February, 1959), 106-107.

2499 SATTIN, Jerry Paul. "Allegory in Modern Fiction: A Study of Moby-Dick, The Brothers Karamazov, and 'Die Verwandlung.'" Ph.D. diss., University of Illinois (Urbana-Champaign), 1978. DA, 39 (1978), 272A. Refers to a novel by Dostoevsky and "The Metamorphosis," a novella by Franz Kafka.

2500 SCHAIBLE, Robert M. "An Annotated Edition of Herman Melville's Redburn." Ph.D. diss., University of Tennessee, 1971. DA, 33 (1972), 2343A.

2501 SCHATT, Stanley, ed. "Bartleby, the Scrivener": A Casebook for Research. Dubuque, Iowa: Kendall-Hunt, 1972.

2501a SCHEER, Steven Csaba. "Fiction as a Theme of Fiction: Aspects of Self-Reference in Hawthorne, Melville, and Twain." Ph.D. diss., Johns Hopkins, 1974. DA, 38 (1977), 791A.

2502 SCHERTING, Jack. "The Bottle and the Coffin: Further Speculation on Poe and Melville." Poe Newsletter, 1 (1968), 22.

2503 SCHIFFMAN, Joseph. "Melville's Final Stage, Irony: A Reexamination of Billy-Budd Criticism." American Literature, 22 (May, 1950), 128-136.

2504 ______. "Critical Problems in Melville's 'Benito-Cereno.'" Modern Language Quarterly, 11 (September, 1950), 317-324.

2505 ______, ed. Three Shorter Novels of Herman Melville. New York: Harper and Row, 1962. Harper's Modern Classics edition. Contains Billy-Budd, Benito-Cereno, and "Bartleby."

2506 SCHLESS, Howard H. "Flaxman, Dante, and Melville's Pierre." Bulletin of the New York Public Library, 64 (February, 1960), 65-82.

2507 ______. "Moby-Dick and Dante: A Critique and Time Scheme." Bulletin of the New York Public Library, 65 (May, 1961), 289-312.

2508 SCHNEIDER, Herbert Wallace. A History of American Philosophy. New York: Columbia University Press, 1946. Melville, pp. 293-301.

2509/10 SCHNEIDER, Joseph L. "Melville's Use of the Vere-Fairfax Lineage in Billy-Budd." Names, 26 (1978), 129-138.

2511 SCHNECK, Dr. Jerome M. "Hypnagogic Hallucinations: Herman Melville's Moby-Dick." New York State Journal of Medicine, 77 (1977), 2145-2147.

2512 SCHOLNICK, Robert J. "Politics and Poetics: The Reception of Melville's Battle-Pieces and Aspects of the War." American Literature, 49 (1977), 422-430.

2513 SCHROEDER, Fred E. H. "'Enter Ahab: Then All': Theatrical Elements in Melville's Fiction." Dalhousie Review, 46 (Summer, 1966), 123-132.

2514 SCHROETER, James. "Redburn and the Failure of Mythic Criticism." American Literature, 39 (November, 1967), 279-297.

2515 SCHROTH, Evelyn. "Melville's Judgment on Captain Vere." Midwest Quarterly, 10 (1969), 189-200.

2516 SCHULTZ, Donald D. "Herman Melville and the Tradition of the Anatomy: A Study in Genre." Ph.D. diss., Vanderbilt, 1969. DA, 30 (1970), 4463A.

2517 SCHUNCK, Ferdinand. Das Lyriche Werk Herman Melvilles. Bonn, Germany: Bouvier, 1976. In German, quotations in English.

2518 SCHWAB, Allen M. "Interrupted Communion with the World: A Study of Herman Melville's Short Fiction." Ph.D. diss., Tufts, 1973. DA, 34 (1974), 5203A-5204A.

2519 SCHWENDINGER, Robert J. "The Language of the Sea: Relationships Between the Language of Herman Melville and Sea Shanties of the Nineteenth-Century." Southern Folklore Quarterly, 37 (1973), 53-73.

2520 SCORZA, Thomas J. "Technology, Philosophy, and Political Virtue: The Case of Billy-Budd, Sailor." Interpretation: A Journal of Political Philosophy, 5 (1975), 91-107.

2521 SCOTT, Nathan A., Jr., ed. The Tragic Vision and the Christian Faith. New York: Association, 1957. "The Vision of Evil in Hawthorne and Melville," by Randall Stewart, pp. 238-263.

2522 SCOTT, Sumner W. D. "The Whaling Background in Moby-Dick." Ph.D. diss., University of Chicago, 1949.

2523 ________. "Some Implications of the Typhoon Scenes in Moby-Dick." American Literature, 12 (March, 1940), 91-98.

2524 SCOTT, Wilbur Stewart, Jr. "Melville's Originality: A Study of Sources in Moby-Dick." Ph.D. diss., Princeton, 1943.

2525 SCOUTEN, Arthur H. "The Derelict Slave Ship in Melville's Benito-Cereno and Defoe's Captain Singleton." Colby Library Quarterly, 12 (1976), 122-125.

2526 SCUDDER, Harold H. "Melville's Benito-Cereno and Captain Delano's Voyages." PMLA, 43 (June, 1928), 502-532. Reprints Chapter 18 of A Narrative by Amasa Delano (Boston, 1817).

2527 ________. "Hawthorne's Use of Typee." Notes and Queries, 187 (October 21, 1944), 184-186.

2528 SEALTS, Merton M., Jr. "Herman Melville's 'I and My Chimney.'" American Literature, 13 (May, 1941), 142-154.

2529 ________. "Melville's Reading in Ancient Philosophy." Ph.D. diss., Yale, 1942. DA, 30 (1969), 1574A-1575A.

2530 ________. "The Publication of Melville's Piazza Tales." Modern Language Notes, 59 (January, 1944), 56-59.

2531 ________. "Did Melville Write 'October Mountain'?" American Literature, 22 (May, 1950), 178-182.

2532 ________. "Melville and the Shakers." Studies in Bibliography, 2 (1950), 105-114.

2533 ________. "Melville's Reading: A Checklist of Books Owned and Borrowed." Harvard Library Bulletin, 2 (Spring and Fall, 1948), 141-163, 378-392; 3 (Winter, Spring, and Fall, 1949), 119-130, 268-277, 407-421; and 4 (Winter, 1950), 98-109. Revised and printed as book, Melville's Reading. Madison: University of Wisconsin Press, 1966.

2534 ________. "Melville's Friend Atahalpa." Notes and Queries, 194 (January 22, 1949), 37-38.

2535 ________. "Melville's Neoplatonical Originals." Modern Language Notes, 67 (February, 1952), 80-86.

2536 ________. "Melville's Reading: A Supplemental List of Books Owned and Borrowed." Harvard Library Bulletin, 6 (Spring, 1952), 239-247.

2537 ________. "The Ghost of Major Melville." New England Quarterly, 30 (September, 1957), 291-306.

2538 ________. Melville as Lecturer. Cambridge: Harvard University Press, 1957. Reprinted Folcroft, Pa.: Folcroft, 1970.

2539 ________. "Melville's Burgundy Club Sketches." Harvard Library Bulletin, 12 (Spring, 1958), 253-267.

2540 ________. "Approaching Melville Through 'Hawthorne and His Mosses.'" Emerson Society Quarterly, 28 (1962), 12-15.

2541 ________. "Melville's 'Geniality,'" in Schulz, Max F., et al., eds., Essays in American and English Literature Presented to Bruce R. McElderry. Athens: Ohio University Press, 1967. Pp. 3-26.

2542 ________. "Melville," in American Literary Scholarship: A Review of Current Scholarship. 1967, pp. 29-47; 1968, pp. 30-49; 1969, pp. 33-55; 1970, pp. 33-54; 1971, pp. 41-58.

2543 ________. "Melville's 'Chimney' Re-examined," in Browne, Ray B., and Donald Pizer, eds., Themes and Directions in American Literature. Lafayette, Ind.: Purdue University Press, 1969. Pp. 80-102.

2544 ________. "A Supplementary Note to Melville's Reading (1966 edition)." Harvard Library Bulletin, 19 (1971), 280-284.

2545 ________. "Melville and Richard Henry Stoddard." American Literature, 43 (1971), 359-370.

2546 ________. The Early Lives of Melville: Nineteenth-Century Biographical Sketches and Their Authors. Madison: University of Wisconsin Press, 1974.

2547 ________. "Mary L. D. Ferris and the Melvilles." Extracts, 28 (1976), 10-11.

2548 ________. "Additions to Early Lives." Extracts, 28 (1976), 11-13.

2549 ________, ed. with Historical Notes. The Piazza Tales and Other Prose Pieces: 1839-1860. Evanston and Chicago: Northwestern University and Newberry Library Press, 1977.

2550 SEARS, Clara Endicott. Days of Delusion: A Strange Bit of History. Boston: Houghton Mifflin, 1924. Melville, Emerson, etc., p. 203. Book is a study of William Miller, a preacher who predicted the world would come to an end in 1843, and who attracted a great deal of attention.

2551 SEDGWICK, Henry Dwight. "Reminiscences of Literary Berkshire." Century, 50 (August, 1895), 562.

2552 SEDGWICK, William Ellery. Herman Melville: The Tragedy of Mind. Cambridge: Harvard University Press, 1944. Reprinted New York: Russell and Russell, 1962.

2553 SEELYE, John Douglas. "The Golden Navel: The Cabalism of Ahab's Doubloon." Nineteenth-Century Fiction, 14 (March, 1960), 350-355.

2554 ________. "The Iridescent Scabbard: Herman Melville's Ironic Mode." Ph.D. diss., Claremont, 1962. DA, 23 (1962), 226.

2555 ________. "Timothy Flint's 'Wicked River' and The Confidence-Man." PMLA, 78 (March, 1963), 75-79.

2556 ________. "'Spontaneous Impress of Truth': Melville's Jack Chase: A Source, an Analogue, a Conjecture." Nineteenth-Century Fiction, 20 (March, 1966), 367-376.

2557 ________. "The Ironic Diagram," in Parker, ed., Recognition of Herman Melville (1967), pp. 347-364.

2558 ________. "The Structure of Encounter," in Vincent, ed., Melville and Hawthorne in the Berkshires (1968), pp. 63-69.

2559 ________. "Ungraspable Phantom: Reflections of Hawthorne in Pierre and The Confidence Man." Studies in the Novel, 1 (Winter, 1969), 436-443.

2560 ________. Melville: The Ironic Diagram. Evanston, Ill.: Northwestern University Press, 1970.

2561 ________. "The Contemporary 'Bartleby.'" American Transcendental Quarterly, 7 (1970), 12-18.

2562 ________, ed. with Introduction. Arthur Gordon Pym, Benito Cereno, and Related Writings. Philadelphia: Lippincott, 1967. Contrasts in Literature series.

2563 ________, ed. The Confidence Man. San Francisco: Chandler, 1968. Facsimile reprint of first edition.

2564 SELDES, Gilbert. The Stammering Century. New York: Day, 1928. Melville, Emerson, passim.

2565 SELSOR, Thomas A. "A Thematic and Structural Analysis of Billy-Budd, Sailor." Ph.D. diss., Wisconsin, 1973. DA, 34 (1974), 5930A.

2566 SELTZER, Leon F. "Camus' Absurd and the World of Melville's Confidence Man." PMLA, 82 (March, 1967), 14-27.

2567 ________. "The Vision of Herman Melville and Joseph Conrad: A Comparative Study." Ph.D. diss., State University of New York (Buffalo), 1967. DA, 29 (1968), 613A-614A.

2568 ________. The Vision of Melville and Conrad. Athens: Ohio University Press, 1970.

2569 SEMMENS, John Edward. "Point of View in the Early and Later Fiction of Herman Melville." Ph.D. diss., Notre Dame, 1965. DA, 26 (1966), 1028.

2570 SENESCU, Betty C. "Melville's Moby-Dick." Explicator, 25 (1967), item 78.

2571 SEQUEIRA, Isaac. "The San Dominick: The Shadow of Benito Cereno." Osmania Journal of English Studies, 10 (1973), 1-6.

2572 SEWELL, Richard B. The Vision of Tragedy. New Haven:

Yale University Press, 1950. "*Moby-Dick* as Tragedy." pp. 92-105.

2573 ________. "Ahab's Quenchless Feud: The Tragic Vision in Shakespeare and Melville." *Comparative Drama*, 1 (Fall, 1967), 207-218.

2574 SHAFER, Robert E. "Teaching Sequence in Hawthorne and Melville," in Leary, ed., *The Teacher and American Literature* (1965), pp. 110-114.

2575 SHANAHAN, Daniel Augustus. "Narcissus Judged: The Decline of Individualism in Fiction Since 1850: Studies in Melville, Conrad, Joyce, and Dostoevsky." Ph.D. diss., Stanford, 1978. *DA*, 39 (1978), 3575A-3576A.

2576 SHAPIRO, Charles, ed. *Twelve Original Essays on Great American Novels*. Detroit: Wayne State University Press, 1958. "A Re-reading of *Moby-Dick*," by Granville Hicks, pp. 44-68.

2577 SHATTUCK, Roger. "Two Inside Narratives: *Billy-Budd* and *L'Etranger*." *Texas Studies in Literature and Language*, 4 (Autumn, 1962), 314-320.

2578 SHAW, Richard O. "The Civil War Poems of Herman Melville." *Lincoln Herald*, 68 (Spring, 1966), 44-49.

2579 SHEEHAN, Peter J. "Strands of the Knot: Ritual Structures in Melville's *Benito Cereno*." *New Laurel Review*, 6 (1976), 23-37.

2580 SHELDON, Leslie E. "'That Anaconda of an Old Man' and Milton's Satan." *Extracts*, 26 (1976), 11.

2581 ________. "Another Layer of Miltonic Allusion in *Moby-Dick*." *Melville Society Extracts*, 35 (1978), 15-16.

2582 SHERBO, Arthur. "Melville's 'Portuguese Catholic Priest.'" *American Literature*, 26 (January, 1955), 563-564.

2583 SHERMAN, Stuart C., J. H. Birss, and Gordon Roper, comps. *Melville Bibliography, 1952-1957*. Providence, R.I.: Public Library of Providence, 1959, for The Melville Society.

2584 SHERRILL, Rowland A. *The Prophetic Melville: Experience, Transcendence, and Tragedy*. Athens: University of Georgia Press, 1978.

2585 SHERWOOD, John C. "Vere as Collingwood: A Key to *Billy-Budd*." *American Literature*, 35 (January, 1964), 476-

484. Refers to Baron Collingwood, vice-admiral and second in command at Trafalgar.

2586 SHETTY, Nalini V. "Melville's Use of the Gothic Tradition," in Chander, Jagdish, and Narindar S. Pradham, eds., Studies in American Literature: Essays in Honour of William Mulder. Delhi, India: Oxford University Press, 1974. Pp. 144-153.

2587 ________. "The Isolato in White-Jacket," in Naik, M. K., S. K. Desai, and S. Mikashi-Punekar, eds., Indian Studies in American Fiction. Dharwar, India: Kamatak University Press; Delhi, India: Macmillan, 1974. Pp. 31-38.

2588 SHIMADA, Taro. "An Essay on Moby-Dick." Pursuit, 1 (December, 1962), 67-83.

2589 SHNEIDMAN, Edwin S. "The Deaths of Herman Melville," in Vincent, ed., Melville and Hawthorne in the Berkshires (1968), pp. 118-143.

2590 ________. "Some Psychological Reflections on the Death of Malcom Melville." Extracts, 25 (1976), 4. Paper read to the Melville Society in San Francisco on December 28, 1975. Complete paper in Suicide and Life-Threatening Behavior, 6 (1976), 231-242. Refers to Melville's son, who died in 1867 of a self-inflicted pistol wound.

2591 ________, ed. Essays in Self-Destruction. New York: Science House, 1967. "Dead to the World: The Passions of Herman Melville," by Henry A. Murray, pp. 7-29.

2592 SHORT, Bryan Collier. "Herman Melville's Poetry: The Growth of a Post-Romantic Art." Ph.D. diss., Claremont, 1971. DA, 32 (1972), 2708A-2709A.

2593 ________. "'Betwixt the Chimes and Knell': Versification as Symbol in Clarel." Extracts, 26 (1976), 4.

2594 ________. "'The Redness of the Rose': The Mardi Poems and Melville's Artistic Compromise," in Robillard, ed., Symposium (1976), pp. 100-112.

2595 ________. "Form as Vision in Herman Melville's Clarel." American Literature, 50 (1979), 553-569.

2596 SHORT, Raymond W. "Melville as Symbolist." University of Kansas City Review, 15 (August, 1949), 38-49.

2597 ________, ed. with Introduction. Four Great American Novels. New York: Holt, 1946. Includes Billy-Budd.

2598 ________, and Richard B. Sewall, eds. A Manual of Suggestions for Teachers Using "Short Stories for Study," 3rd edition. New York: Holt, 1956. "Bartleby, the Scrivener," pp. 46-49.

2599 SHROEDER, John W. "Sources and Symbols for Melville's The Confidence Man." PMLA, 66 (June, 1951), 363-380.

2600 ________. "'Some Unfortunate Idyllic Love Affairs': The Legends of Taji and Jay Gatsby." Books at Brown, 22 (1968), 143-153. Refers to Mardi and The Great Gatsby.

2601 ________. "Indian-Hating: An Ultimate Note on The Confidence-Man." Books at Brown, 24 (1971), 1-5.

2602 SHULMAN, Robert P. "Toward Moby-Dick: Herman Melville and Some Baroque Worthies." Ph.D. diss., Ohio State (Columbus), 1959. DA, 20 (1960), 3731-3732.

2603 ________. "The Serious Function of Melville's Phallic Jokes." American Literature, 33 (May, 1961), 179-194.

2604 ________. "Melville's Thomas Fuller: An Outline for Starbuck and an Instance of the Creator as Critic." Modern Language Quarterly, 23 (December, 1962), 337-352.

2605 ________. "Montaigne and the Techniques and Tragedy of Melville's Billy-Budd." Comparative Literature, 16 (Fall, 1964), 322-330.

2606 ________. "Melville's Timoleon: From Plutarch to the Early Stages of Billy-Budd." Comparative Literature, 19 (Fall, 1967), 351-361.

2607 SHURR, William H. "The Symbolic Structure of Herman Melville's Clarel." Ph.D. diss., University of North Carolina, 1968. DA, 30 (1970), 3477A.

2608 ________. "Melville and Emerson." Extracts, 11 (1972), 2.

2609 ________. The Mystery of Iniquity: Melville as Poet, 1857-1891. Lexington: University Press of Kentucky, 1973. Bibliography of criticism on poetry, pp. 275-279.

2610 ________. "Melville: New Studies of Sources and Methods." Emerson Society Quarterly, 21 (1975), 46-51. Review article.

2611 ________. "Melville and Christianity," in Robillard, ed., Symposium (1976), pp. 129-148.

2612 SHUSTERMAN, Alan. "Melville's 'The Lightning-Rod Man': A Reading." Studies in Short Fiction, 9 (1972), 165-174.

2613 SHUSTERMAN, David. "The 'Reader Fallacy' and 'Bartleby the Scrivener.'" New England Quarterly, 45 (1972), 118-124.

2614 SIEGEL, Mark Andrew. "Dialectics of Consciousness: Melville and the Realistic Imagination." Ph.D. diss., Rutgers, 1977. DA, 38 (1977), 2796A.

2615 SILBERMAN, Donald Joseph. "Form and Point of View in Melville's Fiction." Ph.D. diss., State University of New York (Buffalo), 1965. DA, 27 (1966), 187A.

2616 SILVERMAN, Jay Rose. "The Destruction of the Primitive: A Study of Melville." Ph.D. diss., University of Virginia, 1977. DA, 39 (1978), 888A.

2617 SIMBOLI, David. "'Benito Cereno' as Pedagogy." College Language Association Journal, 9 (December, 1965).

2618 SIMON, Jean. "Recherches australiennes sur Herman Melville." Revue Anglo-Américaine, 13 (December, 1935), 114-130. In French.

2619 ________. "Herman Melville: Marin, metaphysicien, et poète." Ph.D. diss., Paris, 1939. Published Paris, France: Boivin and Cie, 1939. Contains extensive bibliography of translations and foreign sources, pp. 587-602. In French; has not been translated.

2620 ________. La Polynésie dans l'Art et la Littérature de l'Occident. Paris: Boivin and Cie, 1939. Melville, passim. In French.

2621 ________. "Travaux récents sur Herman Melville." Etudes Anglaises, 6 (February, 1953), 40-49. In French.

2622 ________, ed. A Herman Melville Anthology. Paris: Boivin and Cie, 1946. Translated into French by the editor.

2623 SIMONDS, William Edward. "Fiction in the North," in A Student's History of American Literature. Boston: Houghton, Mifflin, 1909. P. 304. Reprinted in Parker, ed., Recognition (1967), p. 149.

2624 SIMPSON, Eleanor E. "Melville and the Negro: From Typee to 'Benito Cereno.'" American Literature, 41 (1969), 19-38.

2625 SIMPSON, Judy Carol Aycock. "The Poetry of Herman Melville with Special Emphasis on the Battle-Pieces." Ph.D. diss., Memorial University of Newfoundland, Canada, 1972.

2626 SINGLETON, Gregory H. "Ishmael and the Covenant." Discourse, 16 (1969), 54-67.

2627 SINGLETON, Marvin. "Melville's 'Bartleby': Over the Republic, A Ciceronian Shadow." Canadian Review of American Studies, 6 (1975), 165-173.

2628 SISTER Cleopatra. "Moby-Dick: An Interpretation." Literary Half-Yearly, 6 (July, 1965), 49-54.

SISTER Mary Ellen see ECKARDT, Sister Mary Ellen.

2629 SKARD, Sigmund. "The Use of Color in Literature." Proceedings of the American Philological Society, 90 (1946), 163-249.

2630 SKERRY, Philip J. "Billy-Budd: From Novella to Libretto." Re: Artes Liberales, 3 (1976), 19-27.

2631 SLATER, Judith. "The Domestic Adventurer in Melville's Tales." American Literature, 37 (November, 1965), 267-279.

2632 SLOCHOWER, Harry. "Freudian Motifs in Moby-Dick." Complex, 3 (Fall, 1950), 16-25.

2633 ________. "Moby-Dick: The Myth of Democratic Expectancy." American Quarterly, 2 (Fall, 1950), 259-269. Reprinted in Stern, ed., Discussions (1960), pp. 45-51.

2634 ________. "The Quest for an American Myth: Moby-Dick," in Slochower, Mythopoesis: Mythic Patterns in the Literary Classics. Detroit: Wayne State University Press, 1970. Pp. 223-245.

2635 SMALL, Julianne. "Classical Allusions in the Fiction of Herman Melville." Ph.D. diss., University of Tennessee, 1974. DA, 35 (1974), 3701A.

2636 SMALLEY, Amos (as told to Max Eastman). "I Killed 'Moby-Dick.'" Reader's Digest, 70 (June, 1957), 172-180.

2637 SMITH, Henry Nash. "The Image of Society in Moby-Dick," in Hillway, ed., Centennial Essays (1953), pp. 59-75.

2638 ________. "The Madness of Ahab." Yale Review, 66 (1976), 14-32. Reprinted in Smith, Democracy and the Novel. New York: Oxford University Press, 1978. Pp. 35-55.

2639 SMITH, Herbert F. "Melville's Master in Chancery and His Recalcitrant Clerk." American Quarterly, 17 (1965), 734-741.

2640 ______. "Melville's Sea Lawyers." English Studies in Canada, 2 (1976), 423-438.

2641 SMITH, Joseph E. A. Bibliographic Sketch of Herman Melville. Pittsfield, Mass.: Evening Journal, 1891. Pamphlet.

2642 SMITH, Kenneth D. "Dramatic Adaptations of Herman Melville's Billy-Budd." Ph.D. diss., Notre Dame, 1970. DA, 31 (1971), 4734A-4735A.

2643 SMITH, Nelson C. "Eight British Reviews and Notices of Melville, 1846-1891." Extracts, 23 (October, 1975), 6-7.

2644 ______. "Melville Reviews in the London Sun." Melville Society Extracts, 36 (1978), 8-12.

2645 SMITH, Paul. "The Confidence-Man and the Literary World of New York." Nineteenth-Century Fiction, 16 (March, 1962), 329-337.

2646 ______. "Benito Cereno and the Spanish Inquisition." Nineteenth-Century Fiction, 16 (June, 1962), 345-349.

2647 SMYTH, Clifford. "A Letter from Herman Melville." International Book Review, 3 (December, 1924), 25, 65.

2648 SNELL, George P. Shapers of American Fiction, 1798-1947. New York: Dutton, 1947. Melville, pp. 60-78.

2649 SNYDER, Oliver. "A Note on Billy-Budd." Accent, 11 (Winter, 1951), 58-60.

2650 SOLOMON, Pearl C. Dickens and Melville in Their Time. New York: Columbia University Press, 1975.

2651 SOLOMONT, Susan, and Ritchie Darling. Bartleby. Amherst, Mass.: Green Knight, 1969. Pamphlet.

2652 SOWDER, William J. "Melville's 'I and My Chimney': A Southern Exposure." Mississippi Quarterly, 16 (Summer, 1963), 128-145.

2653 SPANGLER, E. R. "Harvest in a Barren Field: A Counter-Comment." Western Review, 14 (Summer, 1950), 305-307. Melville criticism of Billy-Budd.

2654 SPANGLER, William. "Rockwell Kent and Moby-Dick." Extracts, 26 (1977), 7-10.

2655 SPECTOR, Robert D. "Melville's 'Bartleby' and the Absurd." Nineteenth-Century Fiction, 16 (September, 1961), 175-177.

2656 SPENGEMAN, William C. "Herman Melville," in Spengeman, The Adventurous Muse: The Poetics of American Fiction, 1789-1900. New Haven: Yale University Press, 1977. Pp. 178-212.

2657 SPILLER, James E. "Review of Billy-Budd, the Play." Saturday Review of Literature, 32 (May 14, 1949), 19-20.

2658 SPILLER, Robert E. "Melville, Our First Tragic Poet." Saturday Review of Literature, 33 (November 25, 1950), 24-25.

2659 ________. The Cycle of American Literature. New York: Macmillan, 1955. Reprinted New York: New American Library, 1957. "Romantic Crises: Melville, Whitman," pp. 89-110.

2660 ________. The Third Dimension. New York: Macmillan, 1965. Melville, passim.

2661 ________. The Oblique Light. New York: Macmillan, 1968. Melville, pp. 27, 73-74, and passim.

2662 ________. Milestones in American Literary History. Foreword by Robert H. Walker. Westport, Conn.: Greenwood, 1977. Consists of 32 reviews by Spiller, 1923-1960. Melville, passim.

2663 ________, et al., eds. Literary History of the United States, 3 vols. New York: Macmillan, 1948. "Melville," by Willard Thorp, Vol. 1, pp. 441-471; "Melville Bibliography," by Thomas H. Johnson, Vol. 3, pp. 647-654.

2664 SPININGER, Dennis J. "Paradise and the Fall as Theme and Structure in Four Romantic Novels: Tieck's William Lovell [in letters, 3 vols. 1795-1796], Chateaubriand's Atala [1801] and René [1802], and Melville's Typee." Ph.D. diss., University of Wisconsin, 1968. DA, 29 (1969), 4469A-4470A.

2665 SPOFFORD, William K. "Melville's Ambiguities: A Re-evaluation of 'The Town-Ho's Story.'" American Literature, 41 (1969), 264-270.

2666 SPRINGER, Haskell S., ed. The Merrill Studies in "Billy Budd." Columbus, Ohio: Merrill, 1970. Contains 25 essays, 1924-1967.

2667 SPRINGER, Norman. "'Bartleby' and the Terror of Limitation." PMLA, 80 (1965), 410-418.

2668 SQUIRE, Sir John Collings. Books Reviewed: Critical Essays on Books and Authors. First appeared weekly in The

Observer (London), 1920. Collected and published as book, New York: Heinemann, 1922. Reprinted Port Washington, N.Y.: Kennikat, 1968. Melville, pp. 214-222.

2669 SRINATH, C. N. "A Note on Melville's Poetry." Literary Criterion (Mysore, India), 11 (1973), 33-40.

2670 STAATS, Armin. "Melville: Moby-Dick," in Lang, Hans-Joachim, ed., Der Amerikanische Roman. Dusseldorf, Germany: Bagel, 1972. Pp. 103-141. Article in English; German publication.

2671 STAFFORD, John. The Literary Criticism of "Young America": A Study in the Relationship of Politics and Literature, 1837-1850. Berkeley: University of California Press, 1952. Melville, passim.

2672 STAFFORD, William T. "The New Billy-Budd and the Novelistic Fallacy: An Essay Review." Modern Fiction Studies, 8 (Autumn, 1962), 306-311.

2673 ________. "A Whale, an Heiress, and a Southern Demigod: Three Symbolic Americas." College Literature, 1 (1974), 100-112.

2674 ________, ed. Melville's Billy-Budd and the Critics. Belmont, Calif.: Wadsworth, 1961. New edition, 1968.

2675 STALLMAN, Robert W., and R. E. Watters, eds. The Creative Reader. New York: Ronald, 1954. Billy-Budd, discussion, pp. 334-338.

2676 STANFORD, Raney. "The Romantic Hero and That Fatal Selfhood." Centennial Review, 12 (1968), 430-454.

2677 STANONIK, Janez. Moby-Dick: The Myth and the Symbol, A Study in Folklore and Literature. Ljubljana, Yugoslavia: Ljubljana University Press, 1962.

2678 ________. "The Sermon to the Sharks in Moby-Dick." Acta Neophilologica (Ljubljana), 4 (1971), 53-60.

2679 ________. "Did Melville Ever See an Albino?" American Literature, 43 (1972), 637-638.

2680 STANTON, Robert. "Typee and Milton: Paradise Well Lost." Modern Language Notes, 74 (May, 1959), 407-411.

2681 STANZEL, Franz K. Narrative Situations in the Novel. Translated by James P. Pusack. Bloomington: Indiana University Press, 1971. Includes Tom Jones, Moby-Dick, The Ambassadors, Ulysses, etc.

2682 STAR, Morris. "Herman Melville's Use of the Visual Arts." Ph.D. diss., Northwestern, 1964. DA, 25 (1965), 2988.

2683 ________. "A Checklist of Portraits of Herman Melville." Bulletin of the New York Public Library, 71 (September, 1967), 468-473.

2684 ________. "Melville's Markings in Walpole's Anecdotes of Painting in England." Papers of the Bibliographic Society of America, 66 (1972), 321-327.

2685 STARBUCK, Alexander. History of the American Whale Fishery. Washington, D.C.: Government Printing Press, 1878.

2686 STARK, John. "'The Cassock' Chapter in Moby-Dick and the Theme of Literary Creativity." Studies in American Fiction, 1 (1973), 105-111.

2687 STARKE, Aubrey H. "A Note on Lewis Mumford's Life of Herman Melville." American Literature, 1 (November, 1929), 304-305.

2688 ________. "Poe's Friend Reynolds." American Literature, 11 (May, 1939), 152-159.

2689 STARKE, Catherine Juanita. Black Portraiture in American Fiction. New York: Basic, 1971. Melville, pp. 158-160.

2690 STAROSCIAK, Kenneth, ed. Herman Melville's Authentic Anecdotes of Old Zack. New Brighton, Minn.: Published by the editor, 1973.

2691 STARR, Nathan Comfort. "The Sea in the English Novel from Defoe to Melville." Ph.D. diss., Harvard, 1928.

2692 STAUFFER, Donald Barlow. A Short History of American Poetry. New York: Dutton, 1974. Melville, pp. 131-137.

2693 STAVIG, Richard Thorson. "Melville's Billy-Budd: A New Approach to the Problem of Interpretation." Ph.D. diss., Princeton, 1953. DA, 14 (1954), 822-823.

2694 STAVROU, C. N. "Ahab and Dick Again." Texas Studies in Literature and Language, 3 (Autumn, 1961), 309-320.

2695 STAWELL, F. M. "Time, Imagination, and the Modern Novelist." Nineteenth-Century and After, 107 (February, 1930), 274-284.

2696 STEDMAN, Arthur. "Herman Melville's Funeral." New York Daily Tribune, October 1, 1891.

2697 ________. "Poems by Melville." Century, n.s., 22 (May, 1892), 104-105.

2698 ________, ed. with Introduction. Typee: A Real Romance of the South Sea. New York: American Publishing Company, 1892.

2699 STEGNER, Wallace, ed. The American Novel: From James Fenimore Cooper to William Faulkner. New York: Basic, 1965. "Herman Melville: Moby-Dick," by Leon Howard, pp. 25-34.

2700 STEIN, Allen F. "Ahab's Turbid Wake and Job's Leviathan." American Transcendental Quarterly, 17 (1973), 13-14.

2701 ________. "The Motif of Veracity in 'Bartleby.'" Emerson Society Quarterly, 21 (1975), 29-34.

2702 ________. "Hawthorne's Zenobia and Melville's Urania." American Transcendental Quarterly, 26 (1975), 11-14. Refers to Melville's poem "After the Pleasure Party."

2703 STEIN, William Bysshe. "The Moral Axis of 'Benito Cereno.'" Accent, 15 (Summer, 1955), 221-233.

2704 ________. "Melville's Poetry: Its Symbols of Individualism." Literature and Psychology, 7 (May, 1957), 21-26.

2705 ________. "The Old Man and the Triple Goddess: Melville's 'The Haglets.'" Journal of English Literary History, 25 (March, 1958), 43-59.

2706 ________. "Melville Roasts Thoreau's Cock." Modern Language Notes, 74 (March, 1959), 218-219.

2707 ________. "Melville and the Creative Eros." Lock Haven Bulletin, 1 (1960), 13-26.

2708 ________. "Melville's Comedy of Faith." Journal of English Literary History, 27 (December, 1960), 315-333.

2709 ________. "The Motif of the Wise Old Man in Billy-Budd." Western Humanities Review, 14 (Winter, 1960), 99-101.

2710 ________. "Billy-Budd: The Nightmare of History." Criticism, 3 (Summer, 1961), 237-250.

2711 ________. "Melville's 'Eros.'" Texas Studies in Literature and Language, 3 (Autumn, 1961), 297-308.

2712 ________. "Melville's Cock and the Bell of St. Paul." Emerson Society Quarterly, 27 (1962), 5-10.

2713 ________. "Melville's Chimney Chivy." Emerson Society Quarterly, 35 (1964), 63-65.

2714 ________. "Bartleby: The Christian Conscience," in Vincent, ed., Melville Annual, No. 1 (1965), pp. 104-112.

2715 ________. "Time, History, and Religion: A Glimpse of Melville's Late Poetry." Arizona Quarterly, 22 (1966), 136-145.

2716 ________. "Melville's Poetry: Two Rising Notes." Emerson Society Quarterly, 37 (1966), 10-13.

2717 ________. The Poetry of Melville's Late Years: Time, History, Myth, and Religion. Albany: State University of New York Press, 1970. Based on earlier published articles by Stein.

2718 ________. "Melville's The Confidence-Man: Quicksands of the Word." American Transcendental Quarterly, 24 (1974), 38-50.

2719 ________. "'The New Ancient of Days': The Poetics of Logocracy," in Robillard, ed., Symposium (1976), pp. 181-192.

2720 STEINMANN, Theodore. "Perverted Patterns of Billy-Budd in The Nigger of the Narcissus." English Studies, 55 (June, 1974), 239-246.

2721 STELZIG, Eugene L. "Romantic Paradoxes of Moby-Dick." American Transcendental Quarterly, 26 (1975), 41-44.

2722 STEMPEL, Daniel, and Bruce M. Stillians. "'Bartleby the Scrivener': A Parable of Pessimism." Nineteenth-Century Fiction, 27 (1972), 268-282.

2723 ________. "The Necessary Angel of Herman Melville: Studies in His Sense of an Ending." Ph.D. diss., Indiana, 1970. DA, 32 (1971), 934A.

2724 STEN, Christopher W. "Bartleby, the Transcendentalist: Melville's Dead Letter to Emerson." Modern Language Quarterly, 35 (March, 1974), 30-44.

2725 ________. "Dialogue of Crises in The Confidence-Man: Melville's 'New' Novel." Studies in the Novel, 6 (Summer, 1974), 165-185.

2726 ________. "Vere's Use of the 'Forms': Means and Ends in Billy-Budd." American Literature, 47 (March, 1975), 37-51.

2727 STENCEL, Michelle M. "Knowledge in the Novels of Herman Melville." Ph.D. diss., University of South Carolina, 1969. DA, 30 (1970), 4956A-4957A.

2728 STERN, Madeleine B. "The House of Expanding Doors: Ann Lynch's Soirees, 1846." New York History, 23 (January, 1942), 42-51.

2729 STERN, Milton R. "Theme and Craft in Herman Melville: Fine Hammered Steel." Ph.D. diss., Michigan State, 1955. DA, 15 (1955), 1859-1860.

2730 ________. "A New Harpoon for the Great White Whale." Clearing House, 30 (May, 1956), 564-565.

2731 ________. "The Whale and the Minnow: Moby-Dick and the Movies." College English, 17 (May, 1956), 470-473.

2732 ________. The Fine Hammered Steel of Herman Melville. Urbana: University of Illinois Press, 1957. Contains extensive bibliography, pp. 252-291.

2733 ________. "Some Techniques of Melville's Perception." PMLA, 73 (June, 1958), 251-259. Reprinted in Stern, ed., Discussions (1960), pp. 114-126.

2734 ________. "Melville's Tragic Imagination: The Hero Without a Home," in LaFrance, Marston, ed., Patterns of Commitment in American Literature. Toronto: Toronto University Press, 1967. Pp. 39-52.

2735 ________. "Moby-Dick, Millennial Attitudes, and Politics," in Cook, ed., Themes, Tones, and Motifs (1968), pp. 51-60. Also printed in Emerson Society Quarterly, 54 (1969), 51-60.

2736 ________, ed. with Introduction. Typee and Billy Budd. New York: Dutton, 1958.

2737 ________, ed. Discussions of Moby-Dick. Boston: Heath, 1960. Reprints 15 essays, principally on Moby-Dick.

2738 ________, ed. Billy-Budd: Sailor. Indianapolis: Bobbs-Merrill, 1975. Contains long introduction, and bibliography; good remarks on Melville's poetry, "The Politics of Melville's Poetry."

2739 STERNLICHT, Sanford. "Sermons in Moby-Dick." Ball State University Forum, 10 (Winter, 1969), 51-52.

2740 STEVENS, Aretta J. "The Edition of Montaigne Read by Melville." Papers of the Bibliographic Society of America, 62 (1968), 130-134.

2741 STEVENS, Harry R. "Melville's Music." Musicology, 2 (July, 1949), 405-421.

2742 STEVENS, Sister Mary Dominic, O.P. "The Con Man: A Study in Herman Melville and Mark Twain." Ph.D. diss., Loyola, c. 1959.

2743 STEVENSON, Robert Louis. In the South Seas. New York: Scribner, 1896.

2744 STEWART, George R. "The Two Moby-Dicks." American Literature, 25 (January, 1954), 417-448.

2745 STEWART, Rachel Whitesides. "The Conditional Mood of Melville's Poetry." Ph.D. diss., University of Colorado, 1975. DA, 36 (1976), 5305A-5306A.

2746 STEWART, Randall. "Ethan Brand." Saturday Review of Literature, 5 (April 27, 1929), 967.

2747 ________. "Hawthorne's Contributions to The Salem Advertiser." American Literature, 5 (January, 1934), 327-341.

2748 ________. Nathaniel Hawthorne. New Haven: Yale University Press, 1948. Melville, pp. 107-112 and passim.

2749 ________. "Melville and Hawthorne." South Atlantic Quarterly, 51 (July, 1952), 436-446. Reprinted in Hillway, ed., Centennial Essays (1953), pp. 153-164.

2750 ________. "The Vision of Evil in Hawthorne and Melville," in Scott, ed., The Tragic Vision (1957), pp. 238-263.

2751 ________. American Literature and Christian Doctrine. Baton Rouge: Louisiana State University Press, 1958. Melville, pp. 89-102. Similar to article "The Vision of Evil...."

2752 ________. "Moral Crisis as Structural Principle in Fiction." Christian Scholar, 42 (1959), 284-289.

2753 ________, ed. The American Notebooks of Nathaniel Hawthorne. New Haven: Yale University Press, 1932. Melville, passim.

2754 ________, ed. The English Notebooks of Nathaniel Hawthorne. New York: Oxford University Press, 1941. Melville, passim.

2755 ________, and Dorothy Betherum, eds. Classic American Fiction. Chicago: Scott, Foresman, 1954. Melville, pp. 180-183.

2756 ________, and Geoffrey Stone. "Herman Melville, 1819-1891: Loyalty to the Heart," in Gardiner, ed., American Classics Reconsidered (1958), pp. 210-228.

2757 STIRLING, A. C., and W. A. Poucher. "Ambergris: Its History, Origin, and Application." Chemist and Druggist, 120 (March 17, 1934), 294-295.

2758 STITT, Peter A. "Herman Melville's Billy-Budd: Sympathy and Rebellion." Arizona Quarterly, 28 (1972), 39-54.

2759 STOCKTON, Eric W. "A Commentary on Melville's 'The Lightning-Rod Man.'" Papers of the Michigan Academy of Science, Arts, and Letters, 40 (1955), 321-328.

2760 STODDARD, Richard Henry. "Herman Melville." New York Mail and Express, October 8, 1891. P. 5.

2761 ________. Recollections, Personal and Literary. New York: Barnes, 1903. Melville, passim. Autobiography, published posthumously.

2762 STOKES, Charlotte F. "Moby-Dick: An Analysis of the Minor Characters." Ph.D. diss., University of Florida, 1973. DA, 35 (1974), 1062A.

2763 STOKES, Gary. "The Dansker: Melville's Manifesto of Survival." English Journal, 57 (1968), 980-981.

2764 STOLL, Elmer E. "Symbolism in Moby-Dick." Journal of the History of Ideas, 12 (June, 1951), 440-465.

2765 STOLLER, Leo. "American Radicals and Literary Works of the Mid-Nineteenth Century: An Analogy," in Browne, Ray B., et al., eds., New Voices in American Studies. Lafayette, Ind.: Purdue University Studies, 1966. Pp. 13-20.

2766 STONE, Albert Edward. "Moby-Dick and Shakespeare: A Remonstrance." Shakespeare Quarterly, 7 (Autumn, 1956), 445-448.

2767 ________. "Melville's Pip and Coleridge's Servant Girl." American Literature, 25 (1963), 358-360.

2768 ________. A Certain Morbidness: A View of American Literature. Preface by Harry T. Moore. Carbondale: Southern Illinois University Press, 1969. Melville, pp. 16-42.

2769 ________. "Melville's Late Pale Usher." English Language Notes, 9 (1971), 51-53.

2770 ________. "American Innocence Revisited: Robert Lowell's

Benito Cereno." Acta Universitatis Carolinae Philologica (Prague), 5 (1971), 117-131.

2771 ________. "A New Version of American Innocence: Robert Lowell's Benito Cereno." New England Quarterly, 45 (1972), 467-483.

2772 ________. "Bartleby and Miss Norman." Studies in Short Fiction, 9 (1972), 271-274. Relates to a story by Thomas Hood.

2773 ________. "The Other Sermon in Moby-Dick." Costerus, 4 (1972), 215-222.

2774 ________. "Whodunit? Moby-Dick!" Journal Pop Culture, 8 (Fall, 1974), 280-285.

2775 ________. "The Buried Book: Moby-Dick a Century Ago." Studies in the Novel, 7 (1975), 552-562.

2776 ________. "The Whiteness of the Whale." College Language Association Journal, 18 (March, 1975), 348-363.

2777 ________. "The Function of the Gams in Moby-Dick." College Literature, 2 (1975), 171-181.

2778 ________. "Ahab Gets Girl, or Herman Melville Goes to the Movies." Literature/Film Quarterly, 3 (1975), 172-181.

2779 ________. "More on Hawthorne and Melville." Nathaniel Hawthorne Journal, 5 (1975), 59-70.

2780 ________. "More on Moby-Dick and 'The Bear.' (Faulkner)" Notes on Modern American Literature, 1 (1977), item 13.

2781 ________. "Moby-Dick and Mailer's The Naked and the Dead." Extracts, 30 (1977), 15-17.

2782 ________. "The Tin Drum and Moby-Dick." Melville Society Extracts, 33 (1978), 22-23.

2783 STONE, Geoffrey. Melville. New York: Sheed and Ward, 1949.

2784 ________, and Randall Stewart. "Herman Melville, 1819-1891: Loyalty to the Heart," in Gardiner, ed., American Classics Reconsidered (1958), pp. 210-228. Also listed under Stewart, Randall.

2785 STONE, Harry. "Dickens and Melville Go to Chapel." Dickensian, 54 (Winter, 1958), 50-52.

2786 STONIER, G. W. "Enigma of a Very Good, Very Bad Writer." New Statesman and Nation, 27 (February 5, 1944), 95.

2787 STOUT, Janis P. "Melville's Use of the Book of Job." Nineteenth-Century Fiction, 25 (1970), 69-83.

2788 ________. "Encroaching Sodom: Melville's Urban Fiction." Texas Studies in Literature and Language, 17 (Spring, 1975), 157-173.

2789 STOVALL, Floyd. American Idealism. Norman: University of Oklahoma Press, 1943. Melville, pp. 67-73.

2790 ________, ed. Eight American Authors. New York: Modern Language Association of America, 1956. Reprinted New York: Norton, 1963. "Melville," by Stanley T. Williams, pp. 207-258. Revised edition, New York: Norton, 1971, ed. by James Woodress. "Melville," by Nathalia Wright, pp. 173-224.

2791 STRACHEY, J. St. Loe. "Review of Raymond Weaver's Herman Melville: Mariner and Mystic." The Spectator (London), 127 (May 6, 1922), 559-560.

2792 STRANDBERG, Victor H. "God and the Critics of Melville." Texas Studies in Literature and Language, 6 (1964), 322-333.

2793 STRAUBEL, Daniel C. "The Projection of Melville and His Concerns as an Author into Mardi." Ph.D. diss., Kent State, 1972. DA, 34 (1973), 2658A.

2794 STRAUCH, Carl F. "The Problem of Time and the Romantic Mode in Hawthorne, Melville, and Emerson," in Strauch, ed., Critical Symposium (1964), pp. 50-60.

2795 ________. "Ishmael: Time and Personality in Moby-Dick." Studies in the Novel, 1 (1969), 468-483.

2796 ________, ed. Special Melville issue. Emerson Society Quarterly, 28 (1962), 2-30.

2797 ________, et al., eds. Critical Symposium on American Romanticism. Hartford: Transcendental, 1964. Also published in Emerson Society Quarterly, 35 (1964), 2-60.

2798 STRICKLAND, Carol Colclough. "Coherence and Ambivalence in Melville's Pierre." American Literature, 48 (1976), 302-311.

2799 STROVEN, Carl, and A. Grove Day, eds. The Spell of the Pacific: An Anthology. Introduction by James Michener. New York: Macmillan, 1949. "The Town-Ho's Story," pp. 49-67; from Typee, "In Typee Valley," pp. 171-184; and "To Ned," pp. 185-186.

2800 STUDIES IN THE LITERARY IMAGINATION. Melville issue, 1969.

2801 STUDIES IN THE NOVEL. Melville issue, 1969.

2802 SUBRAMANI. "The Mythical Quest: Literary Response to the South Seas." Literary Half-Yearly (Mysore, India), 18 (1977), 165-186. Melville, Maugham, and Conrad.

2803 SUITS, Bernard. "Billy-Budd and Historical Evidence." Nineteenth-Century Fiction, 18 (1963), 288-291.

2804 SULLIVAN, J. W. N. "Herman Melville." London Times Literary Supplement, 123 (July 26, 1923), 493-494. Reprinted in Sullivan, Aspects of Science, 2nd Series. New York: Knopf, 1926. Pp. 190-205.

2805 SULLIVAN, Sister Mary Petrus. "Moby-Dick, Chapter 129, 'The Cabin: Ahab and Pip.'" Nineteenth-Century Fiction, 20 (1965), 188-190.

2806 SULLIVAN, William P. "Bartleby and Infantile Autism: A Naturalistic Explanation." Bulletin of West Virginia Association of College English Teachers, 3 (1976), 43-60.

2807 SUMMERHAYES, Donald C. "The Relation of Illusion and Reality to Formal Structure in Selected Works of Fiction by Hawthorne, Melville, and James." Ph.D. diss., Yale, c. 1958.

2808 SUMNER, D. Nathan. "The American West in Melville's Mardi and The Confidence-Man." Research Studies, 36 (1968), 37-49.

2809 ________. "The Function of Historical Sources in Hawthorne, Melville, and Robert Penn Warren." Research Studies, 40 (1972), 103-114.

2810 SUNDQUIST, Eric Joan. "Home as Found: Authority and Genealogy in Cooper, Thoreau, Hawthorne, and Melville." Ph.D. diss., Johns Hopkins, 1978. DA, 39 (1978), 2279A-2280A.

2811 SUSSMAN, Henry. "The Demonstrator as Politician: Melville's Confidence Man," in Weber, Samuel, and H. Sussman, eds., Glyph: Johns Hopkins Textual Studies, Vol. 4 (1979), pp. 32-56.

2812 SUTLIFFE, Denham. "Christian Themes in American Fiction." Christian Scholar, 44 (1961), 304-305.

2813 ________, ed. with Afterword. Moby-Dick. New York: New American Library, 1961.

2814 SUTTON, Walter. "Melville's 'Pleasure Party' and the Art of Concealment." Philological Quarterly, 30 (July, 1951), 316-327.

2815 ________. "Melville and the Great God Budd." Prairie Schooner, 34 (Summer, 1960), 128-133.

2816 SWANSON, Donald R. "The Structure of The Confidence-Man." CEA Critic, 30 (May, 1968), 6-7.

2817 ________. "The Exercise of Irony in 'Benito-Cereno.'" American Transcendental Quarterly, 7 (1970), 23-25.

2818 SWEENEY, Gerard M. "Melville's Use of Classical Mythology." Ph.D. diss., University of Wisconsin, 1971. DA, 32 (1972), 5752A.

2819 ________. "Melville's Hawthornian Bell-Tower: A Fairy Tale Source." American Literature, 45 (1973), 279-285. Reference to the Minotaur story.

2820 ________. Melville's Use of Classical Mythology. Amsterdam: Rodopi, 1975.

2821 ________. "Melville's Smoky Humor: Fire-Lighting in Typee." Arizona Quarterly, 34 (1978), 371-376.

2822 SWEETSER, Margaret S. "Aspects of Melville's Prose Style." M.A. thesis, University of Minnesota, 1948.

2823 ________. "Herman Melville's Conception of the Great Writer and His Experiments in Literary Manners." Ph.D. diss., University of Minnesota, 1952.

2824 TABACHNICK, Stephen E. "T. E. Lawrence and Moby-Dick." Research Studies, 44 (1976), 1-2.

2825 TAKIGAWA, Motoo. "The Relationship Between God and Human Beings in American Literature." Studies in English Literature, 53 (1976), 59-73. In Japanese; abstract in English.

2826 TANDY, Jeannette Reid. "Pro-Slavery Propaganda in American Fiction of the Fifties." South Atlantic Quarterly, 21 (January and April, 1922), 40-50, 170-178.

2827 TANIMOTO, Taizo. "Ahab, a Tragic Hero and the Leading

Character in Moby-Dick." English and American Literature (Tokyo), 7 (October, 1962), 48-67. In English.

2828 ______. "Pierre the Shepherd: The Meaning of Saddle Meadows in Melville's Pierre." Doshisha Literature (Japan), 24 (1966), 23-40. In English.

2829 TANNER, Tony. "Problems and Roles of the American Artist as Portrayed by the American Novelist." Proceedings of the British Academy, 57 (1971), 159-179.

2830 TANSELLE, George Thomas. "Herman Melville's Visit to Galena in 1840." Journal of Illinois State Historical Society, 53 (Winter, 1960), 376-388.

2831 ______. "The First Review of Typee." American Literature, 34 (1963), 567-571.

2832 ______. "A Further Note on 'Whiteness' in Melville and Others." PMLA, 81 (1966), 604.

2833 ______. "Melville Writes to the New Bedford Lyceum: A Letter to W. P. S. Cadwell." American Literature, 39 (1967), 391-392.

2834 ______. "Typee and DeVoto Once More." Papers of the Bibliographic Society of America, 62 (1968), 601-604.

2835 ______. "The Sales of Melville's Books." Harvard Library Bulletin, 18 (1969), 195-215.

2836 ______. "Typee and DeVoto: A Footnote." Papers of the Bibliographic Society of America, 64 (1970), 207-209.

2837 ______. "Textual Study and Literary Judgment." Papers of the Bibliographic Society of America, 65 (1971), 109-122.

2838 ______. "Bibliographic Problems in Melville." Studies in American Fiction, 2 (1974), 57-74.

2839 ______. "Melville in the B.A.L." Extracts, 20 (1974), 7. Refers to Joseph Blanck, Bibliography of American Literature (1955).

2840 ______. "Problems and Accomplishments in the Editing of the Novel." Studies in the Novel, 7 (1975), 323-360.

2841 ______. A Checklist of Editions of Moby-Dick, 1851-1976. Issued on the Occasion of an Exhibition at the Newberry Library Commemorating the 125th Anniversary of Its Original Publication. Evanston and Chicago: Northwestern University Press and the Newberry Library, 1976. 50-page pamphlet.

2842 ______. "The Editorial Problem of Final Authorial Intention." Studies in Bibliography, 29 (1976), 167-211.

2843 ______. "B.A.L. Addenda: Melville." Papers of the Bibliographic Society of America, 72 (1978), 243-245.

2844 TARG, William. Bouillabaisse for Bibliophiles. Cleveland: World, 1955. Melville, pp. 299-307.

2845 TAYLOR, Dennis. "The Confidence Man from 'The Pardoner's Tale' to The Fall." Arizona Quarterly, 31 (1975), 73-85.

2846 TAYLOR, J. Chesley. "Aranda in Benito-Cereno." American Notes and Queries, 12 (1972), 118.

2847 TAYLOR, Kent Hewitt. "Wittgenstein and Melville: A Study in the Character of Meaning." Ph.D. diss., University of California (Santa Cruz), 1976. DA, 38 (1977), 793A.

2848 TERADA, Takehito. "God's Silence--Melville's Character and Works." Ph.D. diss., University of Chikumashobo, Tokyo, 1969.

2849 THAKUR, D. "The Tales of Herman Melville." Literary Criterion (Mysore, India), 8 (1969), 49-53.

2850 THERSITES. "Talk on Parnassus." New York Times Book Review, 54 (May 24, 1949), 7, 27.

2851 THOMAS, Joel J. "Melville's Use of Mysticism." Philological Quarterly, 53 (1974), 413-424.

2852 THOMAS, John L. "Romantic Reform in America, 1815-1865." American Quarterly, 17 (1965), 656-681.

2853 THOMAS, Russell. "Melville's Use of Some Sources in The Encantadas." American Literature, 3 (January, 1932), 432-456.

2854 ______. "Yarn for Melville's Typee." Philological Quarterly, 15 (January, 1936), 16-29.

2855 THOMPSON, Francis J. "Mangan in America, 1850-1860: Michel, Maryland, and Melville." Dublin Magazine, n.s., 27 (July-September, 1952), 30-41.

2856 THOMPSON, G. R. "A Visual Analogue for 'The Cassock' Chapter of Moby-Dick." Extracts, 18 (1974), 1-2.

2857 THOMPSON, Lawrance Roger. Melville's Quarrel with God. Princeton: Princeton University Press, 1952.

2858 ______. "Moby-Dick: One Way to Cut-in." Carrell, 3 (1962), 1-12.

2859 ________, ed. Benito Cereno. Barre, Mass.: Imprint Society, 1972.

2860 THOMPSON, William R. "'The Paradise of Bachelors and the Tartarus of Maids': A Reinterpretation." American Quarterly, 9 (Spring, 1957), 34-45.

2861 ________. "Melville's 'The Fiddler': A Study in Dissolution." University of Texas Studies in Literature and Language, 2 (Winter, 1961), 492-500.

2862 THORP, Willard. "Herman Melville's Silent Years." University Review, 3 (Summer, 1937), 254-262.

2863 ________. "'Grace Greenwood' Parodies Typee." American Literature, 9 (January, 1938), 455-457.

2864 ________. "Redburn's Prosy Old Guidebook." PMLA, 53 (December, 1938), 1146-1156.

2865 ________. "Did Melville Review The Scarlet Letter?" American Literature, 14 (November, 1942), 302-305. Refers to review in Literary World, March 30, 1850.

2866 ________. "Herman Melville," in Spiller, et al., eds., Literary History (1948), Vol. 1, pp. 441-471.

2867 ________. "American Writers as Critics of Nineteenth-Century Society," in Denny and Gilman, eds., American Writer (1952), pp. 90-105.

2868 ________. "Herman Melville," in American Literary Scholarship: A Review of Current Scholarship. 1963, pp. 29-40; 1964, pp. 32-42; 1965, pp. 28-44; and 1966, pp. 25-39.

2869 ________. "Historical Note," in Hayford, et al., eds., White-Jacket (1970), pp. 403-440. Northwestern-Newberry edition.

2870 ________, ed. Representative Selections of Herman Melville. New York: American Book Company, 1938. American Writers Series. "Introduction and Bibliography," pp. i-c.

2871 ________, ed. Moby-Dick. New York: Oxford University Press, 1947.

2872 ________, ed. Billy-Budd and Other Tales. New York: New American Library, 1961.

2873 THURMAN, Howard K. "Herman Melville: Humanitarian and Critic of Politics." Ph.D. diss., University of Iowa, 1950.

2874 THURSTON, Jarvis, et al., eds. Short Fiction Criticism: A Checklist. Denver: Alan Swallow, 1960. Melville, pp. 154-162.

2875 THWING, A. H. The Crooked and Narrow Streets of Boston. Boston: Marshall Jones, 1920. Melville, passim.

2876 TOMLINSON, Henry Major. "A Clue to Moby-Dick." Literary Review, 2 (November 5, 1921), 141-142.

2877 _______. "Travel Books," in Waiting for Daylight. New York: Knopf, 1922. Pp. 28-30.

2878 _______. "Two Americans and a Whale." Harper's, 152 (April, 1926), 618-621. Two Americans are Thoreau and Whitman; the whale is Melville.

2879 _______. "Preface." Pierre, ed. Robert Forsythe, with Introduction by John B. Moore. New York: Dutton, 1929.

2880 _______. The Face of the Earth. Indianapolis: Bobbs-Merrill, 1950. Melville, pp. 114-117. A travel narrative; includes Melville's books he has read, principally Moby-Dick.

2881 TOMPKINS, Jane P. "Studies in Melville's Prose Style." Ph.D. diss., Yale, 1967. DA, 28 (1967), 246A.

2882 TOWNSEND, H. G. Philosophical Ideas in the United States. New York: American Book Company, 1934. Melville, p. 133.

2883 TRACHTENBERG, Stanley. "'A Sensible Way to Play the Fool': Melville's The Confidence-Man." Georgia Review, 26 (1972), 38-52.

2884 TRAVIS, Mildred K. "Mardi: Melville's Allegory of Love." Emerson Society Quarterly, 43 (1966), 88-94.

2885 _______. "Melville's Furies: Technique in Mardi and Moby-Dick." Emerson Society Quarterly, 47 (1967), 71-73.

2886 _______. "Spenserian Analogues in Mardi and The Confidence Man." Emerson Society Quarterly, 50 (1968 supplement), 55-58.

2887 _______. "The Idea of Poe in Pierre." Emerson Society Quarterly, 50 (1968 supplement), 59-62.

2888 _______. "Melville's Furies: Continued in Pierre." Emerson Society Quarterly, 62 (1971), 33-35.

2889 ________. "Toward the Explication of Pierre: New Perspectives in Technique and Meaning." Ph.D. diss., Arizona State, 1970. DA, 32 (1971), 1534A.

2890 ________. "Hawthorne and Melville's Enceladus." American Transcendental Quarterly, 14 (1972), 5-6.

2891 ________. "Echoes of Emerson in Plinlimmon." American Transcendental Quarterly, 14 (1972), 47-48.

2892 ________. "Echoes of Pierre in The Reivers." Notes on Contemporary Literature, 3 (1973), 11-13.

2893 ________. "Fact to Fiction in Pierre: The Arrowhead Ambience." Extracts, 15 (1973), 6-8.

2894 ________. "A Note on 'The Bell-Tower': Melville's 'Blackwood Article.'" Poe Studies, 6 (1973), 28-29.

2895 ________. "Relevant Digressions in Pierre." American Transcendental Quarterly, 24 (1974), 7-8.

2896 TRENT, William P. A History of American Literature, 1607-1865. New York: Appleton-Century, 1903. Melville, pp. 389-391.

2897 ________, ed. Typee. New York: Appleton-Century, 1902.

2898 ________, and John Erskine. Great American Writers. New York: Holt, 1912. Melville, pp. 84-92.

2899 ________, et al., eds. Cambridge History of American Literature, 4 vols. New York: Macmillan, 1917-1921. Reprinted in one-volume edition, 1944. "Poets of the Civil War: The North," by Will D. Howe, Book II, pp. 275-287; "Contemporaries of Cooper," by Carl Van Doren, Book II, pp. 307-325.

2900 TRIMPI, Helen P. "Romance Structure and Melville's Use of Demonology and Witchcraft in Moby-Dick." Ph.D. diss., Harvard, 1966.

2901 ________. "Melville's Use of Demonology and Witchcraft in Moby-Dick." Journal of the History of Ideas, 30 (1969), 543-562.

2902 ________. "Conventions of Romance in Moby-Dick." Southern Review, 7 (1971), 115-129.

2903 ________. "Harlequin-Confidence-Man: The Satirical Tradition of Commedia dell' Arte and Pantomime in Melville's The Confidence-Man." Texas Studies in Literature and Language, 16 (Spring, 1974), 147-193.

2904 TUCKER, Harry, Jr. "A Glance at 'Whiteness' in Melville and Camus." PMLA, 80 (December, 1965), 605.

2905 TUDOR, Stephen. "Four for Melville," a poem. Emerson Society Quarterly, 59 (1970), 3.

2906 TUERK, Richard. "Melville's 'Bartleby' and Isaac D'Israeli's Curiosities of Literature, second series." Studies in Short Fiction, 7 (1970), 647-649.

2907 TUMLIN, John S., Jr. "The Goblet and the Crown: Framing Imagery in the Prose Fiction of Herman Melville." Ph.D. diss., Emory, 1973. DA, 35 (1974), 1066A.

2908 TURCO, Lewis. "American Novelists as Poets: The Schizophrenia of Mode." English Review, 25 (1974), 23-29.

2909 TURLISH, Lewis A. "A Study of Teleological Concepts in the Novels of Herman Melville." Ph.D. diss., University of Michigan, 1969. DA, 30 (1970), 3922A.

2910 TURNAGE, Maxine. "Melville's Concern with the Arts in Billy-Budd." Arizona Quarterly, 28 (1972), 74-82.

2911 TURNER, Arlin. "Recent Scholarship on Hawthorne and Melville," in Leary, ed., The Teacher and American Literature (1965), pp. 95-109.

2912 TURNER, Darwin T. "A View from Melville's 'Piazza.'" College Language Association Journal, 7 (September, 1963), 56-62.

2913 ________. "Smoke from Melville's Chimney." College Language Association Journal, 7 (December, 1963), 107-113.

2914 TURNER, Frederick W., III. "Melville's Post-Meridian Fiction." Midcontinent American Studies Journal, 10 (Fall, 1969), 60-67.

2915 ________. "Melville and Thomas Berger: The Novelist as Cultural Anthropologist." Centennial Review, 13 (1969), 101-121.

2916 TURNER, Lorenzo Dow. Anti-Slavery Sentiment in American Literature Prior to 1865. Washington, D.C.: U.S. Government Association for the Study of Negro Life and History, 1929. Reprinted Port Washington, N.Y.: Kennikat, 1966. Melville, pp. 50-51.

2917 TUTT, Ralph M. "'Jimmy Rose'--Melville's Displaced Noble." Emerson Society Quarterly, 33 (1963), 28-32.

2918 TUVESON, Ernest. "The Creed of the Confidence Man."

Journal of English Literary History, 33 (June, 1966), 247-270.

2919 TYLER, Parker. "Milly and Billy as Proto-Finnegans," in Tyler, Every Artist His Own Scandal: A Study of Real and Fictive Heroes. New York: Horizon, 1964. Pp. 239-255. Milly refers to a character in Joyce's Ulysses.

2920 UJHAZY, Maria. "Herman Melville: From Bowdlerization to Structuralism." Zeitschrift für Anglistik und Amerikanistik (East Berlin), 24 (1976), 265-269.

2921 UNTERMEYER, Louis. "Herman Melville," in Untermeyer, Makers of the Modern World. New York: Simon and Schuster, 1955. Pp. 47-59.

2922 VAHANIAN, Gabriel. Wait Without Idols. New York: Braziller, 1964. "Herman Melville: Fugitive from God," pp. 72-92.

2923 VALENTI, Peter L. "Images of Authority in 'Benito Cereno.'" College Language Association Journal, 21 (1978), 367-379.

2924 VANCE, Thomas H. "Prince Hamlet, Melville, and the Ambiguities," in Weber, Alfred, and Dietmar Haack, eds., American Literature in the Twentieth-Century. Göttingen, Germany: Vandenhoeck and Ruprecht, 1971. Pp. 132-160.

2925 VAN CROMPHOUT, Gustaaf Victor. "Herman Melville's Redburn Considered in the Light of the Elder Henry James' 'The Nature of Evil.'" Revue des Langues Vivantes, 29 (1963), 117-126.

2926 VANCURA, Zdenek. "The Negro in the White Man's Ship: A Critical Triptych." Prague Studies in English, 8 (1959), 73-97.

VANDEKIEFT see Kieft, Ruth M. Vande.

2927 VANDERBILT, Kermit. "Benito Cereno: Melville's Fable of Black Complicity." Southern Review, 12 (April, 1976), 311-322.

2928 VANDERHAAR, Margaret M. "A Re-examination of Benito-Cereno." American Literature, 40 (May, 1968), 179-191.

2929 VAN DER KROLF, J. M. "Zen and the American Experience." *Visva-Bharati Quarterly*, 25 (Autumn, 1959), 122-132.

2930 VANDERWERKEN, David L. "*Trout Fishing in America* and the American Tradition." *Critique*, 16 (1974), 32-40.

2931 VAN DOREN, Carl. "Contemporaries of Cooper," in Trent, et al., eds., *Cambridge History* (1917-1921), Book II, pp. 307-325.

2932 _______. "Mocha Dick," in Van Doren, *The Roving Critic*. New York: Knopf, 1923. Pp. 97-99.

2933 _______. "Mr. Melville's *Moby-Dick*." *Bookman* (American), 59 (April, 1924), 154-157.

2934 _______. "Melville Before the Mast." *Century Magazine*, 108 (June, 1924), 272-277. Refers to *White-Jacket*.

2935 _______. "Lucifer from Nantucket: An Introduction to *Moby-Dick*." *Century Magazine*, 110 (August, 1925), 494-501. Reprinted in Van Doren, *American Criticism, 1926*. New York: Harcourt, Brace, 1926. Pp. 308-325.

2936 _______. "A Note of Confession." *Nation*, 127 (December 5, 1928), 622.

2937 _______. *The American Novel, 1789-1939*. New York: Macmillan, 1940. Revised edition of 1921 publication. Melville, pp. 84-102.

2938 _______, ed. *White-Jacket*. London: World's Classics, 1929.

2939 _______, ed. with Foreword. *Billy-Budd, Benito-Cereno, and the Enchanted Isles*. New York: Readers' Club, 1942.

2940 VANN, J. Don. "A Selected Checklist of Melville Criticism, 1958-1968." *Studies in the Novel*, 1 (1969), 507-535.

2941 _______. "Pickwick and 'Bartleby.'" *Studies in American Fiction*, 6 (1978), 235-237.

2942 VAN NOSTRAND, A. D. "The Linked Analogies of *Moby-Dick*," in Van Nostrand, *Everyman His Own Poet: Romantic Gospels in American Literature*. New York: McGraw-Hill, 1968. Pp. 113-140.

2943 VAN VECHTEN, Carl. "The Later Work of Herman Melville." *Double Dealer* (New Orleans), 3 (January, 1922), 9-20. Reprinted in *Excavations: A Book of Advocacies*. New

York: Knopf, 1926, as "The Confidence Man as Satire on Transcendentalism," pp. 65-88.

2944 VARGISH, Thomas. "Gnostick Mythos in Moby-Dick." PMLA, 81 (June, 1966), 272-277.

2945 VAUGHT, Carl G. "Religion as a Quest for Wholeness: Melville's Moby-Dick." Journal of General Education, 26 (1974), 9-35.

2946 VERNON, John. "Melville's 'The Bell-Tower.'" Studies in Short Fiction, 7 (1970), 264-276.

2947 VERUCCI, Valeria. "'The Bell-Tower' di Herman Melville." Studi Americani, 9 (1963), 89-120. In Italian.

2948 VESSELLA, Carmella M. "Melville on Christmas Day, 1840." American Literature, 49 (1977), 107-108.

2949 VICTOR, Alexander O. "Five Inches of Books." Yale University Library Gazetteer, 22 (April, 1948), 127-128.

2950 ________. The Trying Out of Moby-Dick. Boston: Houghton Mifflin, 1949.

2951 ________. "White-Jacket: An Essay in Interpretation." New England Quarterly, 22 (September, 1949), 304-315.

2952 ________. "And Still They Fall from the Masthead," in Vincent, ed., Melville and Hawthorne in the Berkshires (1968), pp. 144-155.

2953 ________. "Ishmael, Writer and Art Critic," in Browne, Ray B., and Donald Pizer, eds. Themes and Directions in American Literature: Essays in Honor of Leon Howard. Lafayette, Ind.: Purdue Research Foundation, 1969. Pp. 69-79.

2954 ________. The Merrill Guide to Herman Melville. Columbus, Ohio: Merrill, 1969.

2955 ________. The Merrill Checklist of Herman Melville. Columbus, Ohio: Merrill, 1969.

2956 ________. The Tailoring of Melville's White-Jacket. Evanston, Ill.: Northwestern University Press, 1970.

2957 VINCENT, Howard P., ed. Collected Poems of Herman Melville. New York and Chicago: Hendricks House, 1947.

2958 ________, ed. Melville Annual, No. 1 (1965). A Symposium: "Bartleby, the Scrivener." Kent Studies in English. Kent, Ohio: Kent State University Press, 1966.

2959 _______, ed. Melville Annual (1966). Melville and Hawthorne in the Berkshires: A Symposium. Kent Studies in English. Kent, Ohio: Kent State University Press, 1968.

2960 _______, ed. The Merrill Studies in Moby-Dick. Columbus, Ohio: Merrill, 1969.

2961 _______, ed. Twentieth-Century Interpretations of "Billy Budd." Englewood Cliffs, N.J.: Prentice-Hall, 1971.

2962 VIOLETTE, W. L. "Moby-Dick: A Study in Symphonic Prose." Literary Criterion (India), 4 (Summer, 1960), 19-23.

2963 VISWANATHAM, K. "Moby-Dick," in Morris, Robert K., and Irving Malin, eds., The Achievement of William Styron. Athens: University of Georgia Press, 1975.

2964 VITANZA, Victor J. "Melville's Redburn and Emerson's 'General Education of the Eye.'" Emerson Society Quarterly, 21 (1975), 40-45.

2965 VITOUX, Pierre. "'Bartleby': Analyse du rêcit." Delta English Studies, 7 (1978), 173-189.

2966 VOGEL, Dan. "Note: 'The Coming Storm.'" Melville Society Newsletter, 11 (Summer, 1955), 2-3.

2967 _______. "Herman Melville's Shorter Published Poetry: A Critical Study of the Lyrics in Mardi, in Battle-Pieces, John Marr, and Timoleon." Ph.D. diss., New York University, 1956. DA, 17 (1957), 367-368.

2968 _______. "The Dramatic Chapters in Moby-Dick." Nineteenth-Century Fiction, 13 (December, 1958), 239-247.

2969 _______. The Three Masks of American Tragedy. Baton Rouge: Louisiana State University Press, 1974. "Melville and Moby-Dick," pp. 151-159 and passim.

2970 VOGELBACK, A. L. "Shakespeare and Melville's Benito-Cereno." Modern Language Notes, 67 (February, 1952), 113-116.

2971 VON ABELE, Rudolph. "Melville and the Problem of Evil." American Mercury, 65 (November, 1947), 592-598.

2972 VON HAGEN, Victor W. Equador and the Galapagos Islands. Norman: University of Oklahoma Press, 1949.

2973 _______, ed. The Encantadas. Burlingame: California Association of Secondary School Administrators, 1940.

2974 ________, ed. The Green World of the Naturalists. Philadelphia: Greenberg, 1948. "The Enchanted Isles," by Herman Melville, pp. 201-212.

2975 VOSS, Arthur. "Romance, Allegory, and Morality: Nathaniel Hawthorne and Herman Melville," in Voss, The American Short Story. Norman: University of Oklahoma Press, 1973. Pp. 15-46.

2976 VOT, André Le. "Shakespeare et Melville: Le Thème impérial dans Moby-Dick." Etudes Anglaises, 17 (October-December, 1964), 549-563. In French.

2977 WADLINGTON, Warwick P. "The Theme of the Confidence Game in Certain Major American Writers." Ph.D. diss., Tulane, 1967. DA, 28 (1968), 3691A.

2978 ________. "Ishmael's Godly Gamesomeness: Selftaste and Rhetoric in Moby-Dick." English Literary History, 39 (1972), 309-331. Reprinted in Wadlington, The Confidence Game (1975), pp. 73-103.

2979 ________. "Nathanael West and the Confidence Game," in Madden, David, ed., Nathanael West: The Cheaters and the Cheated. Deland, Fla.: Everett-Edwards, 1974. Pp. 299-322.

2980 ________. The Confidence Game in American Literature. Princeton: Princeton University Press, 1975. Melville, pp. 37-178, includes the following essays: "Picaresque and Picturesque: Omoo, Typee, Mardi," pp. 42-72; "Godly Gamesomeness: Selftaste in Moby-Dick," pp. 73-103; "Passion in Its Profoundest: Mardi (Once More), Pierre, 'Bartleby,' and 'Benito Cereno,'" pp. 104-136; "Hidden Suns and Phenomenal Men: The Confidence Man and 'Billy Budd,'" pp. 137-178.

2981 WAGENKNECHT, Edward. "Our Contemporary, Herman Melville." English Journal, 39 (March, 1950), 121-128.

2982 ________. Cavalcade of the American Novel. New York: Holt, Rinehart, Winston, 1952. "The Ambiguities of Herman Melville," pp. 58-81.

2983 WAGGONER, Hyatt H. "A Possible Verse Parody of Moby-Dick in 1865." American Notes and Queries, 2 (April, 1942), 3-6.

2984 ________. American Poets: From the Puritans to the Present. Boston: Houghton Mifflin, 1968. Melville, pp. 227-234.

2985 ________. "Hawthorne and Melville Acquaint the Reader with Their Abodes." Studies in the Novel, 2 (1970), 420-424.

2986 WAGNER, Vern. "Billy Budd as Moby-Dick: An Alternate Reading," in Wallace, A. Dayle, and Woodburn O. Ross, eds., Studies in Honor of John Wilcox. Detroit: Wayne State University Press, 1958. Pp. 157-174.

2987 WAINGER, B. M. "Herman Melville: A Study in Disillusion." Union College Bulletin, 25 (January, 1932), 35-62.

2988 WAITE, Robert George. "'Linked Analogies': The Symbolic Mode of Perception and Expression in Emerson and Melville." Ph.D. diss., University of Kentucky, 1973. DA, 34 (1974), 6668A-6669A.

2989 ________. "Melville's Memento Mori." Studies in American Fiction, 5 (1977), 187-197.

2990 WAKEFIELD, John W. "The Opposing View: A Study of Melville's Style and Thought." Ph.D. diss., State University of New York (Buffalo), 1973. DA, 34 (1974), 6669A.

2991 WALCUTT, Charles C. "The Fire Symbolism in Moby-Dick." Modern Language Notes, 59 (May, 1944), 304-310.

2992 ________. "The Soundings in Moby-Dick." Arizona Quarterly, 24 (1968), 101-116.

2993 WALKER, Franklin. Irreverent Pilgrims: Melville, Browne, and Mark Twain in the Holy Land. Seattle: University of Washington Press, 1974.

2994 WALKER, W. Gregory. "Sperm Whale and Squid." Discovery, 18 (1937), 308-312.

2995 WALKER, Warren S. "A Note on Nathaniel Ames." American Literature, 26 (May, 1954), 239-241. Author of A Mariner's Sketches (1830). See listing.

2996 ________, ed. Twentieth-Century Short Story Explications: Interpretations 1900-1975 of Short Fiction Since 1800. Hamden, Conn.: Shoe String, 1977. Melville, pp. 487-510 plus Supplements I and II.

2997 WALKER, William E., and Robert L. Welker, eds. Reality and Myth: Essays in American Literature in Memory of Richard Croom Beatty. Nashville, Tenn.: Vanderbilt University Press, 1964. "Melville's Plotinus Plinlimmon and Pierre," by Floyd C. Watkins, pp. 39-51.

2998 WALLACE, Robert K. "Billy-Budd and the Haymarket Hangings." American Literature, 47 (March, 1975), 108-112.

2999 WALSER, Richard. "Another Early Review of Typee." American Literature, 36 (January, 1965), 515-516.

3000 WANDER, John Michael. "Cries to the Wilderness: Melville, Hopkins, Eliot." Ph.D. diss., State University of New York (Stony Brook), 1977. DA, 38 (1977), 3461A-3462A.

3001 WARD, Joseph A. "The Function of the Cetological Chapters in Moby-Dick." American Literature, 28 (May, 1956), 164-183.

3002 ________. "Melville and Failure." Emerson Society Quarterly, 33 (1963), 43-48.

3003 WARD, Joseph Thomas. "Herman Melville: The Forms and Forces of Evil." Ph.D. diss., Notre Dame, 1959. DA, 20 (1960), 2786-2787.

3004 WARD, Robert S. "Longfellow and Melville: The Ship and the Whale." Emerson Society Quarterly, 22 (1961), 57-63.

3005 WARNER, Rex, ed. Billy-Budd and Other Stories. London: Lehmann, 1951.

3006 WARNER BROTHERS, Producers. Moby-Dick: Photoplay title, The Sea Beast. New York, 1925.

3007 WARREN, Robert Penn. "Melville the Poet." Kenyon Review, 8 (Spring, 1946), 208-223. Reprinted in Warren, Selected Essays. New York: Random House, 1958. Pp. 184-198. Also reprinted in Stern, ed., Discussions (1960), pp. 127-134.

3008 ________. "Melville's Poems." Southern Review, 3 (1967), 799-855.

3009 ________, ed. Selected Poems of Herman Melville: A Reader's Edition. New York: Random House, 1970.

3010 WASILEWSKI, William Henry. "An Investigation of the Satellite Poems in Melville's Clarel." Ph.D. diss., State University of New York (Binghamton), 1975. DA, 36 (1975), 290A.

3011 ________. "Melville's Poetic Strategy in Clarel: The Satellite Poem," in Robillard, ed., Symposium (1976), pp. 149-159.

3012 WATKINS, Floyd C. "Melville's Plotinus Plinlimmon and Pierre," in Walker and Welker, eds., Reality and Myth (1964), pp. 39-51.

3013 WATSON, Charles N., Jr. "Melville's Agatha and Hunilla: A Literary Re-incarnation." English Language Notes, 6 (1968), 114-118.

3014 _______. "Character and Characterization in the Works of Herman Melville." Ph.D. diss., Duke, 1969. DA, 31 (1970), 372A.

3015 _______. "Melville's Jackson: Redburn's Heroic 'Double.'" Emerson Society Quarterly, 62 (1971), 8-10.

3016 _______. "Melville and the Theme of Timonism: From Pierre to The Confidence-Man." American Literature, 44 (November, 1972), 398-413. Refers to misanthropy, as in Timon of Athens.

3017 _______. "The Estrangement of Hawthorne and Melville." New England Quarterly, 46 (1973), 380-402.

3018 _______. "Melville's Fiction in the Early 1970's." Emerson Society Quarterly, 20 (1974), 291-297.

3019 _______. "Melville's Selvagee: Another Hint from Smollett." Extracts, 20 (1974), 4-5.

3020 _______. "Melville's Israel Potter: Fathers and Sons." Studies in the Novel, 7 (1975), 563-568.

3021 _______. "Premature Burial in Arthur Gordon Pym and Israel Potter." American Literature, 47 (March, 1975), 105-107.

3022 _______. "A New Life of Melville." New England Quarterly, 49 (1976), 627-633. Review of Edwin H. Miller's Melville (1975).

3023 WATSON, E. L. Grant. "Moby-Dick." London Mercury, 3 (December, 1920), 180-186.

3024 _______. "Melville's Pierre." New England Quarterly, 3 (April, 1930), 195-234.

3025 _______. "Melville's Testament of Acceptance: Billy-Budd." New England Quarterly, 6 (June, 1933), 319-327.

3026 WATTERS, Reginald E. "Melville's Metaphysics of Evil." University of Toronto Quarterly, 9 (January, 1940), 170-182.

3027 _______. "Melville's 'Isolatoes.'" PMLA, 60 (December, 1945), 1138-1148. Reprinted in Stern, ed., Discussions (1960), pp. 107-114.

3028 ________. "Melville's 'Sociality.'" American Literature, 17 (March, 1945), 33-49.

3029 ________. "Boston's Salt-Water Preacher." South Atlantic Quarterly, 45 (July, 1946), 350-361. Father Edward Taylor and Father Mapple of Moby-Dick.

3030 ________. "The Meanings of the White Whale." University of Toronto Quarterly, 20 (January, 1951), 155-168. Reprinted in Stern, ed., Discussions (1960), pp. 77-86.

3031 WATTS, Robert A. "'The Seaward Peep': Ahab's Transgression." University Review, 31 (December, 1964), 133-138.

3032 WAUGH, Colton, artist. "Hand-colored lithograph of the Sperm Whale, 12 3/4 by 14 3/4." Buffalo: New York Consolidated Map Company, 1928.

3033 WAY, Brian. Herman Melville: Moby-Dick. London: Arnold, 1978. 64 pp.

3034 WEAKS, Mabel. "Long Ago and 'Faraway': Traces of Melville in the Marquesas in the Journals of A. G. Jones, 1854-1855." Bulletin of the New York Public Library, 52 (July, 1948), 362-369.

3035 ________. "Some Ancestral Lines of Herman Melville as Traced in Funeral and Memorial Spoons." New York Genealogical and Biographical Record, October, 1949. Pp. 194-197.

3036 WEALES, Gerald. "Singing Billy." Ohio Review, 15 (1974), 92-102. Refers to opera based on novel.

3037 WEATHERS, Willie T. "Moby-Dick and the Nineteenth-Century Scene." Texas Studies in Literature and Language, 1 (Winter, 1960), 477-501.

3038 WEAVER, Raymond M. "The Centennial of Herman Melville." The Nation, 109 (August 2, 1919), 145-146. Reprinted in Christman, Henry M., and Abraham Feldman, eds., One Hundred Years of "The Nation": A Centennial Anthology. New York: Macmillan, 1965. Pp. 113-118.

3039 ________. Herman Melville: Mariner and Mystic. New York: Doran, 1921. Reprinted New York: Pageant, 1960. Also reprinted New York: Cooper Square, 1961. Review of Weaver's biography in Catholic World, February, 1922.

3040 ________. "Herman Melville." Bookman (American), 54 (December, 1921), 318-326.

3041 ________. "Herman Melville," in Macy, John, ed., American

Writers on American Literature. New York: Liveright, 1931. Pp. 190-206.

3042 ________, ed. "Billy-Budd" and Other Prose Pieces, in The Works of Herman Melville, Vol. XIII. London: Constable, 1922-1924. First publication of Billy-Budd.

3043 ________, ed. Redburn. New York: Albert and Charles Boni, 1925.

3044 ________, ed. Mardi, and a Voyage Thither. New York: Albert and Charles Boni, 1925.

3045 ________, ed. Moby-Dick. New York: Albert and Charles Boni, 1926.

3046 ________, ed. Shorter Novels of Herman Melville. New York: Liveright, 1928. Reprinted Greenwich, Conn.: Fawcett, 1960.

3047 ________, ed. "Journal of Melville's Voyage in a Clipper Ship." New England Quarterly, 2 (Jan., 1929), 120-139. Refers to 1860 trip to California.

3048 ________, ed. with Introduction. Typee. New York: Limited Editions Club, 1935. Illustrated by Miguel Covarrubias.

3049 ________, ed. Melville's Journal Up the Straits, October 11, 1856--May 5, 1857. New York: The Colophon, 1935. Reprinted New York: Cooper Square, 1971. See also edition by Horsford (1955).

3050 ________, ed. Moby-Dick. New York: Limited Editions Club, 1950.

3051 WEBER, Alfred, ed. with Introduction and Notes. Billy-Budd, Foretopman. Karlsruhe, Germany: Braun, 1961. Translated into German by editor.

3052 WEBER, J. Sherwood, et al. From Homer to Joyce: A Study Guide to Thirty-Six Great Works. New York: Holt, 1959. "Melville: Moby-Dick," pp. 210-218.

3053 WEBER, Walter. Herman Melville: eine stilistische Untersuchung. Basel, Germany: 1937. Study of tropes, similes, etc. In German; has not been translated.

3054 ________. "Some Characteristic Symbols in Herman Melville's Works." English Studies, 30 (October, 1949), 217-224.

3055 WEBNER, Helene L. "Hawthorne, Melville, and Lowell: The Old Glory." Re: Artes Liberales, 4 (1970), 1-17.

3056 WEEKS, Donald. "Two Uses of Moby-Dick." American Quarterly, 2 (Summer, 1950), 155-164.

3057 WEGELIN, Oscar. "Herman Melville as I Recall Him." Colophon, 1 (Summer, 1935), 21-24. On the sale of Melville's library.

3058 WEIDMAN, Jerome. "Moby-Dick: An Appreciation." Holiday, 19 (February, 1956), 50-55.

3059 WEINTRAUB, Rodelle and Stanley. "Moby-Dick and Seven Pillars of Wisdom." Studies in American Fiction, 2 (1974), 238-240. Refers to work by T. E. Lawrence.

3060 WEIR, Charles, Jr. "Malice Reconciled: A Note on Billy-Budd." University of Toronto Quarterly, 13 (April, 1944), 276-285.

3061 WEISERT, John J. "Thomas Edgerton Browne and John Ross Browne in Kentucky." Filson Club Historical Quarterly, 36 (1962), 329-339. J. Ross Browne, 1821-1875, Etchings of a Whaling Cruise (1846), anticipated Melville.

3062 WEISINGER, Herbert, and Adrian H. Jaffe. "Billy-Budd, Foretopman," in The Laureate Fraternity: An Introduction to Literature. Evanston, Ill.: Row, Peterson, 1960. Pp. 142-143.

3063 WEISSBUCH, Ted N. "A Note on the Confidence Man's Counterfeit Detector." Emerson Society Quarterly, 19 (1960), 16-18.

3064 ______, and Bruce Stillians. "Ishmael the Ironist: The Anti-Salvation Theme in Moby-Dick." Emerson Society Quarterly, 31 (1963), 71-75.

3065 WELLS, Daniel A. "'Bartleby the Scrivener': Poe and Duyckinck Circle." Emerson Society Quarterly, 21 (1975), 35-39.

3066 ______. "A Checklist of Melville Allusions in Duyckinck's Literary World: A Supplement to the Mailloux-Parker Checklist." Extracts, 29 (1977), 14-17.

3067 ______. "Melville Allusions in The Southern Literary Messenger." Extracts, 31 (1977), 13.

3068 ______. "Melville Allusions in The American Whig Review." Extracts, 32 (1977), 9-10.

3069 WELLS, Henry W. "Herman Melville's Clarel." College English, 4 (May, 1943), 478-483.

3070 ________. The Modern American Way of Poetry. New York: Columbia University Press, 1943. Reprinted New York: Russell and Russell, 1964. Melville, pp. 78-88.

3071 ________. "An Unobtrusive Democrat: Herman Melville." South Atlantic Quarterly, 43 (January, 1944), 46-51.

3072 WELLS, John F. "Herman Melville's Literary Reputation: 1940-1969." Ph.D. diss., University of Minnesota, 1970. DA, 32 (1971), 2713A.

3073 WELLS, Whitney Hastings. "Moby-Dick and Rabelais." Modern Language Notes, 38 (February, 1923), 123.

3074 WELSH, Alexander. "A Melville Debt to Carlyle." Modern Language Notes, 73 (November, 1958), 489-491.

3075 WELSH, Bernard Howard. "Herman Melville as Magian: Zoroastrianism and Manicheism in the Major Prose Fiction." Ph.D. diss., Auburn, 1972. DA, 34 (1973), 2584A.

3076 ________. "Politics of Race in Benito-Cereno." American Literature, 46 (January, 1975), 556-566.

3077 WENDELL, Barrett. A Literary History of America. New York: Scribner, 1900.

3078 ________, and Chester Noyes Greenough. A History of Literature in America. New York: Scribner, 1904.

3079 WENKE, John. "A Note on Melville and Shakespeare: Two Moments of Truth." Melville Society Extracts, 36 (1978), 7.

3080 WERGE, Thomas A. "The Persistance of Adam: Puritan Concerns and Conflicts in Melville and Mark Twain." Ph.D. diss., Cornell, 1967. DA, 28 (1968), 3653A-3654A.

3081 ________. "Moby-Dick and the Calvinist Tradition." Studies in the Novel, 1 (1969), 484-506.

3082 ________. "Moby-Dick: Scriptural Source of Blackness and Darkness." American Notes and Queries, 9 (1970), 6.

3083 ________. "Melville's Satanic Salesman: Scientism and Puritanism in 'The Lightning-Rod Man.'" Newsletter of the Conference of Christianity and Literature, 21 (1972), 6-12.

3084 WEST, Ray B., Jr. "The Unity of Billy-Budd." Hudson Review, 5 (Spring, 1952), 120-127.

3085 ________. "Primitivism in Melville." Prairie Schooner, 30 (Winter, 1956), 369-385. Reprinted in West, The Writer in His Room. East Lansing: Michigan State University Press, 1968. Pp. 31-47.

3086 WESTBROOK, Max. "The Ontological Critic." Rendezvous, 7 (1972), 49-66. Includes some reference to Melville criticism.

3087 WHEELER, Otis. "Humor in Moby-Dick: Two Problems." American Literature, 29 (May, 1957), 203-206.

3088 WHEELOCK, C. Webster. "Vere's Allusion to Ananias." Extracts, 15 (1973), 9-10.

3089 WHIPPLE, A. B. C. "The Whaleman Novelist," in Whipple, Yankee Whalers in the South Seas. Garden City, N.Y.: Doubleday, 1954. Pp. 40-54.

3090 WHITE, Edgar Walter. "Billy-Budd." Adelphi, 28 (1952), 492-498. Compares novel with opera by Britten.

3091 WHITE, Julie Belle. "A Rhetorical Criticism of Moby-Dick: The Persuasive Campaigns of Ahab, Starbuck, and Ishmael According to Their Substances, Dynamics, and Strategies." Ph.D. diss., University of Minnesota, 1975. DA, 37 (1976), 35A.

3092 WHITE, Morton Gabriel, and L. White. "Bad Dreams of the City: Melville, Hawthorne, and Poe," in White and White, The Intellectual Versus the City. Cambridge: Harvard University Press, 1962. Pp. 36-53.

3093 WHITE, Viola Chittenden. "Symbolism in Herman Melville's Writings." Ph.D. diss., University of North Carolina, 1934.

3094 WHITE, William. "Herman Melville: A New Source." Notes and Queries, 180 (June 7, 1941), 403.

3095 WHITECAR, William B., Jr. Four Years Aboard the Whaleship. Philadelphia: Lippincott, 1864. Excerpt reprinted in McCormick, ed., Life on a Whaler (1960), pp. 106-109.

3096 WIDMER, Kingsley. "The Negative Affirmation: Melville's 'Bartleby.'" Modern Fiction Studies, 8 (Autumn, 1962), 276-286.

3097 ________. "Bartleby," in Widmer, The Literary Rebel. Carbondale: Southern Illinois University Press, 1965. Pp. 48-59.

3098 ________. "The Perplexity of Melville: 'Benito Cereno.'" Studies in Short Fiction, 5 (Spring, 1968), 225-238.

3099 ________. "The Perplexed Myths of Melville: Billy-Budd." Novel: A Forum for Fiction, 2 (Fall, 1968), 23-35.

3100 ________. "Melville's Radical Resistance: The Method and Meaning of 'Bartleby.'" Studies in the Novel, 1 (1969), 444-458.

3101 ________. The Ways of Nihilism: A Study of Herman Melville's Short Novels. Los Angeles: Ward Ritchie Press for California State Colleges, 1970. Based on earlier published three essays listed directly above.

3102 WIGMORE, Douglass. "A Backward Glance o'er Moby-Dick." Extracts, 24 (1975), 7-9.

3103 WILDER, Thornton. "Toward an American Language." Atlantic Monthly, 180 (July, 1952), 31-42. Includes comment on Melville.

3104 WILEY, Elizabeth. "Four Strange Cases." Dickensian, 58 (May, 1962), 120-125.

3105 WILEY, Lulu R. The Sources and Influences of the Novels of Charles Brockden Brown. New York: Vantage, 1950. Melville, pp. 239-243.

3106 WILLETT, Maurita. "The Letter A, Gules, and the Black Bubble," in Vincent, ed., Melville and Hawthorne in the Berkshires (1968), pp. 70-78.

3107 ________. "The Silences of Herman Melville." American Transcendental Quarterly, 7 (1970), 85-92.

3108 WILLETT, Ralph W. "Nelson and Vere: Hero and Victim in Billy-Budd, Sailor." PMLA, 82 (October, 1967), 370-376.

3109 ________, ed. The Merrill Studies in Pierre. Columbus, Ohio: Merrill, 1971. Reprints 24 critical essays.

3110 WILLIAMS, David Park. "Hook and Ahab: Barrie's Strange Satire on Melville." PMLA, 80 (1965), 483-488.

3111 ________. "Peeping Tommo: Typee as Satire." Canadian Review of American Studies, 6 (1975), 36-49.

3112 WILLIAMS, John Brindley. "The Impact of Transcendentalism on the Novels of Herman Melville." Ph.D. diss., USC, 1965. DA, 26 (1966), 1052-1053.

3113 WILLIAMS, Mentor L. "Horace Greeley Reviews Omoo." Philological Quarterly, 27 (January, 1948), 94-96.

3114 _______. "Park Benjamin on Melville's Mardi." American Notes and Queries, 8 (December, 1949), 132-134.

3115 _______. "Two Hawaiian-Americans Visit Herman Melville." New England Quarterly, 23 (March, 1950), 97-99.

3116 _______. "Some Notices and Reviews of Melville's Novels in American Religious Periodicals, 1846-1849." American Literature, 22 (May, 1950), 119-127.

3117 WILLIAMS, Stanley T. "'Follow Your Leader': Melville's 'Benito Cereno.'" Virginia Quarterly Review, 23 (Winter, 1947), 61-76.

3118 _______. "Spanish Influence in American Fiction: Melville and Others." New Mexico Quarterly, 22 (Spring, 1952), 5-16.

3119 _______. The Spanish Background of American Literature, 2 vols. New Haven: Yale University Press, 1955. Melville, Vol. I, pp. 224-227, 394-396, and passim.

3120 _______. "Melville," in Stovall, ed., Eight American Authors (1956), pp. 207-270.

3121 WILLIAMS-ELLIS, Amabel. The Exquisite Tragedy: An Intimate Life of John Ruskin. Garden City, N.Y.: Doubleday, Doran, 1929. Contains reference to Ahab, pp. 266-267.

3122 WILLIS, Samuel. "Private Allegory and Public Allegory in Melville," in Parker, ed., The Confidence-Man (1971), pp. 285-286.

3123 WILLSON, Lawrence. "Yet Another Note on Moby-Dick." Dalhousie Review, 35 (Spring, 1955), 5-15.

3124 WILMES, Douglas Robert. "The Satiric Mode in Melville's Fiction: Pierre, Israel Potter, The Confidence-Man, and the Short Stories." Ph.D. diss., University of Pennsylvania, 1976. DA, 37 (1977), 4360A.

3125 WILNER, Herbert. "Aspects of American Fiction: A Whale, a Bear, and a Marlin." Americana-Austriaca, 58 (1966), 229-246. Edited by Klaus Lanzinger. Stuttgart, Germany: Braumuller, 1966.

3126 WILSON, Edmund. "John Singleton Mosby, 'The Grey Ghost.'" New Yorker, 34 (February 14, 1959), 117-136.

3127 ________. *Patriotic Gore.* New York: Oxford University Press, 1962. Melville, pp. 323-327 and passim. Discusses *Battle-Pieces* and other Civil War poetry.

3128 ________, ed. *The Shock of Recognition.* Garden City, N.Y.: Doubleday, Doran, 1943. Melville, "Hawthorne and His Mosses," with editorial comment, pp. 187-204.

3129 WILSON, Gilbert. "*Moby-Dick* and the Atom." *Bulletin of Atomic Scientists*, 8 (August, 1952), 195-197.

3130 WILSON, G. R., Jr. "*Billy-Budd* and Melville's Use of Dramatic Technique." *Studies in Short Fiction*, 4 (Winter, 1967), 105-111.

3131 WILSON, James D. "Incest and American Romantic Fiction." *Studies in the Literary Imagination*, 7 (1974), 31-50.

3132 WILSON, James Grant, and John Fisk, eds. *Appleton's Cyclopaedia of American Biography*, 7 vols. New York: Appleton, 1887-1901. Enlarged edition, issued 1915; supplementary volumes, 1931.

3133 WILSON, James Southall. "Henry James and Herman Melville." *Virginia Quarterly Review*, 21 (April, 1945), 281-286.

3134 WINTERICH, John T. "Romantic Stories of Books, Second Series, No. 4: *Moby-Dick*." *Publishers' Weekly*, 116 (November 16, 1929), 2391-2394.

3135 ________. "The Compleat Collector." *Saturday Review of Literature*, 7 (1932), 531.

3136 WINTERS, Yvor. *Maule's Curse: Seven Studies in American Obscurantism.* Norfolk, Conn.: New Directions, 1938. "Herman Melville and the Problems of Moral Navigation," pp. 53-89. Reprinted in Winters, *In Defense of Reason.* Denver: Alan Swallow, 1947. Pp. 200-233.

3137 WITHERINGTON, Paul M. "The Art of Melville's *Typee*." *Arizona Quarterly*, 26 (1970), 136-150.

3138 WITHIM, Phil. "*Billy-Budd*: Melville's Testament of Resistance." *Modern Language Quarterly*, 20 (1959), 115-127.

3139 WITTE, W. "The Sociological Approach to Literature." *Modern Language Review*, 36 (1941), 86-94. Melville, passim.

3140 WOLF, George E. "Herman Melville's Experiments in Narration: 1852-1855." Ph.D. diss., University of Connecticut, 1970. *DA*, 32 (1971), 2658A.

3141 WOLFRUM, Max D. "Responsible Failure in Melville." Ph.D. diss., Washington University, 1969. DA, 31 (1970), 1821A.

3142 WOLPERT, Bernard M. "The Herman Melville Revival: A Study of Twentieth-Century Criticism Through Its Treatment of Herman Melville." Ph.D. diss., Ohio State, 1951. DA, 18 (1958), 1800-1802.

3143 WOOD, Ann D. "Herman Melville and the Feminine Fifties." Extracts, 17 (1974), 2.

3144 WOODCOCK, George, ed. Typee. Baltimore: Penguin English Library, 1972.

3145 WOODMANSEE, Martha A. "Melville's The Confidence-Man," in Lohner, Edgar, ed., Der Amerikanische Roman. Berlin, Germany: Schmidt, 1974. Pp. 49-69.

3146 WOODRESS, James, ed. American Literary Scholarship: An Annual Survey. Durham, N.C.: Duke University Press, 1963 to date. See "Melville" section by different authors.

3147 _______, ed. Ph.D. Dissertations in American Literature, 1891-1966. Durham, N.C.: Duke University Press, 1968. Melville, items 1809-1922.

3148 _______, ed. Eight American Authors, new edition. New York: Norton, 1971. "Melville," by Nathalia Wright, pp. 173-224. See also Stovall, ed., Eight American Authors (1956).

3149 WOODRUFF, Stuart C. "Melville and His Chimney." PMLA, 75 (June, 1960), 283-292.

3150 WOODSON, Thomas. "Ahab's Greatness: Prometheus as Narcissus." Journal of English Literary History, 33 (September, 1966), 351-369.

3151 _______. "'Oblivion Lingers in the Neighborhood': The Loss and Recovery of Nineteenth-Century American Literature." Bulletin of the Midwest Modern Language Association, 7 (1974), 26-39. Melville, passim.

3152 WOODWARD, C. Vann. "A Southern Critique for the Gilded Age," in Woodward, The Burden of Southern History. Baton Rouge: Louisiana State University Press, 1968. Pp. 109-140. Melville, passim.

3153 WOOLF, Leonard. "Herman Melville." Nation and Athenaeum, 33 (September 1, 1923), 688.

3154 WRIGHT, Nathalia. "Biblical Allusion in Melville's Prose." American Literature, 12 (May, 1940), 185-199.

3155 ______. "Melville and His Public." *American Notes and Queries*, 2 (August, 1942), 67-71.

3156 ______. "A Source for Melville's *Clarel*: Dean Stanley's *Sinai and Palestine*." *Modern Language Notes*, 62 (February, 1947), 110-116.

3157 ______. "Melville's Use of the Bible." Ph.D. diss., Yale, 1949.

3158 ______. *Melville's Use of the Bible*. Durham, N.C.: Duke University Press, 1949. New edition published New York: Octagon, 1969. Adds Appendix: "Moby-Dick: Jonah's or Job's Whale" (1965), pp. 189-194.

3159 ______. "The Head and Heart in Melville's *Mardi*." *PMLA*, 66 (June, 1951), 351-362.

3160 ______. "Form as Function in Melville." *PMLA*, 67 (June, 1952), 330-340.

3161 ______. "*Mosses from an Old Manse* and *Moby-Dick*: The Shock of Discovery." *Modern Language Notes*, 67 (June, 1952), 387-392.

3162 ______. "The Confidence Man of Melville and Cooper: An American Indictment." *American Quarterly*, 4 (Fall, 1952), 266-268.

3163 ______. "A Note on Melville's Use of Spenser: Hautia and 'The Bower of Bliss.'" *American Literature*, 24 (March, 1953), 83-85.

3164 ______. "*Pierre*, Herman Melville's *Inferno*." *American Literature*, 32 (May, 1960), 167-181.

3165 ______. "An Approach to Melville Through His Themes and Literary Genres." *Emerson Society Quarterly*, 28 (1962), 25-27.

3166 ______. "Moby-Dick: Jonah's or Job's Whale?" *American Literature*, 37 (May, 1965), 190-195.

3167 ______. "Melville and 'Old Burton' with 'Bartleby' as *An Anatomy of Melancholy*." *Tennessee Studies in Literature*, 15 (1970), 1-13.

3168 ______. "Herman Melville," in Woodress, ed., *Eight American Authors*. Revised edition (1971), of 1956 work ed. by Floyd Stovall. Pp. 173-224.

3169 ______. "The Tale of *Moby-Dick*." *Phi Kappa Phi Journal*, 54 (1974), 42-58.

3170 ________. "Herman Melville and the Muse of Italy." Italian Americana, 1 (1975), 169-184.

3171 ________. "The Poems in Melville's Mardi," in Robillard, ed., Symposium (1976), pp. 83-99.

3172 WRIGHT, Ray G. "Herman Melville: The Art of Telling the Truth." Ph.D. diss., Texas A&M, 1971. DA, 33 (1972), 1151A.

3173 WYSS, Hal H. "Involuntary Evil in the Fiction of Brown, Cooper, Poe, Hawthorne, and Melville." Ph.D. diss., Ohio State, 1970. DA, 32 (1971), 1489A.

3174 YAGGY, Elinor. "Pierre: Key to the Herman Melville Enigma." Ph.D. diss., University of Washington, 1946.

3175 ________. "Shakespeare and Melville's Pierre." Boston Public Library Quarterly, 6 (January, 1954), 43-51.

3176 YAGI, Toshio. "Is Ishmael, Ishmael? An Anatomy of Moby-Dick." Studies in English Literature (Tokyo), 54 English No. (1977), 73-94.

3177 YAMAMOTO, Shoh. "The Source and Structure of 'Benito Cereno.'" Studies in English Literature (Tokyo), 49 English No. (1972), 43-54.

3178 YAMAYA, Saburo. "The Stone Image of Melville's Pierre." Studies in English Literature (Tokyo), 34 English No. (1957), 31-57.

3179 ________. "The Inner Struggle in Melville's Pierre." Journal of Humanities, 3 (1958), 101-120.

3180 ________. "Poe, Hawthorne, and Melville's 'Benito Cereno.'" Studies in English Literature (Hosei University), 4 (March, 1961), 21-32.

3181 ________. "A New Interpretation of Melville's Moby-Dick." Studies in English Literature (Tokyo), 38 English No. (1961), 59-81.

3182 ________. "Melville's 'Inland Voyage to Fairyland.'" Essays in English and American Literature, 14 (1961), 185-205.

3183 YANKOWITZ, Susan. "Lowell's Benito Cereno: An Investigation of American Innocence." Yale Theatre, 2 (1968), 81-90.

3184 YANNELLA, Donald J. "Source for the Diddling of William Cream in The Confidence-Man." American Transcendental Quarterly, 17 (1973), 22-23.

3185 _______. "'Seeing the Elephant' in Mardi," in DeMott and Marovitz, eds., Artful Thunder (1975), pp. 105-117.

3186 _______. "Some Recent Melville Studies." Studies in the Novel, 8 (1976), 214-222.

3187 _______. "Melville for Sale." Extracts, 26 (1976), 18-19.

3188 _______, and Kathleen Malone Yannella. "Evert A. Duyckinck's 'Diary': May 29--November 8, 1847," in Myerson, ed., Studies: 1978 (1978), pp. 207-258.

3189 YARINA, Margaret, and Arlene Jackson. "The Dualistic Vision of Herman Melville's 'The Encantadas.'" Journal of Narrative Technique, 3 (1973), 141-148.

3190 YATES, Norris. "A Traveller's Comments on Melville's Typee." Modern Language Notes, 49 (December, 1954), 581-583. Refers to E. K. Drayton, doctor on U.S.S. St. Mary's.

3191 _______. "An Instance of Parallel Imagery in Hawthorne, Melville (Israel Potter), and Frost." Philological Quarterly, 36 (April, 1957), 276-280. Refers to Frost's "The Woodpile."

3192 YEAGER, Henry J. "Melville's Literary Debut in France." Midwest Quarterly, 11 (1970), 413-425.

3193 YELLIN, Jean Fagan. "Black Masks: Melville's 'Benito Cereno.'" American Quarterly, 22 (1970), 678-689.

3194 YODER, B. A. "Poetry and Science: 'Two Distinct Branches of Knowledge' in Billy-Budd." Southern Review (Australia), 3 (1969), 223-239.

3195 YOUNG, Gloria L. "The Sea as Symbol in the Work of Herman Melville and Joseph Conrad." Ph.D. diss., Kent State, 1971. DA, 32 (1972), 6463A.

3196 YOUNG, James Dean. "The Nine Gams of the Pequod." American Literature, 25 (January, 1954), 449-463. Reprinted in Stern, ed., Discussions (1960), pp. 98-106.

3197 YOUNG, Philip. "Melville's Eden, or Typee Recharted," in Young, Three Bags Full. New York: Harcourt Brace Jovanovich, 1973. Pp. 99-112.

3198 YU, Beongcheon. "Ishmael's Equal Eye: The Source of Balance in Moby-Dick." Journal of English Literary History, 32 (March, 1965), 110-125.

3199 ZALLER, Robert. "Melville and the Myth of Revolution." Studies in Romanticism, 15 (1976), 607-622.

3200 ZECK, Gregory R. "The Logic of Metaphor: 'At Melville's Tomb' by Hart Crane." Texas Studies in Literature and Language, 17 (1975), 673-686.

3201 ZEIK, Michael. "The Traditional Element in Herman Melville's Thought with Special Attention to Clarel." Ph.D. diss., Georgetown, 1958.

3202 ZIFF, Larzer. "Shakespeare and Melville's America," in Pullin, ed., Perspectives (1978), pp. 54-67.

3203 ________. "Moby-Dick and the Problem of a Democratic Literature." Yearbook of English Studies, 8 (1978), 67-76.

3204 ZIMMERMAN, Michael P. "Herman Melville in the 1920's: A Study in the Origins of the Herman Melville Revival with an Annotated Bibliography." Ph.D. diss., Columbia, 1963. DA, 25 (1965), 1224.

3205 ________. "Herman Melville in the 1920's: An Annotated Bibliography." Bulletin of Bibliography, 24 (September-December, 1964), 117-120; and (January-April, 1965), 139-144.

3206 ZINK, David D. "Bartleby and the Contemporary Search for Meaning." Forum (Houston), 8 (1970), 46-50.

3207 ZINK, Karl E. "Herman Melville and the Forms: Irony and Social Criticisms in Billy-Budd." Accent, 12 (Summer, 1952), 131-139.

3208 ZIRKER, Priscilla Allen. "The Major and Minor Themes of Herman Melville's White-Jacket." Ph.D. diss., Cornell, 1966. DA, 27 (1966), 1799A-1800A.

3209 ________. "Evidence of the Slavery Dilemma in White-Jacket." American Quarterly, 18 (Fall, 1966), 477-492.

3210 ZLATIC, Thomas David. "Melville's 'Pithy Guarded Cynicism': A Study of His Later Novels." Ph.D. diss., St. Louis, 1974. DA, 36 (1975), 3722A.

3211 ________. "'Benito Cereno': Melville's 'Back-Handed-Well-Knot.'" Arizona Quarterly, 34 (1978), 327-343.

3212 ZOELLNER, Alan Frederick. "The Splendid Labyrinth: Language, Consciousness, and the Contraries in Melville's Later Fiction." Ph.D. diss., Indiana University, 1977. DA, 38 (1978), 6733A.

3213 ZOELLNER, Robert. The Salt Sea Mastodon: A Reading of Moby-Dick. Berkeley: University of California Press, 1973.

3214 ZOLLA, Elêmire. "La strutta e fonti di Clarel." Studi Americani (Rome), 10 (1964), 101-134. In Italian.

3215 ZUPPINGER, Renaud. "'Bartleby': Prometheus Revisited. Pour une problematique de la confiance, ou la 'sortie du souterrain.'" Delta English Studies, 6 (1978), 61-77. In French.

INDEX OF COAUTHORS, EDITORS, TRANSLATORS

SUBJECT INDEX